ACKNOWLEDGEMENT

CU00486845

We wish to thank all the staff and children of schools we have worke
for sharing their ideas and thoughts about mathematics with us and w
would not have been possible. Special thanks to:

THE DEVON NUMERACY PROJECT SCHOOLS
BOVEY TRACEY PRIMARY:
Stefanie Burke*, Colin Butler, Zoe Carnell, Julie Dyer, Sally Egleton, Lucy Gough, Julie Hawkins, Max Quick, Barbara Symcox, David Watson.

COWICK FIRST SCHOOL:
Elizabeth Chadwick*, Jo Donkin, Sally Dyer, Catherine Lawes, Lesley Mold, Jackie Nicolle, Zoe Rhydderch-Evans, Steve Smith, Sue Wake.

KINGSKERSWELL PRIMARY SCHOOL:
Mark Ackers, Lisa Alexander, Nick Burstow, Liz Butler, Alison Foster, Mary Raffell, Graham Rowell, Gill Scholes, Ann Stokes, Maggie Wakely, Debbie Weible*.

WIDECOMBE IN THE MOOR PRIMARY SCHOOL:
Claire Brunsch, Kate Edwards, Kandi Smith*.

*These teachers also participated in the Devon Raising Attainment in Numeracy Project.

THE DEVON RAISING ATTAINMENT IN NUMERACY PROJECT TEACHERS

Dave Ansell	-	Keyham College Road Primary School
Sally Boxall	-	Shute Primary School
Steve Burton	-	Morchard Bishop CE Primary School
Ann Davis	-	Buckland Brewer Primary School
Brian Donahue	-	Lydford Primary School
Angela Folland	-	Our Lady & St Patrick's RC Primary School
Veronica Hindmarch	-	Bishopsteignton Primary School
Annie Holme	-	Heathcoat Primary School
Ann Hume	-	Watcombe Primary School
Linda Naish	-	St David's CE First School
John Norman	-	South Molton Junior School
Angela Perry	-	Okehampton Primary School
Peter Perry	-	Countess Weir Combined School
Vicki Price	-	South Tawton Primary School
Linda Rutkowska	-	Diptford Parochial Primary School
Chris Sargeant	-	Collaton St Mary CE Primary School
Lynne Tidball	-	Whitleigh Junior School
Stephanie Whitcher	-	Chagford CE Primary School
Mary Williamson	-	Meavy CE Primary School

A special thanks to John Slack whose work appears on page 199

CONTENTS

INTRODUCTION   1

MENTAL/ORAL ACTIVITIES   8

Counting   8

Place Value and Ordering   29

Estimating and Rounding   61

Calculating   79

Shape and Space   157

MAIN ACTIVITIES AND PLENARY   173

SAMPLE LESSON PLANS   205

APPENDICES   223

    1. Questions   224

    2. Mental Strategies   226

    3. Writing Frames   229

    4. Photocopiable Resources   233

    5. Useful Addresses   270

GLOSSARY OF MATHEMATICAL TERMS   272

INDEX OF ACTIVITIES   276

INTRODUCTION

Current statements about mathematics and, in particular, those relating to numeracy have not appeared out of the blue and do not proclaim a new path to salvation. On the contrary, they highlight attitudes and beliefs that have existed in mathematics education for many years, and can be traced from the Cockcroft Report (1982) through The Non-Statutory Guidance (1989) to the current National Curriculum (1995).

Central to the work in numeracy is a belief in the fact that mathematics happens in your head. Sometimes it is useful to manipulate pieces of equipment, to model situations with objects or on paper, or to jot down part or all of the process you are engaged in. But, the essential core of any mathematical activity is how you think about it, how you engage in the task, how you use things you already know to find routes to the unknown and how you make sense of these 'solutions' both for yourself and others. This involves a willingness to take risks, to leap into that unknown and explore creatively the ways in which links can be made.

Unfortunately, this creative aspect of mathematics is often obscured by a desire to teach everybody to work in the same way. This is rather like teaching children to paint like Vincent Van Gogh and insisting that they all continue to paint using his techniques and style. We need to introduce children to a variety of styles and techniques - both in art and mathematics - and then let the children use and interpret these in different situations. As one sculpture I create may be heavily influenced by the work of Jean Miro and another may be influenced by Barbara Hepworth, so my seeking to solve 29 + 45 may be influenced by 29 being nearly 30 whilst solving 25 + 17 may be influenced by 17 being 10 + 7. At the same time, others may be influenced differently; by Henry Moore rather than Barbara Hepworth and by 17 being 15 + 2 rather than 10 + 7.

There is a need, therefore, to teach a variety of strategies and to allow children to decide which to use in different contexts. The National Curriculum states quite clearly that the intention is for children to:-

> "Develop flexible and effective methods of computation and recording and use
> them with understanding." (Key Stage 2 Number programme of study)

This will involve developing a critical awareness in mathematics; discussion of whether methods are appropriate and efficient is vital. No one method is the best method in **every** situation. For example, whilst counting on to work out a small difference such as 1003 - 998 is both appropriate and efficient, counting on to calculate a large difference, such as 1003 - 94, is not.

Children deserve to be exposed to the beauty and wonder of mathematics. They should be given opportunities to marvel at the way numbers work and connect, to experience the thrill of discovering patterns and links, to feel the satisfaction of handling and manipulating numbers of all sizes and to share ideas in a supportive and experimental environment. The ideas in this book are intended to help teachers to provide such opportunities for their classes and to seek out the pleasure, excitement, fun and delight in mathematics for themselves.

What is 'mental mathematics'?

As has been said, mathematics happens in our heads. This involves use of the imagination:-

> "The mental faculty which forms images or concepts of external objects not present to the senses and of their relations (to each other or to the subject). The creative faculty of the mind; the ability to frame new and striking concepts."

The New Shorter Oxford English Dictionary

It is important to notice that it is **not** just about remembering facts nor is it solely about having a mental picture of a situation. If we consider it in relation to number then it is about having a sense of number, a feel for how numbers fit together and relate to each other. This sense or feel for mathematics is developed by encountering a rich variety of mathematical experiences. Young children need a wide range of visual images to help them develop their understanding of number and other mathematical concepts. This is where equipment (like hundred squares and number lines) can be useful. The key is variety; the over-use of one form of equipment to the exclusion of others restricts the child's development of a rich network of images. There is also the danger that children can become reliant on a particular piece of equipment or image. This is discussed in the section on resources (see page 4.)

One model for developing mental facility, as used by Askew, Bibby and Brown, (see appendix 5) relies on exploiting the link between known and derived facts:-

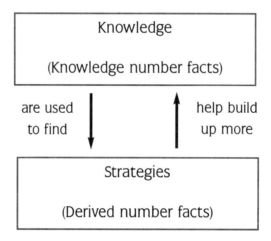

This model suggests that the more you know, the more you can derive and the more you derive, the more you know. This cycle is at the centre of developing mental facility. Unfortunately, some children become stuck with using procedures or fixed methods, which often involve counting objects or marks. A major task for the teacher, in developing children's mental facility, is to move children on from counting to more flexible and efficient strategies based on a range of number facts and properties. A further exploration of this can be found in 'The Devon Raising Attainment in Numeracy Project', a report on research carried out in 1997/98 by a group of Devon teachers (see appendix 5). The introduction of a daily session of mental/oral maths (as recommended in the National Numeracy Project Framework) is an important vehicle for developing mental facility. There are a number of activities that can take place during these sessions and we have tried to provide a wide range of ideas and examples in this book.

Possibilities include:-

Counting in steps of different sizes

Practising the instant recall of number facts

Figuring out new facts from those already known

Discussing ways of remembering facts that need to be learned by heart

Developing and explaining new mental strategies

Discussing which operation and which numbers are needed to solve a problem

Proving or disproving general statements

Developing vocabulary

Revising/reviewing earlier work

It is important that children are exposed to a variety of activities. Sessions should not stagnate nor become daily repetitions of just one activity. They are not intended to be daily tests; tests may be used on occasions but the time is mainly for **teaching**. Whilst the sessions might be directly related to the rest of the lesson there is no need for them to be; they can stand as self-contained 'units'. They may also focus on any aspect of the mathematics curriculum, not just number.

Use of language and questions

Talk is an essential feature of mental mathematics sessions; it is the only way we access how someone is thinking. Children need opportunities to explain and communicate their thoughts, they need to understand why it is important and receive guidance on how to do it. The development of vocabulary is crucial to this and the National Numeracy Project has produced an extremely useful book 'Mathematical Vocabulary' to which every adult working with children in mathematics should have access (see appendix 5).

Teachers' questions provide the means to encourage children's talk and good questioning skills are central to successful mathematics lessons, not just mental/oral sessions. Once very clear objectives for the lessons have been identified and the activities selected to support these, then the teacher's role is very much about provoking thinking and moving the children on through questioning. Spending some planning time considering the questions that will be most effective in meeting the objectives of the lesson has proved to be extremely useful. One of the features of the activities in this book is the identification of questions that could be used to provoke understanding and awareness of connections. We have included a list of useful questions for general use in mathematics in appendix 1. As well as using questions, teachers can make statements for example "When you multiply by ten you always add a nought to the number" for the children to discuss, investigate and prove to be either true or false.

The use of different questions is one way of differentiating during whole class sessions. It is important to involve all the children in these sessions. This can be done by offering a variety of numbers to work with, giving the children digit cards so that they can all respond (for young children who have a very limited understanding of number this could consist of three cards that show '1', '2' and more than '2' - see appendix 4) and creating a culture in the classroom that values everyone's contribution.

Resources

The following resources are recommended for all classrooms:-

Large number squares	(see appendix 4 for small squares)
Large number lines - a variety	(see appendix 4 for small lines)
Calculators	
Digit/number cards	(see appendix 4)
Dienes or similar apparatus for modelling numbers	
Straws or similar material for "bundling'	
Multilink or similar material	
Money - real or plastic	
Place value/arrow cards	(see appendix 4)
Counters	
A variety of dice (i.e. not just six faces and numbered 1 to 6)	
Rulers	
Wall clock	
'Relevant' games	
Different types of mathematical paper (e.g. square paper, square 'dotty' paper, triangular 'dotty' paper)	
Mathematical dictionary	
Pegs and pegboards	
Polydron or similar material	
Place Value Chart	(see appendix 4)
Eigen squares	(see appendix 4)

For other resources, especially those for measures and shape and space, it is not essential for every class to have their own set.

Some of these resources are useful for presenting particular images of number. It is important that none are used exclusively and that there is an awareness of the limitations and dangers associated with each. The aim is to 'force' concepts into the children's heads. The danger is that children may become dependent on pieces of equipment and learn procedures for manipulating that equipment. Remember, developing mental facility is about deriving strategies from things you know not learning procedures in complete isolation. Links and connections need to be made at all times.

Advantages (+) and dangers (-) relating to the use of certain pieces of equipment:-

Hundred Square
+ Provides a graphic image of adding and subtracting tens as moving up and down the grid and so provides the opportunity for 'carving a picture' of adding and subtracting nine and eleven. It is useful for looking at patterns and the relationship between numbers.
- 1 to 100 squares are not good for going through the tens, e.g. from 69 to 71, for large numbers or for negative numbers. There is a need to understand place value to use it effectively. Use of the hundred square can become procedural and divorced from understanding. In other words it can become just another way of counting and about manipulating the apparatus.

Number Lines
+ Provide an ordinal sense of number, i.e. where numbers are in relation to each other. They can promote an emphasis on first the decades then the hundreds as key elements in the structure of number. They provide the idea of continuity of number, that number goes on forever in both directions and that the gaps in between the whole numbers contain other numbers. This provokes an awareness and understanding of negative numbers and decimals. They are also good for estimating and rounding and provide an image for the operations of addition and subtraction.
- Can encourage reliance on counting in ones. They do not give a sense of magnitude nor do they show number patterns easily. Not good for doubling or halving in particular nor multiplication or division in general.

Base 10 (Dienes) Apparatus
+ Provides a cardinal sense of number, i.e. a sense of the size and countability. It provides an image of numbers broken down into hundreds, tens, units, etc. and the relationship between the different parts. It can be useful for forcing awareness of the power of counting in tens, hundreds, etc. It can be used to provide an image for addition as putting together or adding more and subtraction as taking away.
- Problems can occur when used to model an algorithm, such as the method of decomposition, as it encourages reliance on procedure without understanding, stopping the thinking about the mathematics. It takes time to count it out and to use it.

Arrow Cards (see appendix 4)
+ Provide a model for the way that the number names are written as well as a particular way of seeing the structure of the numbers themselves, allowing you to take numbers apart. Powerful illustration of this specific area of place value.
- Limited to place value. Not useful for developing a sense of the size of number nor for working with numbers beyond four digits.

Calculator
+ Useful for the exploration of number and number structure. It can be used to strengthen the idea that, for instance, 123 = 100 + 20 + 3. The constant function can be used to continually add 10 to a number and this helps to illuminate elements of place value. The use of the constant function to repeatedly add or subtract any numbers from a given start number provides many examples of

sequences. Children can then be encouraged to recognise and describe patterns.

Negative numbers can be introduced by inviting children to subtract a large number from a smaller one and explain what happens.

Decimals can be introduced by inviting children to halve numbers on the calculator and explain what happens when you halve an odd number.

Also useful for working on 'real' problems with large or otherwise complicated numbers (e.g. decimals)

− Can be used without understanding and real purpose.

Can be used as a prop for simple calculations than can and should be done mentally.

Results are impermanent - there is a need to record, the steps in a calculation alongside the use of a calculator so that discussion can follow.

Multilink Cubes

+ Useful for modelling small numbers (one-to-one correspondence), comparing and number conservation

− Can encourage reliance on counting in ones. Not good for modelling large numbers.

Money

+ Useful as a context for encouraging counting in twos, fives and tens.

− Many children lack experience and comparative size and value are not consistent.

i.e. 2 pence coin is bigger than 5 pence coin but worth less, causing confusion.

Using and Applying Mathematics

Whilst not all elements of the Using and Applying Mathematics programme of study appear explicity in the National Numeracy Project Framework, all of the work is underpinned by it. Using and applying mathematics as defined in the National Curriculum is the 'how' of mathematics; how children are to experience the elements of number, measures, shape and space and data handling. The importance of **how** children learn mathematics continues to be central to the National Numeracy Project and will need to be a clear element within the structure of the "Numeracy Hour". The three strands of Using and Applying - "Making and Monitoring Decisions", "Communication" and "Reasoning" - are all features of both the mental/oral and the plenary sessions. The list of possible activities for mental/oral sessions in this book includes activities that focus on each of these strands. The plenary provides opportunities for children to reflect on the mathematics that they and others have been involved with, consider the effects of decisions they have made, explain work they have undertaken and discuss patterns and general statements that have arisen through the work.

Assessment

A key element of good assessment is the presence of clear objectives for teaching and learning. The beginning and end sessions of each mathematics lesson are ideal times to assess the children. During the mental/oral sessions, the questions provided alongside activities could be used as assessment questions. The questions that children are asked to answer in the plenary (resulting from the main activity) could also be used for assessment. More formal assessment may come from the independent activities and from asking children to communicate in writing their responses. Writing frames have been used very successfully to help structure children's writing in maths (as well as other subjects) and could be used as an assessment tool (see appendix 3).

The rest of the book

The bulk of this book is a collection of ideas for use in mental/oral sessions. Many of these ideas could be repeated with the same children by changing numbers or varying the questions. We have tried to give an indication of the age range each activity is suitable for but in many cases, especially those relating to calculating, the activities can be used with most ages simply by varying the numbers. The activities are brought together under the headings "Counting", "Place Value and Ordering", "Estimating and Rounding", "Calculating" and "Shape and Space". There are, however, overlaps and it is hoped that the various indexes at the back of the book will help you find activities that fit your needs.

We have also included some examples of activities that can be used by children working without an adult, sample numeracy lesson plans from Devon schools piloting the framework as well as photocopiable resources to support the activities. Many of these could be copied onto transparencies and used with an overhead projector, if one is available, making it easier for all children to view them. A glossary, list of recommended books and details of where to get good equipment complete the book.

MENTAL/ORAL ACTIVITIES
Counting

Children begin reciting number names at a very young age and this is the first step towards counting. However, there are many other things involved in being able to count. These include:-

One to one correspondence - matching one number name to one object as you count, often touching or pointing and saying at the same time.

Seeing numbers in different ways - the ordinal and cardinal aspects of counting so that the object you count as 'three' is the third object you count but if it is also the last object then there are three in the set.

Counting in a systematic way - lining them up, putting them to one side, etc. This helps you to make sure you have counted all the objects and haven't counted any object more than once.

Irrelevance of order - whatever order you count a set in it will still be the same number.

Irrelevance of object - it doesn't matter how big or small the objects are, three boxes and three acorns may look different but there is the same number of boxes as acorns

Conservation - it doesn't matter if the set of objects is spread out, piled up together, held up high, etc. the number stays the same.

'Subitization' - being able to see that there are a certain number of objects on the table without having to count them (we are usually able to do this for up to 6 objects).

It is important to work with young children on activities that focus on these different aspects of counting and also to help them understand that counting forwards involves adding one each time whilst counting backwards involves subtracting one each time.

Once children have gained this understanding of counting it is important to develop other skills. These include counting forwards and backwards starting at different numbers (including counting backwards beyond 0), counting in steps other than one (especially steps of ten) and, later, counting in decimals, fractions and negative numbers. As the children's understanding and ability to count increases it is important to encourage the children to look for the patterns in their counting, to use these to generalise and work with large numbers and to relate counting to addition, subtraction, multiplication and division.

Rhymes

Rhymes are one way that children meet and learn number names and the order of numbers. They can encourage children to find the rhythm of counting, give them confidence, introduce them to large numbers and allow them to look for patterns.

As well as using well known rhymes such as 'Five Little Speckled Frogs', 'One, Two Buckle My Shoe' and 'Ten Green Bottles', it is very easy to generate your own rhymes in a school. An interesting project for older children is to create rhymes that meet given criteria. The following rhymes appear in a poetry book called 'Long, long, long, short, small, big poems' written by children, parents and staff at two Devon schools (see appendix 5).

Eighteen Little Aliens

18 little aliens shining bright and green,
3 crashed their spaceship, then there were 15.

15 little aliens visited earth to pry and delve,
3 went back to Jupiter, then there were 12.

12 little aliens standing in a line,
3 fell down a drain, then there were 9.

9 little aliens playing naughty tricks,
3 got caught, then there were six.

6 little aliens digging up a key,
3 fell down the hole, then there were 3.

3 little aliens wished they hadn't come,
3 went back to the spaceship, then there were none.

No more little aliens here on the planet,
This story can't be true........Or can it?!

Edward and Sue McHugh

Playful Puppies

Two playful puppies
waiting at the door,
Two puppies opened it,
then there were four.

Four playful puppies
eating Weetabix
Two came and joined them,
then there were six.

Six playful puppies
climbing over a gate,
Two were on the other side
then there were eight.

Eight Playful puppies
hiding in a den
Two came to find them,
then there were ten

Jenny and Janet Ellis

Three Little Billy Goats

Three little billy goats
Trotted into town,
One bought some pudding,
One bought a clown.

One bought a pretty dress
A jumper and trousers too,
Put them in a polythene bag
And took them home to chew.

On the way back he met Mr. Troll
Standing by the lake
And he knew he would pass safely,
As he'd bought the troll a cake.

A Reception/Y1 class poem

Hungry Horses

Ten hungry horses went to a fete,
Two got drunk,
Then there were eight.

Eight hungry horses doing magic tricks,
Two did a disappearing act,
Then there were six.

Six hungry horses walking though a door,
Two got shut out,
Then there were four.

Four hungry horses, one lost a shoe,
One went to find it,
Then there were two.

Two hungry horses sitting in the sun,
They both got sunstroke,
Then there were none!

Michelle Rhodes and Hannah Goodliffe

Pass the Basket

AIM: Count reliably a number of objects.

ACTIVITY

Put a pile of acorns, pine cones etc. in the middle of the circle. Pass a basket around the circle and each child in turn adds one to the basket. Everybody counts together as another item is added to the basket. Stop at a suitable number and start to take the items out of the basket, one by one, counting down as it happens.

QUESTIONS

How many are in the basket now?
How many will there be when Nino has added one?
How many have we put in altogether?
How many will we have to take out to make the basket empty?
Who put the first acorn in?
Who put the last one in?
Who is next?
How many do you think it would take to fill the basket?

VARIATIONS/EXTENSIONS

Into KS1, put in two items each time instead of one.

RESOURCES

basket
acorns
pine cones

VOCABULARY

how many
first, second,... last
empty
full
fill
altogether
add
added more
next
less

Number Stories

AIM: Count reliably a number of objects.

ACTIVITY

Using real objects and/or a picture set up a situation. for example, to accompany the Goldilocks story, have three teddy bears and lay out on the floor a tablecloth with items for the teddy bears to have a picnic.

QUESTIONS

Are there enough plates for the bears?
How many sandwiches shall we give each bear?
How many is that altogether?
Is there room for Goldilocks to join them?
What will she need? How many plates are there now?

RESOURCES

tablecloth
plates, etc.
teddy bears

VOCABULARY

how many?
enough
more
altogether

Memory Game

AIM: To accurately count a set of objects; solve simple number problems involving subtraction.

ACTIVITY

Sit the children in a circle. Place a tray in the middle with a number of different objects on it. Ask the children to count them and try to memorise the objects. Then cover the tray and take some away. Ask the children to show you on their fingers how many are missing.

QUESTIONS

How can we make sure we count them all?

Can you count them without touching?

How are you working out how many are missing?

How can we check if we're right?

If there are four on the tray and two are missing, how many did we start with?

If we started with nine and five are left, how many are missing?

Can you show me?

Which objects are missing?

How did you remember them?

VARIATIONS/EXTENSIONS

Children could hold up digit cards to show how many are left/missing.

Children take turns in small groups to hide objects

RESOURCES

tray
up to 10 objects
cloth

VOCABULARY

count
how many?
missing
check
left
digit

Silent Counting

AIM: Count reliably in different contexts.

ACTIVITY

Give each child a set of digit cards or use fingers. Beat a drum (or clap) and count the number of beats together. Once the children understand what they are counting, ask them to count silently in their heads. Each child holds up a digit card or fingers to show the number of beats.

QUESTIONS

How many beats did you count?

What if I had hit the drum one more time - how many beats would that have been?

Can you clap the same number of beats/one more/one less?

VARIATIONS/EXTENSIONS

Let the children lead the activity - give one child a number card- they beat/clap and the others count silently.

Clap/drum with a rhythm, so that the beats are in twos etc.

Bounce a ball and count the number of bounces

RESOURCES

drum

digit cards

VOCABULARY

count

how many?

altogether

more

less

Show Me

AIM: Count reliably a collection of objects; understand and use ordinal numbers.

ACTIVITY

Give each child a small pile of cubes (or other small equipment to count out). Describe different situations that involve a number and ask them to use the cubes to 'show me'. For example:-

Marta has five sisters - show me

Sunil has three biscuits - show me

There are four sweets in a row - show me. The second one gets eaten - show me.

VARIATIONS/EXTENSIONS

Give each child digit cards to put next to the cubes they have counted out. Involve position in the description.

Put the sentence on cards and highlight the number words.

RESOURCES

cubes (or similar)

digit cards

VOCABULARY

first, second, third,...

next to

between

Spot the Mistake

AIM: Know the number names in order when counting forwards and backwards.

ACTIVITY

Give each child a set of digit cards. Count, using a puppet if appropriate, and make a mistake by:-

Missing a number out e.g. 1, 2, 3, 5, 6, 7, 8, 9, 10
Mixing up the order e.g. 1, 2, 3, 4, 6, 5, 7, 8, 9, 10
Repeating a number e.g. 1, 2, 3, 4, 5, 6, 6, 7, 8, 9, 10

Children have to identify the number that has been missed or repeated or the two numbers that have been muddled up. They find the appropriate digit card(s) and hold them up to show the teacher. Vary the numbers according to the ability of the children and count both forwards and backwards.

QUESTIONS

What was wrong with the counting?
Which number was missing?
How do you know?
Where should it have been? Why?
How do you know they were in the wrong order?

VARIATIONS/EXTENSIONS

Let the children lead the counting and make the mistake.
Instead of digit cards have cards with pictures of objects and they have to select the picture that matches the missing number.

RESOURCES

digit cards
puppet (if needed)

VOCABULARY

in between
before
after
one more/less than
order

Body Maths

AIM: Recite the number names in order, read and order numbers and say the number one more or less than a number.

ACTIVITY

Give each child a bib/hat/card with a number on. Together count and the child with that number comes and stands in the line until all the children are standing and the numbers are in order. Count backwards for them to sit down again.

QUESTIONS

Which number do you come after?

Which number is one bigger than you?

Who are your number neighbours?

Do numbers stop at 34?

What if we had everyone in the school in the line, would we reach the end of numbers?

What about zero, who are zero's neighbours?

Do numbers stop at zero?

If you count on three, which number would you reach?

VARIATIONS/EXTENSIONS

Give out the numbers and ask the children to sit next to the number that is one bigger/smaller than them. Progress to sitting next to the number two bigger/smaller - leads to counting in twos and looking at odd and even numbers.

Give out the numbers and ask them to order themselves without any help. Ask them which number they looked for to help them sort out, which number needed to stand still to make it easier for everyone, etc.

Extend the line into negative numbers by using bibs or hats of a different colour.

RESOURCES

number bibs

hats or cards

VOCABULARY

bigger

smaller

more

less

next to

infinity

negative numbers

count on

count back

Number Tiles 1

AIM: Count on or back from any small number, order a set of numbers.

ACTIVITY

Place a number tile on the floor, e.g. 4. Ask a child to lay the 5 tile down. Discuss where the 5 has been put and other options. Do the same for other numbers.

QUESTIONS

Why have you put the five there?
Can anyone think of another reason why the five can go there?
Could the five go anywhere else?
If the four and five are here, where can't the six go? Why?

VARIATIONS/EXTENSIONS

Use tiles that go up in tens rather than ones.

RESOURCES
number tiles

VOCABULARY
before
after
next to
one more
one less
counting

Number Tiles 2

AIM: Count on or back from any small number, order a set of numbers.

ACTIVITY

Put out the number tiles in a line from 0 to 10. Turn them over, except the zero, so that the numbers are hidden. Choose a child and give them a number. They stand on the zero and move on that number of steps. The other children have to hold the number of fingers/number card that matches the number they think the child is standing on.

QUESTIONS

Which number is Samina standing on?
How many steps did she take?
How many steps will she need to take to get back to zero?
How many more steps will she need to reach 10?

VARIATIONS/EXTENSIONS

Start at numbers other than zero and take steps forwards or backwards.

RESOURCES
number tiles
number cards

VOCABULARY
before
after
next to
one more
one less
counting
forwards
backwards
how many?

Imagine a Number

AIM: To develop mental images of numbers and count imagined objects.

ACTIVITY

Ask the children to imagine they have 5 cubes (have a pile of cubes to look at if it helps, or use something other than cubes - counters, toy cars, etc.). Tell them to arrange them in some way in their heads and then describe how they have arranged them to another child/whole class. Can the child/whole class draw/arrange real cubes in the way described to them?

QUESTIONS

Did anyone arrange them in the same way?

Did you imagine different colours?

How many cubes are at the top/bottom?

Did anyone arrange them in a different way?

Can anyone think of a different way to describe this arrangement?

What do you see when you see this arrangement of cubes?

How did you check you had 5?

VARIATIONS/EXTENSIONS

Alter the number - use bigger numbers such as 10 and ask them to arrange them in their heads so that they are easy to count and they can check there are 10.

Give them arrangements of objects on cards and ask them to describe them to the rest of the class/another child so that they can picture what is on the cards and either draw them or arrange real objects.

Imagine picking up a handful of cubes from the pile and putting them in your lap. Imagine placing three on the floor in front of you. Now take another two from your lap and place them on the floor in front of you. Look at what you have - describe it to your partner/the whole class.

RESOURCES

paper
pencil
cubes

VOCABULARY

and
plus
makes
same as
arrange
arrangement
top
bottom
check

Card Count

AIM: Recite and order numbers.

ACTIVITY

Use a pack of playing cards but remove all the picture cards. Sit in a circle and deal each child at least one card. Choose a child to start. The aim is to lay cards in a line starting with an ace (1) and ending with a ten. Cards can only be put down in order and when one line is completed another can be started, until everyone has laid their card. Use a pebble to pass from child to child so that they know when it is their go. Pass the pebble if you can't go, lay your card and pass the pebble if you can. This can be done in silence.

QUESTIONS

Who has a card that could be laid now?

What number will come next?

What number comes before your number?

VARIATIONS/EXTENSIONS

Start at ten and work backwards

Use two or three packs and allow more than one line to be started - if you have an ace you can lay it at any time.

Lay out the numbers in a line but you can add numbers in a domino way - above and below if you want. So, if you have the numbers to five laid and you have a four it could go above the five.

Lay the numbers out so that they go higher, lower.

Use number cards from 0 to 9 rather than 1 to 10.

RESOURCES

playing cards

VOCABULARY

one more

one less

before

after

next

How Many Days in School?

AIM: Count, read and write in figures numbers to at least 100, know what each digit represents and partition two digit numbers into tens and units.

ACTIVITY

Start at the beginning of the school year and count each day the number of days the children have been in your class.

Have a space on the wall to stick up cubes, with the appropriate numeral underneath, and each day add one more. Talk about the ordinal aspect as well - "we have been in school three days" - "this is the third day in school".

When you reach the ninth day tell the children that you are not allowed to put more than nine cubes on the chart - discuss what you can do tomorrow. (This could be a rule left in a letter to the class by a strange visitor or any other device you may want to use!)

Introduce the idea of something else to represent 10 - a 'stick' or 'long'. Add a space next to the existing one for keeping the sticks in. Continue to add one cube each day but now have a numeral underneath each space, one for the sticks and one for the cubes.

QUESTIONS

How many days had we been in school yesterday?

What is one more?

How many days have we been in school today?

How is the number going to change?

How many tens is that and how many ones?

Could we write that as an addition? (e.g. 10 + 3 = 13)

When do you think will be the hundredth day in school? Before or after Christmas? Why?

What happens each time we have nine cubes?

VARIATIONS/EXTENSIONS

Have a 100 party on day 100, involving lots of activities about 10 and 100.

For Y5/Y6 count minutes and hours in school

RESOURCES

base 10 blocks
(e.g. Dienes)
wall space
blu-tack
digit cards

VOCABULARY

units, tens, hundred
one, two and
three digit numbers
numerals
first, second,........
yesterday
today
tomorrow
year
week,
month
days
cubes
how many?
addition

Partner Counting

AIM: Recite in order the number names to at least 100, begin to recognise odd and even numbers.

ACTIVITY

Either with a partner or the whole class with the teacher as a partner, count in ones, taking it in turn to say the next number. Record the numbers each partner is saying, either using a hundred square, number cards or by writing them down.

QUESTIONS

What do you notice about the numbers you are saying?

What about the numbers your partner is saying?

Can you see a pattern on the hundred square?

Who will say the number 71? 86? How do you know?

What about if we went beyond 100 - who would say 101? 1002?

VARIATIONS/EXTENSIONS

Count in tens with a partner - what do you notice about the numbers you are saying? Who will say 120? 310?

Links to:

'Counting Fives', page 23

RESOURCES

hundred square or
number cards

VOCABULARY

odd

even

Counting Cards

AIM: Recite in order the number names to at least 100.

ACTIVITY

Give each child a card with a number on it. The children have to read out their numbers in order as quickly as they can, going both forwards and backwards. Time this and try to beat the time achieved or get within a given time e.g. under a minute.

VARIATIONS/EXTENSIONS

Have cards that start at numbers bigger than 1, e.g. 45 to 88

Use cards going up in twos, tens etc.

(Cards could have numbers on both sides - two different colours relating to two different sets)

RESOURCES

number cards
watch or clock

VOCABULARY

next

before

after

one more

one less

Counting in Tens

AIM: Count on or back in tens starting from any two-digit number.

ACTIVITY

Give children a calculator in pairs. Tell them how to use the constant function to make the calculator count. On most calculators this means +1 = = or + + 1 = =. This will make the calculator keep adding one and you will get the counting numbers. Having done this for counting in ones try the same for tens. Then discuss what would happen if you started at a number other than 0. For example to start at 3 press 3 + 10 into the calculators - what do they think will come next? Ask them to keep pressing = and explain this will add another 10 on each time. In pairs they need to predict, press and record each time. After about two minutes stop to discuss.

QUESTIONS

What do you notice about the numbers you were getting?

What other things do you notice?

What other numbers do you think you would reach if you kept pressing the = button? Would your calculator show 243? 339? Why?

What's the biggest number you can think of that your calculator might show if you kept adding 10?

What if you started with a different number, say 5? What would happen then? What numbers would your calculator show?

What do you think would happen if you started at 104 and subtracted tens? Why?

VARIATIONS/EXTENSIONS

Use the constant function for counting backwards in tens. Discuss what happens when you reach a single digit number. Allow the children to go into negatives. Model this on a number line.

Look at the pattern of numbers that the calculator is producing on a hundred square.

Use the constant function for counting in twos starting at 0 and 1 to extend understanding of odds and evens.

Could be extended into a independent activity during the main part of the lesson.

Links to:

'1, 10, 100, more or less', page 51

RESOURCES

calculators
hundred square
number line

VOCABULARY

counting in tens
adding tens
constant function
hundreds
thousands
millions
negative numbers
odd
even

Counting Steps for Y3/Y4

AIM: Recognise and extend number sequences formed by counting from any number in steps of constant size, extending beyond zero when counting back.

ACTIVITY

Count in threes, fours and fives.

Count in ones, tens and hundreds.

Count in twos and recognise odd and even numbers.

Count in halves and quarters.

Count in steps of 0.5 and 0.1

For each of these the following could be used:-

Count as a class.

Count as a class and on a given signal, e.g. a clap, change from counting forwards to backwards or backwards to forwards.

Count around the class - point to a different child each time to say the next number.

Point to children in turn and they count silently in their heads until you put your palm up and they have to say the number that has been reached.

Give out number cards with appropriate numbers on and call them out in order.

Count quietly but say loudly multiples of six or seven etc.

Play Fizz Buzz - count round the class and for any multiple of five, for example, say "Fizz". For multiples of two say "Buzz" and for multiples of both say 'FizzBuz'.

QUESTIONS

If we start at five and count in twos, what sort of numbers will we say? Will we say 132? Why?

What's the difference between the last two numbers we counted? If we count round the circle in fives, who will say 50?

There are 32 of us in the class today - how many legs, ears, fingers?

Links to:

'Two, Twenty ....', page 45

'1, 10, 100, more or less', page 51

RESOURCES

number cards

VOCABULARY

odd

even

how many?

halves

quarters

multiple

pattern

Counting Fives

AIM: Count in fives forwards and backwards from different numbers.

ACTIVITY

Either with a partner or the whole class with the teacher as a partner, count in fives starting at 0 taking it in turn to say the next number. Record the numbers each partner is saying, either using a hundred square, number cards or by writing them down.

QUESTIONS

What do you notice about the numbers you are saying?

What about the numbers your partner is saying?

Why is this happening?

Can you see a pattern on the hundred square?

Who will say the number 120? 135? How do you know?

What about if we went to bigger numbers - who would say 200? 3005? 401?

How many fives did you count to get to 45?

VARIATIONS/EXTENSIONS

Start at a different number and count in fives together - can you see a pattern? Can you count quickly with a partner in fives starting at 2? 7? etc. Why is it easy?

Links to:

'Partner Counting', page 20

RESOURCES

hundred square

VOCABULARY

multiple

pattern

digit

multiply

divide

Imagine a Line

AIM: Count on or back from different numbers in different size steps.

ACTIVITY

(The children will need to have a lot of experience of number lines before doing this activity.)

Ask the children to imagine they are standing at the beginning of a number line and that the number line stretches out in front of them. They are going to start moving along the number line so that the numbers are getting bigger, looking at the numbers they pass. Allow them to do this for a little while then say that now the numbers start to get bigger more quickly, because they start taking bigger steps - look at the numbers they step on again. Ask them to stop and look at the number they have ended on. Go round the class and ask them to say the number they are on.

QUESTIONS

Who landed on the biggest number?
How did they get there - what size steps were they taking?
Did anyone take different size steps?
Which numbers did you see as you were travelling along your line?
Did anyone see 47? 120? How?
How would you get from the number you ended on to 100? Can you do it in two steps?

VARIATIONS/EXTENSIONS

Move backwards along a line, going into negative numbers.
Take smaller steps involving fractions.

RESOURCES

VOCABULARY

number line
biggest
smallest
steps
along

Pieces of Number Line 1

AIM: Count on or back in ones from any two- or three-digit number.

ACTIVITY

Either use a number line with only some numbers on it, to focus on, or imagine pieces of number line.

Think of/look at the piece of number line that goes from 10 to 20.

Compare it with the piece of number line from 40 to 50.

Think of the piece of number line that goes from 13 to 18. From 23 to 28. From 133 to 138.

QUESTIONS

Which numbers lie on this piece of number line?

What is the same about them? What is different about them?

What is the same about the numbers between 10 and 20 and the numbers between 40 and 50? How are they different?

How does the piece of number line from 13 to 18 help you think about the piece from 113 to 118? From 343 to 348?

Links to:

'Pieces of Number Line 2', page 27

RESOURCES

blank number line
numbers

VOCABULARY

between
same
different
compare

Counting Races

AIM: Recognise and extend number sequences formed by counting from any number in steps of constant size, extending beyond zero when counting back.

ACTIVITY

Split the class in half. Agree a starting number - one half of the class is to count in ones whilst the other half of the class counts in tens. Start and stop the counting together.

QUESTIONS

Will each group stop on the same number? Why?

Why is counting in tens quicker?

Will both groups count 20? 32?

Can you give a number that only your group will count? Why?

Can you give a number that neither group will count? Why?

VARIATIONS/EXTENSIONS

Split into smaller groups and have a variety of steps -

e.g. twos, fives, halves, quarters, etc.

Give the groups a starting card and a finishing card and hold these up when they finish.

RESOURCES

number cards

VOCABULARY

counting in tens
sequences
steps
continue
count up to

Counting Steps for Y5/Y6

AIM: Recognise and extend number sequences formed by counting from any number in steps of a constant size, extending beyond zero when counting back.

ACTIVITY

Count in sixes, sevens, eights, nines from different starting numbers forwards and backwards.

Count in steps of 0.1 and 0.01 forwards and backwards.

Count in steps of different sizes starting at a negative number, forwards and backwards.

Count in quarters, tenths etc. forwards and backwards.

For each of these the following could be used:-

Count as a class.

Count as a class - on a given signal, e.g. a clap, change from counting forwards to backwards or backwards to forwards. Count around the class - point to a different child each time to say the next number.

Point to children in turn and they count silently in their heads until you put your palm up and they have to say the number that has been reached.

Give out number cards with appropriate numbers on and call them out in order.

Count quietly but say loudly multiples of six or seven etc.

Play Fizz Buzz - count round the class and for any multiple of six, for example, say "Fizz". Multiples of nine say "Buzz" and multiples of both six and nine say "FizzBuzz".

QUESTIONS

If we start at five and count for one minute in steps of a quarter, where do you think we will reach? Do you think we will finish on a number bigger or smaller than one hundred? Why?

Will we say the number 41? 6.3? ‾24? Why?

What's the difference between the last two numbers?

If we start at five and count forwards in eights which number shall we stop at if we want to count back in nines and reach five? Why? What other numbers would work?

RESOURCES

number cards

VOCABULARY

negative

tenths

hundredths

multiples

difference

Pieces of Number Line 2

AIM: Count on or back in decimals.

ACTIVITY

Use a number line marked in ones or marked every 0.5

Talk about counting in tenths.

QUESTIONS

Which numbers lie between 0 and 1?

What is the same about them?

What is different about them?

What about the numbers between 3 and 4?

What is the same about the numbers between 0 and 1 and the numbers between 3 and 4? How are they different?

How does the piece of number line from 1 to 2 help you think about the piece from 101 to 102? From 341 to 342?

Links to:

'Pieces of Number Line 1', page 25

RESOURCES

number line

VOCABULARY

between

same

different

compare

Place Value & Ordering

"All things have special places where they belong, including numbers"

(girl aged 8)

Understanding place value and how numbers fit together to form the number system is central to developing a feel for number. A sound understanding is also required if pupils are to become efficient and effective at mental and written calculations.

Teaching children standard written algorithms before they have developed this feel for number can inhibit development of mental facility. Pupils whose 'diet' consists of pages of vertically written sums may learn to 'see' numbers as strings of separate digits rather than view them holistically and may perform calculations without understanding. There is, therefore, a danger that children will fail to recognise when their answers are unreasonable and will be dependent on written methods leading to inappropriate use, for example.

$$\begin{array}{r} 0\ 9\ 9 \\ 1\ {}^{1}0\ {}^{1}0\ {}^{1}0 \\ -\quad\quad 7 \\ \hline 9\ 9\ 3 \end{array}$$

They may also be unable to solve number problems in different contexts. Working from right to left, as we do when calculating using vertically written sums, also conflicts with how many people calculate mentally, starting with the largest part of the numbers first.

Presenting sums horizontally encourages children to treat numbers more holistically. Base 10 materials when accompanied by the use of arrow cards (see appendix 4) are useful in helping children to visualise numbers and to gain a feel for their size and how they are made up. Number lines can also help children develop an awareness of place value and our number system (see appendix 4). However children should be encouraged to see that numbers can be partitioned in a variety of ways and not just in terms of hundreds, tens and units. For example, being taught to treat 69 as 60 and 9, or 70 less 1, or 50 and 19, may provide a better understanding of number structure and help children to develop more effective mental strategies.

Part of developing a feel for numbers is the ability to order numbers in a range of contexts and to understand infinity. Activities involving number lines can help children to develop a sense of the ordinality and continuity of our number system.

One reason children may experience difficulties with place value is because the naming of numbers doesn't mirror the place value system. Unfortunately, spoken and written English do not underline the patterns that are present in our counting system. Below one hundred number names are idiosyncratic and can be confusing to children especially as the second decade numbers are spoken in reverse order. For example, 13 is spoken as 'thirteen' and not as 'ten-three' (as it would in the Japanese counting system). This is why children often reverse the 'teens' numbers.

When you reach numbers above a hundred the visual and aural patterns become clear, so we should expose children to big numbers from as early as possible. Not only do pupils enjoy handling larger numbers but they are empowered by them, for example counting aloud, in hundreds, thousands or millions helps them to spot the patterns that exist in our number system and to make their own connections.

It is important that children understand the effect of multiplying and dividing by 10,100, etc. Learning a quick rule "When multiplying by 10, just add a nought" without understanding will cause problems later on, for example when multiplying decimals.

Many of the following activities can be done in the context of measures.

More than the 3 Billy Goats Gruff

AIM: To order objects by size and number.

ACTIVITY

Extend the story of 'The 3 Billy Goats Gruff' to include 10 goats using 10 children of different sizes as the goats. Give each one a numbered bib to wear and mark areas at the front of the class as the fields and the bridge. As you re-tell the story ask the children to respond to questions you ask them using their fingers.

QUESTIONS

Which goat is second in line?

Show me which goat is sixth in line?

Which goats are between the seventh and tenth goats?

How do you know?

If the third goat has gone across the bridge how many are on the other side now?

Which goat is before the tallest goat?

Which goat is behind the tallest goat?

Which goat is behind the second smallest?

Which goat will be the last to cross the bridge?

How many will have crossed then?

If the fourth goat has crossed over, who will be next?

VARIATIONS/EXTENSIONS

Ask the children to order themselves in terms of size and distribute the bibs among the others who then have to come out and find the right 'goat' to give their bib to. Get them to imagine being in a queue. Ask how many people there are, who's in front, who's behind, etc.

This links to the measures particularly regarding the language of length.

RESOURCES

large numerals 1-10 on bibs/cards

VOCABULARY

order

first, second, third, ...

behind

in front

last

before

in between

numerals

digits

number words

one to ten

biggest

smallest

medium

middle

sized

largest

tallest

shortest

taller

shorter

More or Less Towers

AIM: To order numbers of objects and understand more or less.

ACTIVITY

Give the children a set of cubes each. The teacher turns over two digit cards, chooses one herself and shows the other to the children. The children make a tower with the matching number of cubes and the teacher makes a tower to match her number. Compare their two towers and repeat for different numbers.

QUESTIONS

How can you make sure you've counted correctly?

Is your number smaller or larger than seven?

Who has got fewer cubes?

Have you got more or fewer than me?

How do you know?

How many more/fewer have you got?

How could you work it out?

What's the difference between the length of your tower and mine?

How many cubes longer is it?

Is your tower the same as the person next to you? If not, why not?

VARIATIONS/EXTENSIONS

Could be used as an activity with a focus group during the main part of the lesson.

Make a set of towers matching the numbers 1 to 9. Order these as a staircase and consider how many more or fewer each tower is compared to others.

RESOURCES

digit cards
cubes

VOCABULARY

more
less
fewer
bigger
smaller
longer
shorter
difference
how many?
same as

Hanging out the 'Washing'

AIM: Reading and ordering numbers; matching ordinal and cardinal numbers.

ACTIVITY

Hand the numeral cards and picture cards to different children. Ask the children with number one and number ten to come out and peg their numbers on the line. Ask the children holding the other numerals, out of sequence, to come up and peg up their cards. Repeat, with the children holding the picture cards.

QUESTIONS

Where do you think six should be? Why?

Which number will come before five? after?

What will go between three and five? How do you know?

How do you know that's the right place?

How many objects are on that card?

Which card has got one more/one less object on it?

How could we show zero?

VARIATIONS/EXTENSIONS

Give out old birthday/Christmas cards and ask the children what number they can see in the card and to write it on the back with a picture. Peg them on the line and then ask others to 'spot' what the number is. Once all have been worked out then they can order them.

This can be extended into the main part of the lesson as an independent activity by asking the children to choose a number and draw a picture to go with it. These can be used in future activities.

Use for different sections of the number line.

RESOURCES

string

pegs

numeral cards 1 to 10

pictures of objects

VOCABULARY

one, two, three, ..., ten

order

between

bigger

smaller

match

how many?

first

second

more

less

Higher/Lower

AIM: To know and use language of highest, lowest and order numbers.

ACTIVITY

Give each child 3 cards from a packs of 1-30 cards, and ask them to arrange in order, lowest to highest. Then ask the children to hold up their highest cards and compare. Repeat for lowest cards. Then call out a number and say 'lower'. Those with numbers lower than this, hold them up. Call out a different number and say 'higher'.

QUESTIONS

Show me your highest cards.

Who's got the highest of the high cards?

Who's got the lowest of the high cards?

Show me your lowest card.

Who's got the lowest low card?

Who's got the highest low card?

Can we read them out in order starting from the lowest to the highest low card?

How do you know you've got the lowest/highest card?

Is the highest low card, higher than the lowest high card?

How do you know?

VARIATIONS/EXTENSIONS

Deal out a set of digit cards to the children in a circle. The first child calls out their number and the second child holds up their card and shouts 'lower' or 'higher' depending on their number. Continue around the circle. Give a starting number and a rule, e.g. "12, higher". The first child holds up their card if its higher, (than lays it on the floor), so does the second child if their card is higher than that. Continue until there are no higher cards left. Then the rule becomes lower.

RESOURCES

set of cards numbered 1-30

VOCABULARY

high

low

higher

lower

highest

lowest

in between

order

What's the Biggest Number?

AIM: To develop awareness of infinity and name large numbers.

ACTIVITY

Ask the children to give you a big number. Then ask if they know a bigger number than this. Which is the biggest number they can say, read, think of? Write them on the board.

QUESTIONS

What does the number start with? How do you know?

What does the number end with? How do you know?

What is one more than that number?

How would you write it? How do you know?

Does anyone know a number in the hundreds? Thousands?

Can you give me an even bigger number than that? How much bigger is that?

Do you know what that number looks like?

What is the biggest number?

If you started counting in ones how far could you go? How long do you think it would take? Would you ever reach the biggest number?

What's 1 and 1?

What's 100 and 100?

What's 1000 and 1000?

Do you see a pattern?

How far can you go?

VARIATIONS/EXTENSIONS

Ask the children to collect different numbers from magazines, newspapers, etc. and make a display. Can they locate the smallest/largest numbers, and give numbers higher or smaller than this? Link to large numbers in their every day experience such as house numbers, the lottery, etc.

Links to 'Toy Story' where Buzzlightyear says, 'To infinity and beyond'.

RESOURCES

different collected numbers (e.g. from newspapers, magazines, signs, labels, etc).

VOCABULARY

bigger
biggest
pattern
hundreds
tens
thousands
millions
one more
one less
infinity

First in Line

AIM: Match ordinal and cardinal numbers.

ACTIVITY

Ask the children to get into lines of 6. Run through their order, so they know which number they are. Next, throw the dice. Children who match the number thrown, collect a counter/cube, eg if a 2 is thrown, each second child in a line collects a counter. Continue, say, until a number's come up 10 times. Ask the children then in each line, to order themselves so that the one with the most counters is in front.

QUESTIONS

Who's first in line?
Who's sixth in line?
If a 5's been thrown, which children will collect a counter?
How do you know?
If we had 10 children in a line what other numbers would we have to be able to throw to make it fair?
How do you know you're standing in the right place?
If you've got fewer cubes than Joshua, where will you stand, behind or in front?
Which number do you think will be thrown most often? Why?

VARIATIONS/EXTENSIONS

Use a set of digit cards 1-10, to generate the number and extend the lines to 10 children.
Use a die marked in 2's (i.e. with 2, 4, 6, 8, 10 and 12 marked on faces) and allocate an even number from 2 -12 to each child.

RESOURCES

large foam dice
cubes or counters

VOCABULARY

first, second, ...
number names
most
least
in front of
behind
next
fair
most often
likely

Make a Two Digit Number

AIM: To know what each digit in a two-digit number represents and partition into tens and units.

ACTIVITY

Give each pair of children a tens/unit card, nine 10ps, nine 1ps, nine rods/longs and nine unit cubes.

The teacher tells the class a two-digit number or writes one on the board.

One child makes the number using the coins, the other uses the base 10 equipment and the card. Each child checks their partner's total.

QUESTIONS

How many tens are there in 53?

Which digit in 69 is the units?

Which is bigger, five tens or forty units?

How many pennies make 10p?

How many units make 10?

If the number was 50, would you need any 1ps? Why?

How many units in 3 tens? How do you know?

What is the connection between how you make the number with cards, money and base 10 blocks?

VARIATIONS/EXTENSIONS

Use an abacus. Make a number, using apparatus, and ask the children to write the number. Extend to larger numbers.

RESOURCES

set of coins

base 10 blocks

(e.g. Dienes)

digit cards

VOCABULARY

place value

units

tens

coins

value

worth

the same as

how many?

pennies

Match Me

AIM: To read and write three digit numbers, partition into hundreds, tens and units.

ACTIVITY

Sit the children in a U-shape facing the teacher. Give each pair a set of arrow cards (see appendix 4), paper and pencil. Tell the children that you are going to make a three digit number using the dienes apparatus and that you want them to show you what the number is using the arrow cards and write it down. Choose a pair to read out the number written down and they then come to the front and make the next number. When the children have completed five numbers, ask them to order them.

QUESTIONS

How many units are there in this number?

How many tens? How many hundreds?

Which number is the biggest?

How do you know?

If you tried to make 306 would you use any tens? Why?

What number would you make with the cards 200, 50 and 6?

VARIATIONS/EXTENSIONS

Use dice to generate the three digits.

RESOURCES

base 10 blocks
(e.g. Dienes)
digit cards
arrow cards

VOCABULARY

hundreds
tens
units
order
place value

Matching Number Names to Numerals

AIM: To read numbers and number names.

ACTIVITY

Sit the children in a circle. Hold up and read aloud the number name cards and ask the children to read them aloud as a class. As certain number words are read out, ask the children in pairs to show the number on their fingers.

Next, hand out the cards, and also give out the set of digit cards 0 to 20. Ask the children to find their partner and sit by them.

QUESTIONS

Name me three numbers beginning with a 't'.

Name me two numbers beginning with an 'e'.

Give a number that comes after a number word beginning with an 'f'

Before one beginning with an 's'.

How do you know you are showing the correct number?

Which ones are easiest to remember? Why?

What could help us to remember?

What letter does 3 begin with? 30? 300? What do you notice? Can you link any other numbers in the same way?

VARIATIONS/EXTENSIONS

Read the number names silently and show the number on fingers.

Have number names and dots on one side, numerals on the other.

Have a set of cards showing ten, twenty, thirty, ..., one hundred.

RESOURCES

flash cards of number names

number cards 0-20

VOCABULARY

number names

zero, one, two, ...

digit

numeral

figure

match

beginning

after

Odd/even

AIM: To recognise odd and even numbers.

ACTIVITY

Give pairs of children a pile of multilink cubes. Call out a number between 0 and 10 and ask them to make it with a tower of cubes and then try to split it into 2 equal towers. For each number you call out write it on the board and ask the children to keep a record of which numbers can/can't be split into 2 equal towers. Write up 2 column headings and ask children to come up and write up their findings. Discuss results.

8 can be split

QUESTIONS

What do you notice about all the towers that you can split?

If a number doesn't divide equally into 2, what's left over?

What patterns can you find by looking at the numbers?

Can you predict whether or not there will be one cube left over before you split the tower?

How do you know whether a number's odd or even?

How can you make an odd number into an even number? An even number into an odd number?

Is the number 52 odd/even? How do you know? What about 104? 1004?

VARIATIONS/EXTENSIONS

Roll a die. In pairs, one child collects odd numbers, the other even numbers. In 10 throws who has collected the most? What about after 20 throws ?

Links to:

'Partner Counting', page 20

RESOURCES

multilink
paper
pencils

VOCABULARY

odd
even
equal
pattern
remainder
share
divide
half
one left over

Negative Numbers

AIM: To understand and use negative numbers.

ACTIVITY

Give each child (or pair) a calculator and a number below 20 to key in. Demonstrate how to use the constant function (-1 = = or - - 1 = = will usually work), to repeatedly subtract one. Tell them to continue past zero and write down the sequence. Discuss the numbers and place on a class number line.

QUESTIONS

What do you see in the display as you subtract 1 from zero?
Why do you think this happens?
Is negative 3 more or less than zero?
How do you know?
How could we get from a negative number to a positive number? Would we have to add or subtract?
Can you think of a place where you've seen negative numbers?
What do they mean?
Can you see a pattern in the numbers? What would come next if we continued to subtract one? How do you know? What do you think will happen if we keep subtracting 10 instead of 1? 2 instead of 1?

VARIATIONS/EXTENSIONS

In pairs one child keys in a single digit and their partner has to predict how many times they will have to press the '=' sign before the calculator gets to zero and then how many times to reach a given negative number. Can they see a connection and a quick way of predicting the number of presses needed?

Give a starting number, eg 30 and a finishing number, eg -20. In pairs with one calculator the children take turns to subtract a number from 1-9. The winner is the first to reach -20.

Link negative numbers to a thermometer scale and calculating changes in temperature.

Links to:
'Below Zero', page 44

RESOURCES
calculators

VOCABULARY
digit
negative numbers
positive numbers
constant function
subtract
add
pattern

'Air' Numbers

AIM: Begin to use and understand the language of place value and order numbers.

ACTIVITY

Ask children to close their eyes and imagine the number five hundred and sixty two, drawn in the air in front of them. Ask them which digit is on the left and which is on the right, and tell them to swap these two numbers. Share with a partner what the number says now. Imagine rearranging the digits to make the largest and smallest numbers.

QUESTIONS

What number did you get when you swapped the hundreds and units?

Where is the hundreds digit?

Where is the tens?

What digit is on the right?

What is it?

What's the largest/smallest number you can make? How do you know?

VARIATIONS/EXTENSIONS

Use larger numbers

RESOURCES

VOCABULARY

hundreds

tens

units

order

digits

largest

smallest

Ordering Numbers to 100

AIM: To read and order numbers, know what each digit represents.

ACTIVITY

With the children in a circle, hand out several cards to each child from a shuffled pack of 0-100 cards. First ask the children, in pairs, to order their cards. Then name a starting number and an end number and ask children to come out and place their cards in order. Repeat for different sections of the number line. For example, start number 35, end number 50. The children with those numbers lay them on the floor and then go round the circle with children placing the appropriate numbers in between 35 and 50 in turn.

QUESTIONS

How are you ordering your cards?

Which is the smallest/largest number? Show me! How do you know?

Who's got a number with 5 tens in it? 3 units?

Show me a number between 83 and 97.

Show me a number less than 49 but greater than 19.

Which numbers could go between 25 and 44?

How many numbers are there between 19 and 31? How could you check?

What number would come next after 100? After 200?

How could we order the cards differently?

What comes before zero?

How did you decide where to lay your card?

Does anyone think it should be moved? Why?

VARIATIONS/EXTENSIONS

Order the cards according to different criteria, eg those children with a 3 in the units column, come and place their cards in order. Look at the tens pattern. Use sets of cards higher than 100, less than zero, decimals.

RESOURCES

set of cards 0-100

VOCABULARY

compare

order

smallest

largest

number names one, two, three, ...

hundred

digit

unit

tens

less

greater than

between

Below Zero

AIM: Understand and use negative measurements in context.

ACTIVITY

Draw a thermometer on the board and mark the day's temperature, eg 18°C. Ask the children a range of questions, for example what the temperature would be if it dropped 20° overnight, or what it would be if it rose by 15°?

Ask the children in pairs to think of a question and write it down. Then work out the answer, write it on the other side and then swap with another pair. Run through some of the questions and ask children to explain their methods. Make a display of the questions.

QUESTIONS

If the temperature was 6°C and dropped overnight to ⁻15°C, by how many degrees had it fallen?

If it was 12°C and rose by 9°C, what would the temperature become?

If the temperature fell by 25°C and it was initially ⁻15°C, what would it be? How can you check?

What if the scale was in intervals of 5? If the level fell by four marks, what would it be?

Have you got a quick way of working out, when the temperature drops, where it will end up?

VARIATIONS/EXTENSIONS

Link to the depth of the sea, to going in a lift, and bank accounts.
Use different scales measured in intervals of 10 or 100.

Links to:

'Negative Numbers', page 41

RESOURCES

paper
pencils
thermometer (drawn)

VOCABULARY

negative numbers
temperature
rise
fall
thermometer

Two, Twenty,..........

AIM: To use and recognise pattern in number.

ACTIVITY

Start counting in twos with the children from zero. Write up part of the sequence on the board. Ask the children how you could use this to count in twenties. Show them how they can use their fingers to count in twenties if they get stuck.

Write up the pattern underneath the twos sequence. Discuss what is the same and what is different about the numbers and why.

Repeat but count in two hundreds, then two thousands. Discuss the patterns and link to addition, subtraction, multiplication and division

QUESTIONS

What is 2 add 6? 20 add 60? 200 add 600?

What is 80 subtract 20? How do you know?

How does knowing how to count in twos help you to count in higher numbers?

How does counting help you to calculate?

What do the zeros on the ends of the numbers tell you?

How many groups of two hundred make a thousand?

What patterns can you use?

How could knowing how to count in fives help you count in fifties?

VOCABULARY
pattern
tens
hundreds
thousands
counting
calculate
add
subtract
groups

Which is Biggest?

AIM: To read and write whole numbers and know what each digit represents, to use addition strategies.

ACTIVITY

Draw up or give out photocopies of the following grid:

□ □ □ + □

□ □ + □ □

□ □ + □ + □

□ + □ + □ + □

Write four digits on the board. Ask the children to make the largest total for each of the digit arrangements.

Repeat for a different set of digit cards, and share and discuss findings with the class.

QUESTIONS

Which is the most important digit? why?

What strategies are you using? How did you decide where to put the numbers?

How do you know that your total for an arrangement is the largest?

Are you working systematically?

How would you make the smallest total each time?

Is there more than one way to get the largest total in each case? Why?

VARIATIONS/EXTENSIONS

Use 5 digit cards and investigate how many different grid arrangements you could make.

Links to:

'Trigits', page 54

RESOURCES

blank grids

VOCABULARY

digits

place value

addition

total

More or Less Inequalities

AIM: To use and understand the inequality sign, compare numbers and know the position of a digit represents its value.

ACTIVITY

Give each child a sheet with inequality grids on it. (see overleaf)

For example: □ □ □ □ < □ □ □ □

□ □ □ > □ □ □

The teacher either selects a card from a set of 0-9 cards or throws a ten sided die. The children place the number on the grid aiming to make the statement true.

QUESTIONS

Is your statement true? How do you know?

What number do you have on the right?

Does anyone have a different number?

How did you decide where to put the numbers?

Do you think you will always get it right?

Which spaces are the most important? Why?

What strategies are you using?

VARIATIONS/EXTENSIONS

Use for larger numbers or decimals. This can be extended into the main part of the lesson as an independent activity. Children work in pairs and can either work collaboratively to make the statement true (or false!) or have one side each to complete in turn. Encourage them to extend it for themselves.

RESOURCES

sets of digit cards 0-9

'Inequality Grids' sheet

VOCABULARY

inequality

more

less

greater than

less than

place value

position

digit

thousands

hundreds

tens

units

Inequality Grids

Number Sequences

AIM: To recognise and extend number sequences

ACTIVITY

Sit children in a circle and deal out several cards to each child from a pack of 0-100 cards. From another pack place in the middle, sections of number sequences, eg:

35, 37, 39,	4, 11, 16, 22
42, 46, 50,	12, 15, 18

Go around the circle asking children to try to continue the sequences in both directions. When they can't go they have to take a card from a centre pile. Continue until someone has been able to place all their cards.

QUESTIONS

How do you know whether you can place your card or not?

What's the rule?

What are you counting on/back in?

Can you predict the first one in the sequence?, the tenth?

What else do you know about this sequence of numbers?

VARIATIONS/EXTENSIONS

Let the children make up the sequences in the middle of the circle.

Write 10 different sequences down on pieces of paper and pass around the circle for children to continue.

Organise the children into small groups who challenge each other to work out and continue their own sequences.

RESOURCES

sets of 0-100 cards

VOCABULARY

number sequence

patterns

predicting

equal steps

rule

Rectangular Numbers

AIM: To recognise prime numbers.

ACTIVITY

Draw 2 unlabelled columns on the board. Using the numbers 11 to 30, place all prime numbers in one column, and the rest in the other, eg:

11	13		12	14	15	16
17	19		18	20	21	22
23	29		24	25	26	27
			28	30		

In pairs ask children to choose one number from each column and to see if they can arrange the numbers as a rectangle either by drawing or using cubes or counters. Ask them to find as many different rectangular arrangements as possible.

Share and discuss findings on the board and describe what prime numbers and factors are. Prime numbers are only divisible by themselves and one. The number 15 is not prime but has 4 factors (1,3,5,15).

QUESTIONS

How are you organising your work?
How do you know if you've found them all?
How many cubes are in a row? Column?
Can you spot a pattern?
Why are some numbers harder to make rectangles with?
Can you predict how many rectangles you could find for the number 33? 143?
How do you know?

VARIATIONS/EXTENSIONS

This activity can be extended into the main part of the lesson.

RESOURCES

squared paper
cubes or counters

VOCABULARY

prime
factor
multiple
divisible by
rectangular numbers

1,10,100 More or Less

AIM: Read and write the numbers 1,10,100 more or less than a given number.

ACTIVITY

Write ten 3/4 digit numbers on the board. Ask children to choose one and write down the numbers 1 more and 1 less, and then share on the board. Repeat but ask them to write down and read out the numbers 10 more and 10 less, and then 100 more and 100 less. As the numbers are recorded on the board, ask other children to read them aloud and discuss in pairs what's happening.

QUESTIONS

Can you spot a pattern?

Which numbers are hardest to work out? Why?

When does the tens digit change to zero as we say the number ten more? Why?

If we say the number one more, and then follow with the number ten more, what happens to the number? What is this the same as?

What if we do ten more and one less? What is this the same as?

Could you work out the number twenty more, two hundred more, quickly? What do you notice?

VARIATIONS/EXTENSIONS

Sit children in a circle and at different points give out 10 pieces of paper with the same starting numbers on. All children have a pencil, and as the teacher calls out a function, eg 10 more/100 less, so the child with the paper writes the new number down and passes to the next child. Stop at various intervals and ask children to read the numbers out to check if they're the same.

In team groups children take turns to say a number 1/10/100 more or less than a number on the board. The others have to work out what the original number was.

Extend to adding and subtracting 1000 or 10000.

Links to:

'Counting in Tens', page 21

'Counting Steps for Y3/Y4', page 22

RESOURCES

paper
pencils

VOCABULARY

unit
ten
hundred
thousand
more
less
add
subtract

What is it's Value?

AIM: To read and write numbers, know what each digit represents and partition into thousands, hundreds, tens and units.

ACTIVITY

Give pairs of children a small version of the place value chart and a set of arrow cards. Have a large version of the place value chart on the board.

Write a range of 3, 4 and 5 digit numbers on the board. Ask a child to choose one and read it out whilst another indicates the relative values of the digits on the class chart. In pairs the children overlay their arrow cards to show the number. Record the partitioning on the board.
For example, 5304 = 5000 + 300 + 4 Repeat for other numbers.

QUESTIONS

What happens as you go across the chart?
What is the pattern as you go down or up through a column?
Why do you think we read numbers from left to right?
What does 'zero' do in a number?
Which numbers are hardest to write in figures?
Could you read a 6 figure number?
What if we continue moving upwards through a column but off the chart? What would be the value of the digit then?
What is 6906 made of?

VARIATIONS/EXTENSIONS

This can be extended into the main part of the lesson as an independent activity. With younger children use it to practise counting and to reinforce the pattern between counting in ones, hundreds and thousands. In pairs children choose their own numbers and take turns using their place value charts and arrow cards.
Use the chart to multiply or divide by 10, 100, 1000, etc.

Team Games - In teams of 4, children roll 3/4 dice to generate numbers. Each team writes their number on the board, constructs it on the place value chart, makes it with the arrow cards and writes down the component parts
eg. 5432 = 5000 + 30 + 2. If they're correct, they win a point.

Links to:

'How Close Can You Get?' page 185
'Blanks', page 57

RESOURCES

place value chart
(see appendix 4)
arrow cards
(see appendix 4)

VOCABULARY

place value
partition
thousand
hundred
ten
unit
figure
column
digit

In Between

AIM: To understand that between any two numbers there is an infinite number of fractional and decimal numbers.

ACTIVITY

Draw a blank number line on the board and mark a number at each end. Ask the children for two numbers in between and mark them on. Then ask for two numbers in between these two. Repeat until there are no whole numbers left.

For example:-

Give me two numbers between 60 and 85, between 61 and 75,...

QUESTIONS

What's happening to the two numbers each time?

How far can we go before there are no whole numbers left?

Although we have run out of whole numbers what numbers do you know that are between 71 and 72?

If we magnified the section of the number line between 71 and 72 how many more numbers do you think we could mark in?

What could we call the intervals on the line between 71 and 72?

Can you always find two numbers between two numbers?

VARIATIONS/EXTENSIONS

Link to measurement and estimation, for example ask the children to name something that is a metre long, 0.1m, 0.01m, etc. Mark two numbers on a line and ask the children to estimate where the half-way point is. Then half-way between the new point and the first number, e.g 10 and 30.

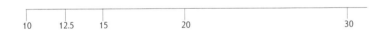

RESOURCES

VOCABULARY

between

number line

fraction

decimal

infinity

Trigits

AIM: To order and read and write 2 & 3 digit numbers, to work systematically.

ACTIVITY

Tell the story of the 'trigits', a race of tiny people who only knew the digits 1,2,3, and who cycled everywhere. Unfortunately, their bikes kept being stolen, but because no-one had a record of the bikes it was hard to trace them. The trigit police came up with an idea, whereby each bike could have a registration number.

Ask the children to work out what two digit numbers they could make where the digits weren't repeated, and order them. Then ask what numbers they would make if digits could be repeated. Ask them to keep a record of all their numbers. As children find others they can write them on the board.

QUESTIONS

What 2 digit numbers can you make?

Which numbers have 3 tens? 3 units?

Which is the largest/smallest?

How do you know if you've found them all?

Can you read your numbers out in order?

Have you found a pattern?

Can you work systematically?

What if the numbers were 4, 5 and 6?

VARIATIONS/EXTENSIONS

This can be extended into the main part of the lesson as an independent activity.

Repeat for three digit numbers.

Can they predict how many numbers they could make if they used four digits, five digits?,....... What if they could repeat them?

Link to real-life contexts such as telephone numbers, car registration plates, 'PIN' numbers etc.

Links to:

'Which is biggest?' page 46

RESOURCES

digit cards

HTU base boards

paper

pencils

VOCABULARY

hundreds

tens

units

digits

place value

order

largest

smallest

Guess the Number in my Pocket

AIM: Recognise and use properties of numbers.

ACTIVITY

Tell the children you've got a secret number in your pocket, and that they are to try to guess it within 10 questions. Draw a number line in intervals of 10 on the board, marking the beginning and end of the range, e.g. 0 to 100 or use a hundred square. Ask the children to write down questions to ask, thinking about what they know about numbers that could help find the hidden number quickly, for example, 'Is it bigger than 50?' Choose children to ask a question, give your answer and if appropriate invite the child out to mark on the number line numbers that they now know can't be the secret number. The child that guesses correctly takes over and writes down their secret number. If it isn't guessed within 10 questions, they reveal the number.

QUESTIONS

What numbers do you think it's between?

How does asking if it's odd or even help?

If it's in the 5 times table what digits could it end in?

What do you think is the maximum number of questions you should need to ask?

If you know it's odd, can it be in the 2 times table?

What are good questions to ask? Why?

What are bad questions? Why?

VARIATIONS/EXTENSIONS

Write statements on the board about a hidden number. Children have to work out what the number is.

Children choose their own secret number for a friend.

Increase/decrease the size of the number, include negative numbers and decimals.

Choose a rule e.g. numbers that are square numbers or prime numbers or multiples of 4, etc. Draw a chart on the board and ask the children to give you a number. Write the number in the appropriate column. The children have to try and find your rule.

Links to:

'What's That Number', page 88

'Number Talk', page 99

'What's That Number 2', page 101

'Number Detectives', page 132

RESOURCES

paper

pencil

VOCABULARY

odd

even

pattern

greater than

less

between

times table

properties

Multiplying & Dividing by 10 and 100

AIM: To multiply and divide by 10 and 100.

ACTIVITY

Give each pair a calculator and remind them how to programme the calculate to multiply by ten.

(For most calculators either $\boxed{\text{x}}\ \boxed{\text{x}}$ 10 = = or $\boxed{\text{x}}$ 10 = = will do this)

Ask the children to key in a single digit and use the constant function to multiply by 10. Whilst one child presses $\boxed{=}$ key on the calculator, their partner writes down the sequence of numbers. Repeat but multiply two digit numbers by ten. Also try numbers with one decimal place.

QUESTIONS

What patterns are you noticing?

What does each extra zero represent?

How far could you go on your calculator?

Can you come up with a rule for multiplying by ten? Does it work for all numbers?

What if you multiply by 10 and then divide by 10?

Can you predict what multiplying by 100 would do? Dividing by 10?

VARIATIONS/EXTENSIONS

Multiply by 100 or divide by 10 or 100.

Multiply or divide by 0.1 or 0.01

Children put a number into their calculator and ask their partner to predict what the number would be if they multiplied by 100 or divided by 100, etc. If they guess correctly they score a point.

RESOURCES

calculators

VOCABULARY

multiply

divide

rule

generalise

Blanks

AIM: To partition numbers into thousands, hundreds, tens and units.

ACTIVITY

Write up 10 numbers on the board, partition into their component parts but omit some of the numbers.

Eg $56321 = \square + 6000 + \square + 20 + 1$

$89035 = 80000 + \square + \square + 30 + 5$

$4963 = 4000 + \square + 60 + \square$

Ask children to choose 3 numbers and decide what is missing.
Ask them then to come out and fill in the missing numbers on the board, explain their methods and show the number, using the place value chart (see appendix 4).

QUESTIONS

How do you know whether you're right or not?
What's the quickest way to check?

VARIATIONS/EXTENSIONS

In pairs children give each other questions to work out.
Give pairs of children a calculator each. They key in a 4 digit number and have to try to get their calculator to display zero by subtracting from one place value column at a time. For example, the display reads: 4025 To get it to zero, first 4000, then 20, then 5 has to be subtracted.

Links to:

'What's It's Value?' page 52

RESOURCES

place value chart
(see appendix 4)

VOCABULARY

partition
place value
thousands
hundreds
tens
units

Three in a Line

AIM: To read, write and order decimals to two decimal places.

ACTIVITY

Put a 0 to 10 number line where everyone can see it. Draw □•□□ on the board and get the children to do the same on paper. You are going to take numbers from a pack of 0-9 digit cards. The first number is the teacher's to write in one of her empty boxes, the second is for children to write in one of theirs. Repeat in turn until the numbers are complete.

Write your numbers on the number line and choose one of the children's to write on in a different colour. For example

> Teachers ②•⑨⑥
>
> Children ③•⑤⑧ ⎫
>   ⑧•③⑤ ⎬ Select one
>   ⑤•⑧③ ⎭

Repeat to make new numbers. The object is to try and get three of your numbers in a line without one of your opponent's being in the way.

For example

QUESTIONS

What different numbers could you have made?

Which is largest/smallest?

Which is closest to the number you already have on the line?

How are you deciding where to put your digits?

Which digit card is the most important? Why?

When do the numbers become difficult to order?

What strategies do you use in order to try and win?

What happens to the value of the digit as you move it one place to the right?

VARIATIONS/EXTENSIONS

This can be extended into the main part of the lesson as an independent activity for children to play in pairs

Use dice to generate the random numbers

Use place value cards to support less able

RESOURCES

digit cards
number lines
paper

VOCABULARY

tenths
hundredths
units
decimal point
number line
estimation
closest

Decimals & Fractions

AIM: Order a set of fractions and decimals, know decimal equivalents of tenths and hundredths.

ACTIVITY

Hand out a fraction/decimal card to each child. In turn ask children come out and arrange themselves in order. Equivalent fractions stand or kneel behind each other. Then they can take turns placing their cards correctly on the number line:

eg | 0.25 | | 0.5 | | 0.75 | | 0.95 |

| $\frac{1}{4}$ | | $\frac{5}{10}$ | | $\frac{75}{100}$ | | $\frac{95}{100}$ |

QUESTIONS

How are you working out where to stand?

Are you nearer to zero or 1?

Where will 0.5 stand? 0.25?

If the number line is only marked in tenths how many intervals will we need to mark to show hundredths?

How can you work out which decimals and fractions are equivalent?

What if we magnified a hundredth section of the number line and divided it into ten?

What would each interval be worth?

How could we write a thousandth as a decimal?

What fractions are more difficult to order? 'Why?'

VARIATIONS/EXTENSIONS

Children have their own number lines on which to order sets of fractions and decimals.

Use to show the links between percentages, fractions and decimals e.g.

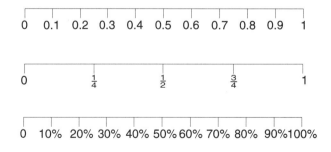

RESOURCES

set of decimal cards to 1 or 2 decimal places
set of fractions mainly in tenths and hundredths but include quarters, thirds, fifths, etc:
blue tac
class blank number line

VOCABULARY

fractions
decimals
tenths
hundredths
quarters, fifths, etc
equivalent
intervals

Quick Factors

AIM: Know and recall factors of numbers.

ACTIVITY

Hand out a set of digit cards 0-10 to each child. Write up some 3,4,5 and 6 figure numbers on the board. Point to each number in turn and ask the children to hold up a card which is a factor of the number. Give 5 seconds for them to respond and then ask children to explain how they worked it out, and discuss the properties of the numbers.

QUESTIONS

How do you know it's a factor?

What's special about the last digit?

What's a quick way of predicting if a number is divisible by 3?

If a number's divisible by 2, will it also be divisible by 4?

How can you check?

Which factors are the easiest to spot? Why?

If 5 is a factor of a number, what do we call that number?

How do you know if a number is prime or not?

How could you work out the total number of factors?

VARIATIONS/EXTENSIONS

Ask the children to devise sets of question and answer cards on factors that groups can play.

Investigate a test of divisibility by 7, 11 or 13.

RESOURCES

class set of 0-10 cards

VOCABULARY

factors

prime

even

odd

multiple

properties

divisible

Estimating and Rounding

There are two important aspects to estimating, the need for experience and the understanding that what is required is a range. If a child is asked if an elephant would fit through the classroom door, it will depend on their experience of an elephant. If their only experience is a cuddly elephant they have at home then they will say 'Yes'. Therefore, it is important that part of estimating is giving the children experiences which they can use to help revise their estimates.

Children often misunderstand what is being asked of them when estimating and think that what is required is an exact answer. In fact, estimating is about a range; it often helps to consider the statement 'I think there are at least __ but no more than ___'. Making estimates more accurate involves reducing the range. It also involves rounding; accuracy of estimating could be to the nearest hundred, million, etc. For example "I think that, to the nearest thousand, there were 89 000 people at Wembley for the cup final."

We have included a number of activities that involve looking at sheets of dots. This links to counting work and in particular subitization, i.e. seeing numbers of objects without counting them. We have included activities relating to subitization in this section and related photocopiable sheets appear in appendix 4.

Many of the activities in this section can be done in the context of different measures.

Pile of Cubes

AIM: Give a sensible estimate of up to 100 objects, understand the vocabulary of estimation.

ACTIVITY

Make a pile of cubes (or any other object).

Make statements about the pile and ask the children whether they agree or disagree with them, starting from the obvious.

For example:-

There is only one cube in the pile.

There are more than 1 million cubes in the pile.

The pile has fewer than ten cubes in it.

The pile has more than ten cubes in it.

The pile has at least twenty cubes in it.

The pile has no more than eighty cubes in it.

The pile has fifty-five cubes in it.

Sort the statements into those that everyone agrees with, those that everyone disagrees with and those that there is a split on. Use this to develop the idea of a range, that the number of cubes is somewhere between two numbers.

QUESTIONS

Which statements were easiest to decide you agreed with? Why?

Which were easiest to decide you disagreed with? Why?

Which statements did you have to think about for longer? Why?

Are there any of the statements that you are not sure whether you agree or disagree with? Why do you think that is?

Would it help you to see what a pile of ten cubes looks like?

How does that help?

Why are there some statements we don't all agree on and some we do?

VARIATIONS/EXTENSIONS

Let the children come up with statements for a pile of objects - in pairs make a statement they think everyone **will** agree with or everyone **will** disagree with. Then move onto making statements they think people **might** disagree about.

Vary the objects in the pile; compare two piles and discuss which statements are easier for one pile than the other and why.

RESOURCES

cubes or other objects

statements on cards

VOCABULARY

estimate

estimation

agree

disagree

too many

too few

more than

less than

might

at least

fewer

no more than

About Half

AIM: Recognise and estimate one half of objects and sets of objects

ACTIVITY

Collect a number of items - piece of paper, length of string, ball of plasticine, cup of water, pot of acorns, etc. Discuss the two important things about halving - you end up with two pieces or sets and they are the same size. Look at the paper - where would you cut to cut it in half? Can you approximate, without folding. Either let a number of children have a go or do it in pairs.

Discuss how you are going to check if the paper has been cut in half, or how close to halves you have. Check.

QUESTIONS

How can we check if the two pieces are halves?

How could we have made sure we cut it in half?

Is there more than one way we could have done it?

How are we going to check the estimated halves of the other objects?

What are you doing when you estimate halfway along the length of string?

Do you do something different with the plasticine? Why?

VARIATIONS/EXTENSIONS

Extend into the main part of the lesson by giving the children a variety of items to halve.

RESOURCES

variety of objects and sets of objects to halve

paper

scissors

VOCABULARY

half

estimate

check

length

weigh

same

match

count

On the Mat

AIM: Give a sensible estimate of up to 100 objects.

ACTIVITY

Unfold or unroll a mat/scarf/piece of fabric and lay it on the floor. Ask the children how many children could stand on the mat together? What's the fewest they think will fit and the most?

Try it out - how are they going to decide if any more can fit on? Having stood on the mat discuss how many could sit on it.

QUESTIONS

How many children do you think will fit on the mat?
Will it make a difference if they hold onto each other?
Will every bit of mat be stood on?
What about if the children sat down - would you fit more or fewer? Why?
How could we fit on the most children?
How could we cover the mat with the fewest children?
What about a different mat - do you think more or fewer children will fit on it? Why?
How many cats do you think would fit on the same mat? Teddy bears? Elephants? Why?

VARIATIONS/EXTENSIONS

Use a variety of mats, etc. of different shapes and sizes and discuss arranging the children on standing, sitting, lying, etc.
Cover with sheets of paper; this links to the idea of area.

RESOURCES

mats or pieces of fabric

VOCABULARY

most
more
fewest
fewer
fit
cover
area

Early Blank Lines

AIM: Make and justify estimates.

ACTIVITY

Use two blank number lines (strips of card) the same length and mark the ends 0 and 10.

Ask a child to put the marker where they think 6 would be on one of the lines and another to do the same on the other line. Compare the two lines by placing one below the other. They won't be exactly the same but does that mean they can both be good estimates?

QUESTIONS

How did you decide where to put your marker?

Why are the markers in different places?

Can they both be good estimates?

Does anyone think 6 is in a different place?

Could this marker be showing 6?

Why not?

VARIATIONS/EXTENSIONS

Move the marker along the line from zero and ask them to put up their hand when they think it has reached 6. Make a mark when the first child puts up their hand and another when the last child puts up their hand. This is the range for the class.

Links to:

'Blank Lines', page 71

RESOURCES

strips of card markers

VOCABULARY

estimate

approximately

close to

near to

How Many Dots?

AIM: Recognise the number of objects in a group without having to count in ones.

ACTIVITY

Use cards with a small number of dots on (less than 7 to start with - see appendix 4) arranged in different ways. Flash these at the children so that they see the dots but don't have long enough to count them in ones. Ask them to show you how many dots there were using either fingers or number cards.

QUESTIONS

How many dots did you see?

What did they look like to you? How were they arranged?

Did anyone see them differently?

Did anyone see them as more than one group?

Can you describe the groups?

VARIATIONS/EXTENSIONS

Rather than dots on card held up, use an overhead projector and either dots on transparencies or counters placed on the projector.

Cards with more dots on can be used for estimating.

Links to:

'How Many Dots Now?', page 69

RESOURCES

cards with dots

(see appendix 4)

number cards

VOCABULARY

how many?

arranged

differently

Round the Line

AIM: Make and justify estimates and round to the nearest ten or hundred.

ACTIVITY

Use a number line marked in tens. Ask children to estimate positions of different numbers, marking them with an arrow, and explain why they have placed the arrow where they have.

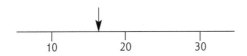

For example the arrow above is placed to show approximately where 18 is.

QUESTIONS

Where will 25 be?

How do you know it is there?

Can anyone give another reason why it is there?

What about 32?

Which decade number is it nearest to? Does anyone think it should be moved? Why?

If that is where 32 is, where is 42? How did you decide?

Can anyone give a different reason why it should be there?

What about 58? Does knowing approximately where 32 is help us find approximately where 58 is? How?

VARIATIONS/EXTENSIONS

Number line going up in hundreds.

Number line showing only 0 and 10 but extending beyond 10.

Links to page

'Round the Line Again', page 72

RESOURCES

number line

arrows

VOCABULARY

estimate

approximately

nearest

decade

Rounding Bingo

AIM: Round any two-digit number to the nearest ten and any three-digit number to the nearest hundred.

ACTIVITY

Each child draws for themselves a two by two grid and writes a decade number of their choice in each of the squares. Two digit numbers are then read out. The children can cross out a number on their grid if the number read out rounds to that decade number.

For example, if I draw and fill in my grid as below:-

10	40
70	30

When the number 39 is called out I can cross off 40 because 39 is 40 to the nearest 10

When all the numbers are crossed out call 'bingo' or another agreed word.

QUESTIONS

What number could have been called so that you could cross off 50?
How many numbers do I need to read out so that all the decade numbers can be crossed off?
What if I call out 45? 65?

VARIATIONS/EXTENSIONS

Fill the grid with hundreds and round three-digit numbers to the nearest hundred.
Use the rule that the numbers should be rounded up or down rather than to the nearest.

Links to:

'Rounding Bingo 2', page 74

paper
pencils
two digit numbers

VOCABULARY

rounding up
rounding down
nearest ten
nearest hundred
decade

How Many Dots Now?

AIM: Use the vocabulary of estimation and estimate up to 500 objects.

ACTIVITY

Use cards with dots on, some random, some arranged in patterns.
(see appendix 4 for samples). Show the cards to the children and ask
them to estimate the number of dots on the card, using the sentence 'I
think there are at least __ dots but no more than __ dots'.

QUESTIONS

How did you estimate - did anything help you?

How big is your range?

Would it help if you saw ten spots the same size? How?

Would you now like to revise your estimate?

Which cards did you find easier to estimate for? Why?

Which cards did you have the smallest range for? Why?

How could we calculate the number of dots on the card?

VARIATIONS/EXTENSIONS

Rather than dots on card held up, use an overhead projector and have
dots on transparencies.

Links to page

'How Many Dots?' page 66

RESOURCES

cards with dots
(see appendix 4)

VOCABULARY

how many?

arranged

estimate

revise

range

This Container Holds ....

AIM: Make and justify estimates up to 500, organise counting of a large number of objects so that checking is easy.

ACTIVITY

This can be broken down into parts and used over more than one session, or extended into the main teaching activity.

Group the children in small groups and give each group a container with a lid on it, filled with beads, cubes, dice, playing cards, buttons, cotton reels, straws, match sticks, etc. (a different object for each container).

Each group has a short time (1 minute) to estimate how many are in the container, completing the sentence:

'We think there are at least ___ and no more than___'

Swap the containers and repeat until every group has estimated for each container.

Discuss how the estimates could be improved - would taking the lid off and counting the top layer help? Would counting out ten of the objects out help? Revise estimates accordingly.

Each group counts the contents of one container - discuss first ways of doing this so that the number can be checked and people don't lose count. Compare totals with the estimates.

QUESTIONS

What is the least/most you think the container will hold? Why?

How could we improve our estimates? Why does this help?

How are you going to count the objects? Does anyone have a different way? Why is that a good way of counting them?

How will you check how many there are?

Which objects/containers did you find easier/more difficult to estimate? Why?

VARIATIONS/EXTENSIONS

Use the same object in a variety of different containers - focus here will be on the comparative capacity of the containers.

Use the same container with different objects - focus here will be on the comparative volume of the objects.

Links to:

'How many Minutes Have You Lived?', page 202

RESOURCES

containers with lids various objects e.g. beads, cubes, straws, etc.

VOCABULARY

least
most
estimation
range
capacity
volume
compare

Blank Lines

AIM: Make and justify estimates and round to the nearest ten or hundred.

ACTIVITY

Give each child a strip of card and an elastic band or a paper clip. The band/paper clip is for marking positions on the card.

Imagine the strip of card is a number line running from 0 to 100. Put your marker approximately where 60 would be. Compare it with a neighbour. They won't be exactly the same but they should be close to each other. Discuss positions that are acceptable and ones that are not and why not.

QUESTIONS

How did you decide where to put your marker?

What other numbers might your marker be on?

Turn your number line around - what number are you on now?

If the line was from 0 to 10, what number would you be on? From 0 to 1000? From 300 to 400?

Move your marker to 23. How accurate do you think you are?

Do you think you are accurate to the nearest ten? What range would that mean your markers falls within?

Could this marker be showing 23?

Why not?

VARIATIONS/EXTENSIONS

Place the number lines next to each other on the floor to compare the markers - use a numbered piece of card to find the range of the estimations. How big is the range?

Use rulers turned over and mark numbers using it as a 0 to 30 line (or metre sticks for 0 to 100). Turn over to find out how accurate you were.

Links to page

'Blank Lines 2', page 73

'Early Blank Lines', page 65

RESOURCES

strips of card

rubber bands or paper clips

VOCABULARY

estimate

approximately

accurate

position

nearest ten

range

Round the Line Again

AIM: Make and justify estimates and round to the nearest ten, hundred or thousand and numbers with up to two decimal places to the nearest tenth or whole number.

ACTIVITY

Use a number line marked in ones. Ask children to estimate positions of different numbers, marking them with an arrow, and explain why they have placed the arrow where they have.

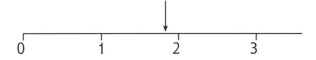

For example the arrow above is placed to show approximately where 1.8 is.

QUESTIONS

Where will 2.5 be?

How do you know it is there?

Can anyone give another reason why it is there?

What about 3.2?

Which whole number is it nearest to?

Does anyone think it should be moved? Why?

If that is where 3.2 is where is 4.2? How did you decide?

Did anyone do something different?

What about 5.8?

Does knowing approximately where 3.2 is help us find approximately where 5.8 is? How?

Which whole number is it nearest to ?

VARIATIONS/EXTENSIONS

Number line going up in tenths, hundreds or thousands.

Using number line showing only two numbers e.g. 1 and 2, 320 and 330, etc. but extending beyond these numbers in both directions..

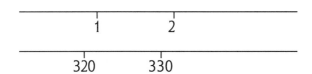

Links to:

'Round the Line', page 67

RESOURCES

number line

arrows

VOCABULARY

estimate

approximately

nearest

tenth

rounding

THINK MATHS!

Blank Lines 2

AIM: Make and justify estimates and round to the nearest tenth or hundredth.

ACTIVITY

Give each child a strip of card and an elastic band or a paper clip. The band/paper clip is for marking positions on the card.

Imagine the strip of card is a number line running from 0 to 1. Put your marker approximately where 0.6 would be. Compare it with a neighbour. They should be close to each other, though not necessarily in exactly the same position. Discuss positions that are acceptable and ones that are not and why not.

QUESTIONS

How did you decide where to put your marker?

What other numbers might your marker be on?

Turn your number line around - what number are you on now?

If the line was from 0 to 0.1, what number would you be on? From 0 to 10 or 0 to 100? From 3 to 4?

What if your number line was twice as long - what number would it be on now?

Move your marker to 2.3. How accurate do you think you are? Do you think you are accurate to the nearest whole number? What range would that mean your markers falls within?

Could this marker be showing 2.3?

Why not?

VARIATIONS/EXTENSIONS

Place the number lines next to each other on the floor to compare the markers - use a numbered piece of card to find the range of the estimations. How big is the range?

Links to:

'Blank Lines', page 71

RESOURCES

strips of card

rubber bands or paper clips

VOCABULARY

estimate

approximately

accurate

nearest tenth

nearest whole number

Rounding Bingo 2

AIM: Round any three or four digit number to the nearest ten, hundred or thousand and numbers with two decimal places to the nearest tenth or whole number.

ACTIVITY

Each child draws for themselves a two by two grid and writes numbers of their choice, between one and ten, in each of the squares. Numbers with one or two decimal places are then read out. The children can cross out a number on their grid if the number read out rounds to that whole number.

For example, if I draw and fill in my grid as below:-

5	3
2	8

When the number 2.85 is called out I can cross off 3 because 2.85 is 3 to the nearest whole number.

When all the numbers are crossed out call 'bingo' or another agreed word.

QUESTIONS

What number could have been called so that you could cross off 3?
How many numbers do I need to read out so that all the whole numbers can be crossed off?
What if I call out 4.5?

VARIATIONS/EXTENSIONS

Fill the grid with hundreds or thousands and read out three or four digit numbers and round to the nearest hundred or thousand.
Fill the grid with numbers between 4 and 5 with one decimal place and read out numbers with two decimal places that need to be rounded to nearest tenth.
Use the rule that numbers are to be rounded up or rounded down rather than the nearest.

Links to:

'Rounding Bingo', page 68

RESOURCES

paper
pencils
number cards

VOCABULARY

rounding up
rounding down
nearest tenth
nearest hundred
nearest thousand
tenths
decimal places

How Many?

AIM: Make and justify estimates of large numbers.

ACTIVITY

Ask the children to imagine how many people you could seat comfortably in the school hall (or books you could pack in a large box you have, or chairs you could stack in the classroom, etc.). Come up with a range from the whole class:-

'We think that at least ___ and no more than ____people could sit comfortably in the hall'

Discuss how this estimate could be made more accurate, without actually filling the hall with people.

Look at the range and ask what number falls in the middle of it. If this was the estimate, how accurate do they think it is. Will it be correct to the nearest ten? hundred? thousand?

QUESTIONS

What is the fewest and the most you think will fit?

How could we make the range smaller/our estimate more accurate?

What is the median of our range?

How accurate is that likely to be?

Links to:

'How Many Minutes Have You Lived?', page 202

RESOURCES

VOCABULARY

least

more

range

median

estimate

estimation

Jar of Mung Beans

AIM: Make and justify estimates of large numbers, use the vocabulary of estimation.

ACTIVITY

Fill a glass jar with mung beans or similar (make the beans quite small ones) and ask the children to estimate the number of beans in the jar, completing the sentence:-

"I think there are at least ___ beans and no more than ___ in the jar"

Give ten children some beans from the jar and ask them to count out ten each and put these in a dish. Discuss how many beans will be in the dish and return any extra ones to the jar. Show the children what 100 mung beans look like - can they use this image they now have of 100 mung beans to revise their estimate?

QUESTIONS

How big is the range of your estimate?
How could you make your range smaller?
Do you want to change your estimate? How?
How can you use the 100 mung beans to help you estimate better?
Have you made your range smaller or bigger? Why?
How could we find out approximately how many there are without counting them all?

VARIATIONS/EXTENSIONS

Tell the children the number of beans it takes to fill one container. How many do they think it would take to fill other given containers? Can they use the information they have been given to estimate?
Links to volume and capacity.

Links to:

'Grains of Rice', page 203

beans in a jar
dish

VOCABULARY

range
least
most
estimate
estimation
approximately
volume
capacity

Calculation Approximation

AIM: Approximate results of calculations by rounding.

ACTIVITY

Give the children a calculation, such as 375 ÷ 79 to approximate by rounding. Discuss the different ways this could be done and the different answers you get. This may include 360 ÷ 90, 400 ÷ 80, 375 ÷ 75. Discuss which of these answers will be closest and whether the answer is going to be nearer to 4 or 5.

QUESTIONS

Does rounding the numbers to the nearest ten make an approximation easy? The nearest hundred?

What approximations could we use? What answer do they give? How close do you think this is?

Which approximation will be closest? Why?

Which approximation will be furthest away? Why?

VARIATIONS/EXTENSIONS

Ask questions about the answer without working it out - for example if the calculation is 16 **x** 23, as well as approximating by rounding, ask:-

What can you tell me about the answer to the calculation?

Will it be odd or even? How do you know?

How many digits will the answer be? How do you know?

What do you think will be the first digit? the last digit? Why?

Can you give me a number that won't be the answer? How do you know?

Follow it up with the children writing scenarios that fit each approximation as an independent activity

Links to:

'It went like this', page 113

RESOURCES

VOCABULARY

approximation
rounding
nearest ten
nearest hundred
odd
even
digits

Calculating

When working on aspects of calculating, there are a number of considerations to keep in mind:-

* Lots of opportunities for explaining and discussing different strategies need to be provided. All methods should be valued but there should also be a discussion of the appropriateness and effectiveness of the different methods used. Methods should be modelled (on the board if appropriate) for the class to see, either by the child or the teacher.

* Different strategies need to be taught, building on what the children already know. For instance, children need to be able to add on ten in one step if they are to be taught the strategy for adding on nine that uses "add on ten and subtract one". If they are still adding on tens by counting in ones, they will not be ready for this strategy. All children will not absorb all strategies but by exposing them to a variety, and teaching the strategies by linking them to things the children already know, you will encourage flexibility. (For a list of strategies see appendix 2).

* It is important to link the inverse operations from the start. Addition and subtraction should be seen as two sides of the same coin, not two totally separate operations. As far as is possible, links should be made in all lessons that focus on addition and subtraction. The same can be said for multiplication and division.

* Checking should also be a feature of calculating, from the beginning. Children need to be taught different ways of checking (see appendix 2).

* Subtraction needs to be understood as 'difference', 'take away' and "how many to add to make, division as 'sharing', 'repeated subtraction' and "how many to multiply by to make"?

* Contexts are important. Children need to meet numbers in a variety of situations and make decisions about the mathematics that is needed to find a solution. Many of the activities could be set in the context of measures and data-handling.

If children find it hard to focus on the strategy and are only interested in the answer, try giving them some calculations with the answers and ask them how they would have gone about solving the problem.

Many of the ideas and activities that follow are suitable for different age groups and abilities if the numbers used are varied, e.g. one, two or three digit whole numbers, fractions, decimals, negatives numbers, etc. We have tried to indicate this as appropriate. Many of the activities can be done in the context of different measures.

When the Doorbell Rang .....

AIM: Begin to solve problems involving division.

ACTIVITY

Retell the story of 'The Doorbell Rang' by Pat Hutchins, modelling the biscuit sharing with the children sitting around a picnic cloth. Give twelve children a number, 1 to 12. As you tell the story, the children come out in order.

For example:-

First Dermot and Geeta sat down to have some biscuits.

There were twelve. How many will they have each? How can we share them between these 2 plates?

Then two more children arrived just as they were about to eat them. How could we share the twelve biscuits now? etc.

Ask the children to draw pictures to show how the biscuits are shared each time. Model some recording for them.

QUESTIONS

How can we share them out so that it is fair?

If Kostas has 5 and Renu has 7 is that fair?

How many biscuits will 4 children get each if we give them an equal share?

If three children have 3 biscuits each, how many is that altogether?

Are there enough biscuits for 6 people to have 3 each?

Could we share 12 biscuits equally between 5 people? Would any be left over? How do you know? Can you show them?

VARIATIONS/EXTENSIONS

Set up other scenarios referring to both division and multiplication when asking questions

RESOURCES

'The Doorbell Rang' by Pat Hutchins
picnic cloth
12 plates
pack of biscuits

VOCABULARY

share
equal
fair
number
digit

What Do I Do?

AIM: Solve word problems involving numbers in real-life contexts, choose and use appropriate operations to solve a problem.

ACTIVITY

Read a word problem to the class and discuss the mathematics involved. Make sure a range of problems are used, varying where the unknown quantity appears e.g.

$$3 + 6 = ?$$
$$? + 6 = 9$$
$$3 + ? = 9$$

To increase the difficulty use combinations of operations, larger numbers and problems that contain too much information so that the children must select the relevant numbers as well as the appropriate operation(s). Examples for all years appear on the following pages.

QUESTIONS

How are you making sense of the problem?
Which numbers do you need to use? Why?
What does the answer mean?
How do you know which operation(s) you need to use?
How do you know if your answer is right?
Can you think of another way of solving the problem?
What could you use to help you?

VARIATIONS/EXTENSIONS

Write up a calculation like 24 - 13 = 11 and ask the children to devise story problems that may have given rise to the calculation.

Links to:

'It went Like this', page 113

RESOURCES

word problems
(see following pages)

VOCABULARY

how many?
altogether
difference
compare
change
total
cost
sum
plus
add
minus
subtract
more
less
fewer

Miscellaneous Word Problems

Fabrizio had 3 apples. Naomi gave Fabrizio 5 more apples. How many apples does Fabrizio have now?

Carl has 3 balloons. His sister Whitney has 5 balloons. How many more balloons does Whitney have than Carl?

Jung had 5 pencils. How many more pencils does she have to put with them so she has 7 pencils altogether?

Tom has 8 smarties. Erin has 6 smarties. How many smarties fewer does Erin have than Tom?

Omar went to get 2 more cookies. Now he has 5 cookies. How many cookies did Omar have in the beginning?

Lee has 6 pet fish. Carol has 2 more fish than Lee. How many fish does Carla have?

Shoila has 8 marbles. Jakob has 5 marbles. How many more marbles does Jakob have to get to have the same as Shoila?

The postwoman delivered 9 letters to our house on Monday. On Tuesday she delivered three less. How many letters did she deliver on Tuesday?

Amman had 8 marbles. Then he gave 5 marbles to Preet. How many marbles does Amman have now?

Jin-ming has 14 flowers. Eight of them are red and rest are yellow. How many yellow flowers does Jin-Ming have?

Winston had 11 sweets. He lost some. Now he has 4 sweets. How many sweets did Winston lose?

Niki has 12 pet mice. Seven of them are white and the others are brown. How many brown mice does she have?

Deirdre had a box of chocolates. She ate 6 of them and still had 10 left. How many did she have to start with?

There are eleven boys and twelve girls in a class. How many children are there in the class?

Polly has 7 teddies. Salman has 3 teddies. How many teddies would Polly need to lose to have as many as Salman?

There are 26 children on a coach. If 15 of them are boys, how many are girls?

Lin is twenty years old. Her sister Lauren is eight years old. What is the difference between their ages?

Camara is eight years old. His sister is twelve. How much older is his sister than him? Megan is eleven years old. Her brother is seven. How much younger is her brother than her?

In one shop a toffee bar costs 23 pence. In another, the same toffee bar costs 18 pence. What's the difference in their price?

Miscellaneous Word Problems

There are 9 boys on a soccer team. Two more join the team. Now there is the same number of boys as girls on the team. How many girls are on the team?

The difference between my favourite number and my friend's is 8. If my favourite number is 12, what could my friend's favourite number be?

Peter buys 4 lollies at 6 pence each. How much does he spend?

Anna spends 30 pence on buying chews. If each chew costs 3p, how many chews does she buy?

There are 5 cars in a car park. If each car has four wheels, how many wheels do the cars have altogether?

Three cats have 4 kittens each. How many kittens are born in total?

Athos helps his mum sort out the sock drawer. He counts 25 socks. How many pairs of socks can he make?

Jung helps his dad make some buns. He fills 3 rows of a cake tray. If 4 buns are in each row, how many buns does he make altogether?

There is the same number of boys as girls in a class. If there are 30 children in the class, how many boys are there?

Kate scored a double eight and a double two on the dartboard. What was her total score?

Max had 3 friends. Each friend had 2 pets. If Max had 3 pets, how many pets did they have in total?

Jack plants 4 rows of carrots. If he puts 9 carrots in each row, how many carrots does he plant?

Shyamm has a bag of sweets. If he has 20 altogether and shares them equally between himself and 3 friends, how many do they each get?

26 people arrive at a restaurant for a party. If each table can seat 4 people, how many tables will be needed?

230 children are going on a trip. Each bus can seat 50 children. How many buses will be needed?

Five friends are going out for lunch. They each order a coke and a cheeseburger. The bill comes to £10. How much does each friend pay if they share the bill?

Etsuko has 12 marbles. She gives her brother a quarter of them. How many does she give him?

Francoise helps her dad collect the hens' eggs and put them into boxes. If each box can hold 6 eggs and there are 32 eggs, how many boxes will she need?

Chews cost 5p each and lollies 8p each. If I buy 2 chews and a lolly, how much will I spend?

Miscellaneous Word Problems

The price of my comic is 35p and the local paper is 30p. If I buy both, what will the total cost be?

Mariko has £1.15 saved in her piggy bank. Her brother has £1.50 saved. How much more does Mariko have to save to have the same as her brother?

I spend 25p on a packet of crisps and 16p on an apple. How much do I spend altogether?

I buy an orange for 20p and a banana for 17p. I give the shopkeeper a 50 pence piece. What coins might I get as change?

I get £1.50 a week pocket money and my friend gets 50p less than me. How much does my friend get?

Nelson has 15p less than Lynton. If Lynton has 70p, how much does Nelson have?

I have a £1 coin to spend. I buy a can of coke for 45p. How much change will I get?

Ann has 40p. Her mum gives her 2 twenty pence coins. How much does she now have?

I have 35 pence in silver coins in my pocket. What's the fewest number of coins I could have?

Liz had fifty pence in change in her pocket. Later when she counts it again she finds she has lost some. If she only has 34p now, how much has she lost?

In my pocket I have a 10 pence coin, two 5 pence coins, a 2 pence coin and a 1 pence coin. How much money do I have?

Roberto is 152cm tall. If his sister is 29cm taller, how tall is his sister?

An ice cream costs 75p. I have a fifty pence coin, a ten pence coin and two 5 pence coins. Do I have enough? How do you know?

Tom jumps a distance of 1 metre, 35 centimetres. If Greg jumps 19 centimetres more, how far has he jumped?

My sister and I like toffees. Each toffee costs 2p. If I buy 6 and my sister buys 8, how much more money than me does she spend?

Ben is 19 years old. If his mum is 25 years older than him, how old is his mum?

Alex paid for a book with 3 pound coins. If he gets twenty five pence change, how much was the book?

It takes three 50g weights and one 20g weight to balance the sugar. How much sugar is there?

If a jam doughnut costs 18p and a ring doughnut costs 21p and I spend 60p, what doughnuts did I buy?

Lottie leaves the house at half past five. Her dad tells her that she must be home by nine o' clock. How much time is she allowed out for?

Miscellaneous Word Problems

My train is running an hour and a half late. If it is due now is 6.10pm, at what time should the train arrive?

There are 6 weeks before my birthday and 3 weeks and 2 days before my sister's. How many days are there between my birthday and my sister's?

My favourite number is 32. If the difference between my number and my friend's lucky number is 19, what might my friend's number be?

A school has 196 boys and 135 girls. How many pupils does it have in total?

Paul plants 175 flowers. If 70 of them are red, 39 are blue and the rest are yellow, how many yellow flowers does he plant?

Kate has 134 marbles in her collection. If her brother wins another 18 he will have the same as her. How many does he have?

A carpenter needs to cut 36cm off a length of wood which is 2.5 metres long, in order to have the right length. How long is the length he needs?

A book costs £3.99 and a comic costs 40p. If Tim buys both and pays for them with a £5 note, how much change will he get?

The thermometer reads 25°C today. In January the lowest temperature recorded was ¯7°C. What is the difference in temperature between today's and January's lowest?

I have £3.25 in change in my purse. If all the coins are silver, what coins could I have?

There are 205 animals on a farm. 95 are cows, 17 are horses and the rest are sheep. How many sheep are there?

Kazuo has £10 to spend. He buys 3 books at £1.99 each. How much change will he get?

Naiko has £2 to spend. He wants to buy as many chocolate bars as he can. If each bar costs 24p, how many can he buy?

John helps his father buy some cookies. If they fill $4\frac{1}{2}$ trays and each tray can hold 18 cookies, how many cookies do they make?

There are 26 cars in a car park and 3 motorbikes. If each car has 4 wheels, how many wheels are there altogether?

A farmer has 300 metres of fencing to go around the outside of his field. If the field is square, how much fencing will be needed for one edge?

A farmer has 25 chickens and 45 cows. How many legs do the animals have altogether?

A school is planning a concert. They put 240 chairs in 8 rows. How many chairs are there in one row?

If I have six 50p pieces and three 5p coins in my pocket, how much money do I have?

Miscellaneous Word Problems

If my book is 375 pages long and I'm able to read, on average, 24 pages a night, how many nights will it take me to finish the book?

In our school there are 3 times as many boys as girls. If there are 364 children in the school and 18 adults, how many children are girls?

Meena has £1000 saved. She spends a fifth of it on a new suit and another £300 on a holiday. How much does she have left?

Mamadou is counting the hours until his dad comes home from sea. There are still $8\frac{1}{2}$ days to go. How many hours has Mamadou left to wait?

392 children are going on holiday. If each coach can take 56 children, how many coaches will be needed?

Nimala throws three darts and scores a double 9, a double 18 and a treble. If her score is 101, which treble did she throw?

Jodie's dad weighs 104kg and her mum weighs 60kg. If Jodie weighs a quarter of their combined weight, what does she weigh?

Ichiro bought an ice cream and 2 packets of crisps for £1.50. Annetta bought 2 ice creams and 2 packets of crisps for £2.40. How much does a packet of crisps cost?

Alex buys 2 packets of crisps and an ice cream for £1.40. Rae buys 5 packets of crisps and an ice cream for £2.30. How much is a packet of crisps?

4,400 people attend a Lighthouse Family concert at a ticket price of £18 each and programmes cost £5. If it costs the organisers £30,000 to stage the concert, how much profit do they make?

Our lounge measures 6 metres by $4\frac{1}{2}$ metres. How big is the area we need to carpet?

Paula has some coins. She has twice as many 50p pieces as 20p coins and three times as many 10p coins as 5p coins. If the total value of her coins comes to £10, how many of each type of coin does she have?

Millie, Martin and Mohammed took a holiday job picking strawberries. Every time Millie filled 8 punnets Martin had filled 10 and Mohammed 5. How many punnets will Martin have filled when Millie has filled 328 punnets?

The combined weight of 3 body builders is 339kg. If the heaviest is 120kg and another is $\frac{19}{20}$ of his weight, what is the weight of the third body builder?

For a concert, they arrange 325 chairs in 13 rows. Due to popular demand they take an extra 20% bookings and have to increase the seating by the same amount. How many chairs will there be in each row now, if the number of rows stays the same?

A baby is three and a half days old. Her twin is 302,040 seconds old. Which baby was born first and how many minutes older is she?

Miscellaneous Word Problems

Every day a machine makes 200,000 paper clips which are packed into boxes. If a full box holds 120 paper clips, how many full boxes can be made from 200,000 paper clips?

A man ran the half marathon in fifty-six minutes. If the race was 21000 metres, how many metres did he run on average per second?

An expensive suit is reduced in a sale by 15% to £850. What was the original price of the suit?

A 750g box of shreddies contains an average of 16 servings. How many grammes of shreddies are there in one serving? If a 750g box lasts me only 10 servings on average, how many more grammes of shreddies am I having per serving?

A customer had a restaurant meal at a specially reduced rate of 25% for eating early. The restaurant makes a service charge of 10% on all meals. The waiter made out the bill by first working out the service charge on the meal and then a 25% reduction. The customer argued that too much was being charged and the waiter should have reduced the cost of the meal first. Who was right? The original cost of the meal was £12.60.

There are 155 children having lunch. 126 have a cheeseburger and 67 have chicken burgers. Everyone has either one or both. How many children have both?

There are people and horses in a field. If you count 11 heads and 36 legs, how many people and how many horses are in the field?

What's that Number?

AIM: Count on or back in tens and ones; explain methods and reasoning about numbers.

ACTIVITY

Use a large hundred square and either turn one number over or cover one number. Tell the children to think of six reasons for knowing which number is hidden.

1	2	3	4	5	6	7	8	9	10
11	12	13	14	15	16	17	18	19	20
21	22	23	24	25	26	27	28	29	30
31	32	33	34	35	36	37	38	39	40
41	42	43	44	■	46	47	48	49	50
51	52	53	54	55	56	57	58	59	60
61	62	63	64	65	66	67	68	69	70
71	72	73	74	75	76	77	78	79	80
81	82	83	84	85	86	87	88	89	90
91	92	93	94	95	96	97	98	99	100

For example, if the number is 45 the children might say 'I know it's 45 because:-

    It comes between 44 and 46
    It is ten bigger than 35
    It is ten smaller than 55
    It is one less than 46
    It is the next odd number after 43
    It is two more than 43', etc.

QUESTIONS

What can you always say about the number above or below?
What can you always say about the number to the left or right?
Can you say which number it is twenty more than? Thirty less than? How?

Links to:

'Guess the number in my pocket', page 55
'Add and Adjust', page 106
'What's that number 2?' page 101

RESOURCES
hundred square

VOCABULARY
between
bigger
smaller
more
less
odd
even
add
subtract
left
right
above
below

Hidden Numbers

AIM: Know by heart pairs of numbers with a total of ten.

ACTIVITY

Using a pot and ten cubes, count the cubes into the pot so that everyone is sure there are ten in there. Then tip the pot over so that some cubes can be seen and some are hidden under the pot. This may work best on an overhead projector. Model recording the situations as addition and subtraction sentences using appropriate symbols.

QUESTIONS

How many cubes can you see?

How many cubes are hidden?

How do you know how many are hidden?

Can anyone give me an addition sentence to go with this?

Can anyone give me a subtraction sentence to go with

VARIATIONS/EXTENSIONS

Instead of using a pot and cubes use cards with a picture on each side with spots that total ten. Show the children one side and ask 'How many spots can I see?'

Links to:

'Ladybird Spots', page 176

RESOURCES

pot

cubes or counters

overhead projector

VOCABULARY

how many?

total

addition

subtraction

Line Jumps

AIM: Understand addition and subtraction and the relationship between addition and subtraction; investigate a general statement about familiar numbers.

ACTIVITY

Have a large number line, or number tiles, on the floor from zero to 10. Ask a child to stand on zero and jump forwards five. Then jump forwards another three. Model the movements by recording them as number sentences on the board.

QUESTIONS

Where do you think Michaela will land? Why?

How many will she have to jump to get back to zero? How do you know?

If she jumped twenty forwards, how many would she have to jump to get back to zero?

What about if she jumped a hundred forwards, how many to get back to zero?

When someone jumps forward and then jumps forward again, how do you know where they will land?

Do you have to count every step? Why?

Can you work out where they will end up without counting? How?

What happens if we jump forwards zero? Backwards zero?

What happens if the number we jump backwards is greater than the number we jumped forwards?

Where do we land if we start at three and jump on four? What about starting at four and jumping on three? What do you notice?

Does this always happen?

If you jump on four, how many more will you need to jump on to get to ten? How do you know?

VARIATIONS/EXTENSIONS

Children do their own recordings of the jumps.

Children give instructions, for example two jumps to get to 7.

Links to:

'Ladybird Spots', page 176

RESOURCES

number line or number tiles

VOCABULARY

zero, one, two, three, ...

forwards

backwards

how many more?

count

greater

Starting Big

AIM: Develop mental calculation strategy for addition of putting the larger number first

ACTIVITY

Before children can use this strategy they have to be clear about the commutative aspect of addition, i.e. that 4 + 5 = 5 + 4.

To explore this have two pots and some number cards. Choose two numbers, one for each pot, and count the matching number of cubes into each pot. Look at the numbers and ask does it matter which pot you count first if you are going to count them all? If some of the children need convincing let them count them and then swap the pots round and let them count them again.

Then use bigger numbers and no cubes to help them generalise. For example if 40 + 1 = 41 then what is 1 + 40? (Hold up the pots to represent the two numbers each time, reinforcing that you are adding together the same numbers each time). What about 100 + 1 and 1 + 100?

Write up some additions such as:-

$$7 + 4$$
$$3 + 22$$
$$5 + 14$$
$$23 + 4$$

Ask the children to work these out by putting one number in their head and counting on the other number. Then ask the children to explain what happened when they did each one and model it on a number line. For example:-

3 + 22

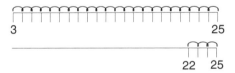

QUESTIONS

Which ways was quicker?
Why is it quicker to start from the largest number?
When you count on, how do you remember where you are?
Can you count in steps bigger than one? Is this quicker?
Which numbers is this useful for?

VARIATIONS/EXTENSIONS

Add single digit numbers to three digit numbers

Links to:

'So that means', page 100

RESOURCES

number line

VOCABULARY

count on
add
addition
largest number
same as

Halving and Doubling Sticks
AIM: Know that doubling and halving are related.

ACTIVITY

Sit children in a circle. Give each pair a card from 1 to 10 and either 20 multilink cubes or beads and a string. Call out 'Double it' and the children have to quickly double their number and show the double with their beads or multilink. Repeat with 'halve it'. Discuss what they notice. Swap cards and try different numbers.

QUESTIONS

What is doubling the same as?
How do you know if you've doubled your number correctly?
How can you check?
What do you notice if you double a number and then halve it? Why is this?
What if you halve a number first and then double it?
Which numbers are hard to halve? Why?
What do you have to imagine when you halve an odd number?
What do you notice about the numbers that are doubles?
Which double facts do you know off by heart?

VARIATIONS/EXTENSIONS

Extend the numbers.
Play as a game with children competing in groups to work out the doubles/halves in the shortest time. Some can have apparatus, others do it in their head.

Links to:

'Pair of Hands', page 94
'Dotty Doubles', page 102

RESOURCES

cards from 1-10
cubes or beads

VOCABULARY

halve
double
odd
even
remainder
half

More or Less Moves

AIM: Understand more or less; add and subtract 1 and 10 to any two-digit number.

ACTIVITY

Sit children facing a large hundred square. Choose a number. Ask the children to say the number one more/less, ten more/less. Point out the patterns in direction. Repeat but with the children giving the starting numbers.

QUESTIONS

What happens to the numbers as we move vertically upwards one square?

What if we move two squares to the left? How many more or less is this number?

Which digit changes when we move down/up the square?

Which digit changes when we move left or right? Is it always the same? Where is it different? Why?

What number is one more than 69?

How do you know?

What number is two less than 50?

What is 19 and 10 more? 28 and 3 less?

What is 15 add 10? 25 subtract 10?

What do you notice?

VARIATIONS/EXTENSIONS

Give each pair a hundred square and use counters to mark the new numbers.

Hand out a number card to each child. In pairs ask them to write down their numbers and the numbers one less/more, ten less/more. Children then pass their cards on. Discuss the patterns in the numbers.

Links to:

'Add and adjust', page 106

RESOURCES

hundred square

VOCABULARY

add
subtract
digit
tens
units
more
less
patterns
vertical
horizontal

Pairs of Hands

AIM: Begin to understand the language of multiplication.

ACTIVITY

Sit the children in a circle. Tell them that they're going to do some counting in twos with their hands. Start them off, by putting your hands in the air one at a time and saying 'one' silently and 'two' loudly. Continue round the circle. When all hands are in the air ask how many pairs there are. Repeat for different numbers of children.

QUESTIONS

Which numbers do we say silently? Loudly?

What do you know about these numbers?

How many pairs of hands will be up when we get to the number 12?

How did you work it out?

Do you need to count every hand?

What's a quicker way?

If 7 pairs of hands are in the air how many hands is that?

If there are 21 hands in the air, how many pairs can we make?

Three pairs is six hands, if we doubled this number of hands, how many pairs would we have? How did you work it out?

VARIATIONS/EXTENSIONS

Repeat using feet and count back in twos as well as forwards. Show how you can use fingers to represent twos.

Use hands and feet to introduce multiples of 4.

Links to:

'Halving and Doubling Sticks', page 92

'Body Multiples', page 109

RESOURCES

VOCABULARY

counting in twos

two, four, six, ...

how many?

sets of

pairs

groups of

odd

even

How Much?

AIM: Recognise all coins and find totals.

ACTIVITY

Have a range of cards with coins on.

Show the children the card, briefly, and ask how much the coins are worth.

Use cards with a collection of single coins, for example a 5p, a 10p and a 50p, cards with collections of one type of coin for example three 10ps and cards with collections of two or more types of coins, for example two 5ps and three 20ps.

QUESTIONS

How did you work it out?

Which coin(s) did you start with? Why?

Did anyone start with a different coin? Why?

Can you see a quick way of finding the total?

Can you show how you did it on the board?

What other coins could we use to make the same total?

VARIATIONS/EXTENSIONS

Tell the children different amounts that you have in your piggy bank and ask them to volunteer different sets of coins that it could contain.

Links to:

'Spending Money', page 97

RESOURCES

cards with pictures of coins

coins

VOCABULARY

money

coin

pence

pound

price

cost

Countdown

AIM: Know by heart addition and subtraction facts for all numbers to 20.

ACTIVITY

Choose one child to countdown from ten. Each time they say a number either the child or the teacher points at another child who must say the partner number that adds to it to make ten.

Ten	Zero
Nine	One
Eight	Two
etc.	

QUESTIONS

What do you notice about the numbers?

Why is this happening?

What would happen if we started at a different number?

VARIATIONS/EXTENSIONS

Start at twenty and ask for the partner number to make twenty, or any number below twenty.

Rather than work on bonds for ten and twenty, get the children to add or subtract a constant number, for example:-

Countdown and add five

Teacher	Response
"Ten"	"Fifteen "
"Nine"	"Fourteen"
"Eight"	"Thirteen"
etc	

Randomly choose numbers rather than counting up or down.

Links to:

'Grid Totals', page 98

'Clapping Numbers', page 115

'Ladybird Spots', page 176

RESOURCES

VOCABULARY

add

partner

total

number fact

number bond

Spending Money

AIM: Find totals, give change and work out how to pay.

ACTIVITY

Have a number of items with price labels. Make the prices suitable to the children - less than 10p, prices under a pound or prices including pounds. Ask a variety of questions that focus on different ways of paying, change when paying too much and totals when buying more than one item.

QUESTIONS

What coins could you use to give the exact money to pay for this item?

How do you know?

Could you use different coins?

How many pennies would you have to pay if it cost 12p? 32p? 99p?

If I paid £1 how much change would I get?

How did you work it out?

Did anyone work it out in a different way?

Which way is best for these numbers?

How many lollipops could I buy if I have 50p? How did you work it out?

Would I have any money left?

VARIATIONS/EXTENSIONS

Use a number line to model giving change by adding on.

Links to:

'How Much?' page 95

RESOURCES

priced items

coins

number line

VOCABULARY

money

coin

pence

pennies

pound

price

cost

buy

sell

pay

change

how much?

Grid Totals

AIM: Know by heart addition and subtraction facts.

ACTIVITY

Each child draws a small two by two grid and puts a single digit number, of their choosing, into each box.

6	3
2	8

The teacher picks a number card and calls it out. If the child has a number that, added to the number called out, makes ten they can cross it off.

For example, if the teacher calls out 'four' the six on the grid above could be crossed off as 4 + 6 = 10.

When a child has crossed off all their numbers they can call 'Bingo' or another agreed word.

VARIATIONS/EXTENSIONS

This can be varied for any age group. Instead of single-digit numbers put in two-digit numbers and they are looking for the number called out to add to their number to make a multiple of ten.

Alternatively, write in numbers less than one with one decimal place, for example 0.6, 0.8, 0.2 and 0.5 and then call out similar numbers, with the children looking for pairs that total 1. Vary this with any number with one decimal place, looking for pairs that add together to make a whole number, or numbers with two decimal places with hundredths called out, this time looking for totals with only one decimal place.

Links to:

'Countdown', page 96
'Grid Totals 2', page 114
'Clapping Numbers, page 115

paper
pencils
a set of number cards

VOCABULARY

single digit
two digit
total
multiple
tenths
hundredths

THINK MATHS!

Number Talk

AIM: Use and understand the vocabulary of number, use tests of divisibility.

ACTIVITY

Give each child a set of digit cards. Ask them to choose one card and then ask a question about their number, for example:- 'Is your number odd?'

Then ask all the children who answer yes to 'show me'. The questions depend on the age of the children.

You could ask the children to make a two or three digit number rather than a single digit number and ask questions in the same way. After a one or two questions let them change their chosen number.

QUESTIONS

Is your number smaller/bigger than 4?

Is it odd/even?

Is it a prime number?

Is it the square root of 25?

Is it a multiple of 3?

Is it divisible by 2?

Is it a factor of 24?

Is it 30 rounded to the nearest 10?

Discuss which numbers fit and which don't and why.

VARIATIONS/EXTENSIONS

Ask the children to choose a card from their set of digit cards. The teacher writes a number on the board and asks the children to show their number if it is a factor of this number.

e.g. teacher write 234 on the board

child shows '3' because 3 is a factor of 234

Links to:

'Guess The Number in my Pocket', page 55

'Number Card Pairs', page 139

RESOURCES

digit cards

VOCABULARY

odd

even

prime

square

square root

multiple

divisible

factor

rounded

So that Means

AIM: Understand and use the relationship between addition and subtraction.

ACTIVITY

Have two small towers of cubes, one bigger than the other. Tell the children that you are not going to actually count the number of cubes in each tower but instead pretend how many there are. Ask them some additions that you know they will know, for example:-

If this tower is 10 and this one is 5 how many do I have altogether? (Indicate which tower you are referring to each time and bring them together at the end of the question) So we can write that as 10 + 5 = 15.

Explore this for a few examples, modelling the number sentence in each case and allowing the children to volunteer some numbers they can add together.
Then ask 'Can we use these to help us find some subtractions?'
Use one of the examples:-

If 10 and 5 made 15, what happens if I have the 15 then remove the 5? What do I have left? So 15 - 5 = 10
If 20 and 30 made 50, so I have 50, what am I left with if I take away the 20? What about if I took the 30 instead?
So 50 - 20 = 30 and 50 - 30 = 20.

Keep exploring but sticking with numbers the children are confident in adding. Let them use bigger numbers that they are happy with:-

If 100 and 50 make 150, what am I left with if I subtract the 50 from 150?

Keep using the two towers as physical representations of the numbers to force awareness of the link between addition and subtraction.

QUESTIONS

Can you give me an addition you know and then tell me a subtraction that goes with it?
If I tell you that 97 + 64 = 161 what else can you tell me about those numbers? Can you give me a subtraction to go with it?

VARIATIONS/EXTENSIONS

Use two sticks of wood of different lengths rather than towers and cubes. Relate the questions to length.

Links to:

'Starting Big', page 91

RESOURCES

cubes
sticks of wood

VOCABULARY

make
made
total
add
subtract
take away
together

What's that Number 2?

AIM: Count on or back in ones and tens; explain methods and reasoning about numbers.

ACTIVITY

Use a large hundred square and turn over or cover all the numbers. Invite a child to tell you a number they are going to turn over/uncover, or ask for someone to turn over/uncover a given number. Repeat with other numbers.

QUESTIONS

Is that number in the top half or the bottom half? How do you know?

Is it near the end of a line or near the middle? Why?

How did you find your number?

Did you use any of the numbers we can already see to help you?

Now we can see 36, does it help us find other numbers quickly? Which numbers? Why?

Which card is a good one to turn over first ? Why?

VARIATIONS/EXTENSIONS

Use the computer program 'Monty' from the 'SlimWam II' disk (see appendix 5)

Links to:

'Guess the Number in my Pocket', page 55

'What's that Number?', page 88

'Number Detectives', page 132

RESOURCES

hundred square

VOCABULARY

between

more

less

add

subtract

left

right

above

below

middle

Dotty Doubles

AIM: To develop mental imagery and use double facts to calculate near doubles.

ACTIVITY

Hold up a series of flash cards with dots (from 4 to 20) arranged in doubles or doubles plus one. Give the children 3 seconds to look at the card and then ask them how many dots there were. Share and discuss how they see the dots and model the children's explanations on the board.

For example:-

I know it's 13 because I saw double 6 and 1 more.

QUESTIONS

How can you work out the totals without counting all the dots?

Which patterns do you see vertically? horizontally?

Which double facts do you know off by heart? How?

How does knowing your double facts help you work out other numbers?

Are there other ways the dots could be arranged to make the numbers easier to see?

Eleven is double 5 add 1. What other double is near to it and how would you use it?

VARIATIONS/EXTENSIONS

Use to focus on odd and even numbers. Encourage the children to arrange numbers on peg boards and to visualise larger numbers in dot form.

Investigate arranging in two rows, three rows etc. and look for number patterns.

Links to:

'Halving & Doubling Sticks', page 92

'Doubling Patterns', page 130

'More Doubles', page 179

RESOURCES

dotty cards
(see opposite)

VOCABULARY

near doubles
patterns
double facts

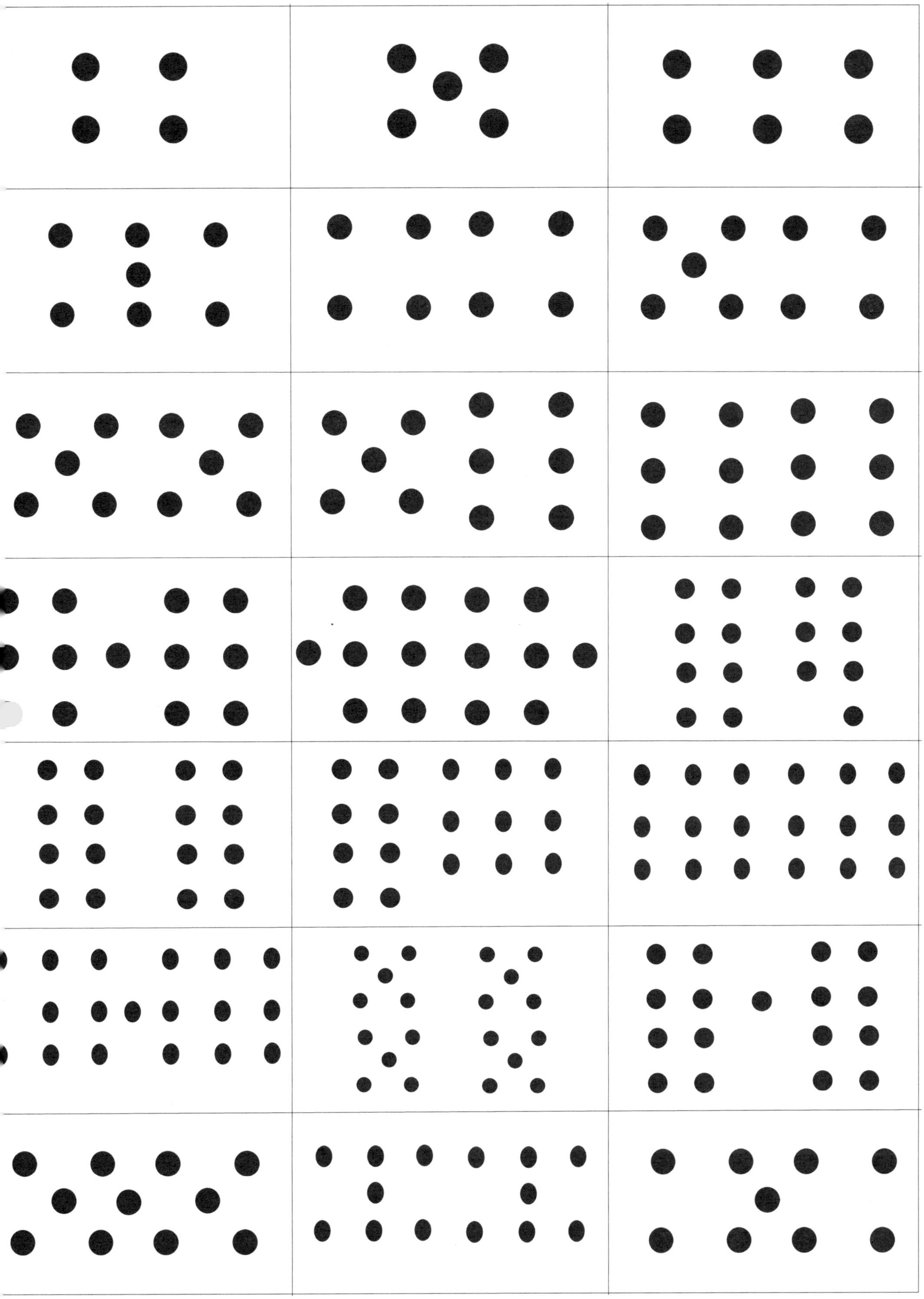

Sharing People

AIM: To understand the idea of a remainder. Recognise division as sharing equally.

ACTIVITY

Organise children in a 'U' shape facing 3 empty tables. Ask 13 children to see if they can arrange themselves so that there's the same number at each table. Encourage the others to predict whether or not it can be done. Record on the board the division and discuss what it means.

   13 ÷ 3 = 4 reminder 1

Illustrate the repeated subtraction of 3 from 13 on a number line

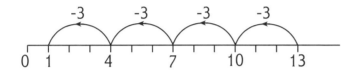

QUESTIONS

Why can some numbers be divided equally and not others?

What's special about these numbers?

Can 11 be shared out into 3 equal groups?

How do you know?

What do you think will be the remainder if 15 people tried to divide themselves equally between the 3 tables?

What do 3 groups of 3 make?

What about 6 groups of 3?

What does this tell us about the numbers 9 and 18 then?

Can you predict whether 30 people could be shared into 3 equal groups? 60? What about 300? Can you explain how you know?

VARIATIONS/EXTENSIONS

Extend to investigating whether numbers are divisible by 4, 5, 6, 7, etc and identifying factors

RESOURCES

number lines

VOCABULARY

division

share

equal group

remainder

repeated

subtraction

factors

Totalling Up

AIM: Recognise different values of coins, use knowledge of 2, 5 and 10 times tables in solving problems involving money.

ACTIVITY

Hand out containers containing different amounts of money in 10p, 5p, 2p and 1p coins. Say it's money collected from refreshment sales at a school disco and needs counting. In small groups ask them to count each amount, deciding which way would be best. Deliberately give different assortments of coins to different groups.

eg give one group lots of bronze coins, give another lots of 10ps.

Ask each group to sort the coins out and total up each amount separately before finding the overall amount, keeping a record as they go. Ask them to think about quick ways of adding it up. Model their methods on the board.

QUESTIONS

What did you use to help you count the money?

Why did some groups take longer than others?

What makes the counting easier?

How did you keep track?

Did anyone put their coins in groups? Why?

What strategies did you use?

What facts did you know that helped you?

Did you spot any patterns whilst totalling up the money?

Why do you think we have different coins?

Did you check your results? How?

Can you explain/show me how you calculated the total amount?

VARIATIONS/EXTENSIONS

This can be extended into the main part of the lesson as an independent activity.

Play a money game with 2 dice; one standard 1-6 die and the other with fares marked as follows - 2p, 2p, 5p, 5p, 10, 10p. Children take turns throwing the dice, finding the product and collecting that amount of money, e.g. if you roll at '3' and a '5p', collect 3 lots of 5p i.e. collect 15p. The first to £1.00 wins.

This can be extended to calculating multiples of 20p and 50p.

Investigate equivalents, e.g. How many 2p's make 50p?.

RESOURCES

containers

collections of 10p, 5p, 2p and 1p coins.

VOCABULARY

total

amount

money

multiplication

addition

pound

penny

ten pence

Add and Adjust

AIM: Add or subtract 9, 19, 29, ... or 11, 21, 31, ... by adding/subtracting 10, 20, 30, ... and adjusting by 1.

ACTIVITY

Each child or pair of children needs a hundred square and two counters. They should be familiar with the layout of a hundred square and know that moving from left to right adds in ones, from top to bottom adds in tens, from right to left subtracts in ones and from bottom to top subtracts in tens.

Start on a given number, for example 19. Ask them to put one counter on 19 then add on nine and place the other counter on the number they finish on. Ask them to add on nine again and move the first counter to the new number:-

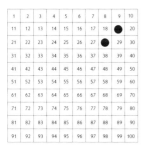 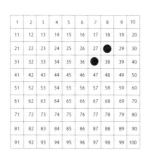

QUESTIONS

Can you see a pattern?

What happens each time? Why does it happen?

Can you predict where the counter will end up next?

Now ask them to start again but this time to add ten and subtract one.

So if you start at 19, adding ten gives 29, subtracting one gives 28.

What do you notice about this pattern?

Why is it the same?

Can you use this to add nine quickly to different numbers?

Can you do it without the hundred square?

VARIATIONS/EXTENSIONS

Use the same strategy for subtracting 9 and adding and subtracting 11.

Links to:

'Around the hundred square', page 133

'What's that number', page 88

'More or Less Moves', page 93

RESOURCES

hundred squares
counters

VOCABULARY

pattern
predict
add
subtract
adjust

Bridging Through Ten

AIM: Bridge though 10 or 20 then adjust as a mental calculation strategy for addition and subtraction, count up through the next multiple of 10.

ACTIVITY

Choose a single-digit number and discuss the different ways it can be split into two numbers. For example seven is:-

        6 + 1
        5 + 2
        4 + 3

Look at a number of calculations and ask which of the different ways of seeing seven is useful in each case. Use a number line to model. For example, for the calculation 26 + 7, it may be useful to see the seven as 4 + 3, taking 26 up to the next multiple of ten and then adding the remaining three.

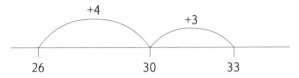

(It is possible that children will give alternatives which are equally valid such as seeing seven as 6 + 1 because knowing double six is twelve, then add the extra one.)

Explore different single digit numbers in different calculations.

QUESTIONS

What is the next multiple of ten after 26?

What must you add to 26 to get to the next multiple of 10?

How do you know? How can you use this strategy for subtracting?

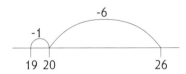

For example, to do 26 - 7, subtract 6 then adjust by subtracting 1.

For which calculations is this not a good strategy? Why?

Links to:

'Addition Chains', page 135

'Bridging Through Ten 2', page 136

RESOURCES

number line

VOCABULARY

total
add
subtract
multiple

Aim for the Target

AIM: Use knowledge of number facts and place value to add/subtract a pair of numbers mentally.

ACTIVITY

Decide on a target number, for example 50. Throw two dice and the children decide which number they will use as the tens and which the units. Then throw a die and the children have to decide whether to add to or subtract from their number, recording their new number.

Continue this until the target number is reached. For example, if the target is 30 and the two numbers thrown at the start are 2 and 4, one pair might decide to start with 24 and another 42.

Then, a 3 is thrown

24 + 3 = 27	42 - 3 = 39

Followed by a 6

27 + 6 = 33	39 - 6 = 33

and so on.

QUESTIONS

Which number did you choose to start with? Why?

Which number was closest to the target?

If you were on 29 and the number thrown was 4 would you decide to add or subtract? Why?

Is there more chance of getting to the target number from 33 than from 25? Why?

VARIATIONS/EXTENSIONS

Use dice with more than six sides. Have a three digit target number and add or subtract two digit numbers.

Links to work a probability.

RESOURCES

paper
pencils
dice

VOCABULARY

add
subtract
chance

Body Multiples

AIM: To understand the operation of multiplication and associated vocabulary, counting in 5s and 10s.

ACTIVITY

To warm up count aloud forward and backwards in fives, then tens, using a hundred square to prompt, pointing out the patterns in the units column.

Then, with the children in a circle, count in fives using fingers. Put one hand up and then another saying 5, 10, ... and continue around the circle. Stop at various points and ask how many groups or sets of fingers are in the air. Encourage children to predict before they count, linking multiplication with division

QUESTIONS

There are 50 fingers in the air, how many hands would that be?

If there are 4 hands up, how many fingers in total will there be?

If five and five makes ten, how many sets of five will make twenty?

How do you know? How many fingers are on 2 hands? 6 hands?

How can you check? What patterns can you hear? See?

What do four groups/sets of 5 make?

What does double five make? Double 20?

How many sets of 5 is this? How many sets of 10 make 100?

How many people would we need to show 100 fingers?

How do you know?

What else could we use to show and count in groups of five or ten?

VARIATIONS/EXTENSIONS

Use toes, children having to imagine they can see the five on each foot.

Combine feet and hands to extend visualising larger numbers.

Links to:

'Pairs of Hands', page 94

'Multiplication Monsters', page 127

RESOURCES

hundred square

VOCABULARY

patterns

five, ten, fifteen, ...

groups

sets

predict

how many?

double

Mental Jumping

AIM: To reinforce multiplication facts for 2, 5 and 10 tables and understand multiplication as repeated addition.

ACTIVITY

Ask the children to close their eyes and imagine jumping from zero in steps of two, along a number line to 20. Ask them to share and discuss with a partner the numbers they land on and how many jumps they took. Repeat for jumps of 5 and 10. Ask them to remember the numbers they landed on more than once and to work out why.

Tell the children that the numbers they landed on when counting in equal jumps from zero are called multiples.

Draw a number line on the board or use the class number line and ask a child to draw in the jumps of two from zero to 20, whilst the children record in pairs on their own number lines. Repeat for jumps of 5 and 10. Ask how many equal jumps of 2 make 20 and how they worked it out. Show that the further along the line we go the more steps of 2 were added.

Ask how many lots of 2 would get them to the number 24, 30, etc. Show number sentences to accompany the images, for example:-

Ten lots of two gets us to 20.

We can record this as

$2 \times 10 = 2 + 2 + 2 + 2 + 2 + 2 + 2 + 2 + 2 + 2 = 20$

Ask the children in their pairs to write down number sentences to accompany their number line showing steps of 5 and 10.

QUESTIONS

If you jump from zero in steps of 5 would you land on 12? How do you know?

What patterns can you spot in the numbers as you jump?

Which numbers do you land on more often? Why is that?

Which numbers didn't you land on? Why?

Can you predict whether or not you would land on 44 when jumping in fives?

What about 89?, etc.

What are the only odd numbers you land on? Why?

How many jumps of 5 would you take from zero to land on 50?, 100? How do you know?

If we started at 25 and jumped back in twos would we land on zero?

VARIATIONS/EXTENSIONS

This can be extended into the main part of the lesson as an independent activity or with the whole class. Investigate common multiples of numbers. Ask children to start at zero and jump first in 2s, then 3s, 4s, etc., each time marking the numbers they land on with a counter. Use different colours for different jumps. Discuss which numbers have several counters. Investigate factors of a number such a 20 by repeatedly jumping backwards in equal steps of 2, 3, 4 etc. Show the link between repeated subtraction and division.

RESOURCES

number lines
class number line

VOCABULARY

repeated addition
multiplication
multiple
equal
times tables
digit
lots of

True or False?

AIM: Explain methods and reasoning about numbers.

ACTIVITY

Write a variety of number sentences on cards to hold up. The children have to decide whether they are true or false and need to be able to justify their decision.

Encourage the children to use a number of different strategies including use of approximations, knowledge of odd and even numbers, inverse operations and number bonds.

For example:

I know $17 + 15 = 41$ is false because $7 + 5 = 12$ so the number must end in 2. Or because two odd numbers added together make an even number and 41 is not even. Or the answer must be less than 40 because $20 + 20 = 40$ and 17 and 15 are both less than 40.

I know $2.5 \times 5 = 125$ is false because the answer is between 10 (2×5) and 15 (3×5). Or when you have an odd number of halves you still have a half left over so the answer must have a half in it. Or because $125 \div 5 = 25$.

I know $634 \div 5 = 127$ is false because only numbers ending with 5 or 0 are divisible by 5.

I know $312 \times 6 = 1877$ is false because two even numbers multiplied together make an even number. Or because 6×2 is 12 so the answer must end with a 2.

QUESTIONS

Is the statement true or false? How do you know?
Can anyone give another reason why it is false?
Do you need to do the whole calculation to prove it is false? Why not?
Can you prove it is true? How?

VARIATIONS/EXTENSIONS

Make statements about numbers which could be true or false and ask the children to either justify or disprove for example 'all multiples of ten end with a zero'. Discuss how to change the false ones to make them true. Include statements that are partly true, such as 'Odd numbers added together always make an even number' (three odd numbers don't!) 'When you multiply by ten you put a 0 on the end' (not with decimals!) Give examples for which it works and doesn't work to help try and clarify what needs changing to make the statement true.

RESOURCES

statements on cards

VOCABULARY

added together
subtracted
multiplied
divided
divisible
odd
even
total
approximately
between
less than
more than

What Number Am I Holding?

AIM: Understand and use the relationship between addition and subtraction, multiplication and division.

ACTIVITY

Give each child a set of number cards and keep a set for yourself. Select one of the cards and then tell the children, for example:-

"I have picked a number that when you add seven to it you get fifteen. What number am I holding?"

"I have picked a number. There is a difference of four between this number and ten. What number am I holding?"

The children select the number they think you have chosen and then, on a given signal, all show you their numbers.

QUESTIONS

How did you work it out?
Did anyone do it differently?

VARIATIONS/EXTENSIONS

Make the statement more complicated with combinations of operations, for example:-

"I have picked a number that when I double it and add ten makes twenty-nine. What number am I holding?"

Use the digit cards to form two-digit numbers as well as single digit and introduce the decimal point card so that you can do examples with numbers with one decimal place.

Links to:

'Around the class', page 117

RESOURCES

number cards

VOCABULARY

add
subtract
multiply
divide
double
halve
difference

It Went Like This

AIM: Use all four operations to solve problems involving numbers in 'real life'.

ACTIVITY

Write up a calculation such as

65 + 23 = 88 or 76 - 41 = 35 or 14 x 6 = 84 or 363 ÷ 3 = 121

and offer the children a number of scenarios that involve these numbers. For example, for 65 + 23 = 88, scenarios that could be discussed are:

I had sixty-five pounds and then I won twenty-three pounds in a raffle so I had eighty-eight pounds altogether.

My sister is twenty-three and my mum is sixty-five, making my grandmother eighty-eight.

You owed me 65p then I lent you another 23p so now you owe me 88p.

I needed eighty-eight pounds to buy a coat. I already had sixty-five pounds so I needed another twenty-three pounds.

I thought there were sixty-five sweets in the jar and my friend thought there were twenty-three so we decided eighty-eight as this was the average.

(The first, third and fourth are all possible. The second and fifth are not!)

QUESTIONS

Could this be the calculation for this situation? Why?

If not, what is the calculation for this situation?

Could a different number sentence be written for the same situation? Why?

Can you give me a situation in which this would be the calculation?

Can you give me a situation that involves these numbers but for which this is not an appropriate calculation?

VARIATIONS/EXTENSIONS

Put a calculation on the board and ask the children in pairs to come up with two situations that involve these numbers - one for which the calculation is appropriate and the other for which it is not. Put a list of words up on the board for the children to use in their scenarios, directing them to use them if you want them to practice the language, or using them as a prompt. This could be used as an independent activity in the main part of the lesson.

Links to:

'What do I do?' page 81

'Calculation Approximation', page 77

RESOURCES

VOCABULARY

calculation

add

subtract

multiply

divide

total

more

less

fewer

difference

how many?

altogether

same

Grid Totals 2

AIM: Know by heart addition and subtraction facts.

ACTIVITY

Each child draws a small two-by-two grid and puts a number less than twenty, of their choosing, into each box.

6	8
12	5

The teacher picks two number cards and calls out the numbers. The children must total these numbers and if they have it on their grid, cross it off.

For example, if the teacher calls out 'Four' and 'Eight' the number twelve can be crossed off on the grid above.

When a child has crossed off all their numbers they can call 'Bingo' or another agreed word.

QUESTIONS

Which numbers can't you make? Why?

Which is the lowest/highest number we can make?

Which numbers are easiest to make? Why do you think that is?

What if we had to total three numbers? What would change?

What is a quick way of adding three numbers together?

How do you know you're right?

VARIATIONS/EXTENSIONS

Again, this can be varied for any age group by making the numbers multiples of ten and the numbers called out all multiples of ten, numbers with one or two decimal points or negative numbers. Instead of drawing two cards the teacher could draw three cards or throw three dice, which could be the standard six-sided dice or dice with as many as twelve sides.

Alternatively, use a larger grid and children are aiming to get three or four in a row.

Links to:

'Grid Totals', page 98

'Ladybird Spots', page 176

RESOURCES

paper

pencils

a set of number cards

or dice

VOCABULARY

single digit

two digit

total

multiple

tenths

hundredths

Clapping Numbers

AIM: Know by heart addition and subtraction facts for all numbers to 20, number pairs that total 100; use knowledge of number facts.

ACTIVITY

Everybody claps their hands and then taps their thighs in a steady rhythm. On the first clap the teacher says a number below ten and on the next clap the class reply with the partner number that adds to the teacher's number to make ten. For example:-

Teacher: Six	Clap hands
	Tap thighs
Class: Four	Clap hands
	Tap thighs
Teacher: Eight	Clap hands
	Tap thighs
Class: Two	Clap hands

QUESTIONS

Can you use the numbers that are partners for ten to find partners for a hundred?

VARIATIONS/EXTENSIONS

This can be varied for any age group:-

Numbers that add to make twenty

Numbers that add to make 100

Decimals that add to make 1 or 10

Constant number added, e.g. add five to every number

Teacher claps a number of times and the children reply with the number of claps needed to make ten.

Links to:

'Countdown', page 96

'Grid Totals', page 98

RESOURCES

VOCABULARY

add

total

Corner Numbers

AIM: Add several small numbers, solve number problems and puzzles, use knowledge of multiplication and division facts.

ACTIVITY

Draw a shape on the board and in the centre write a number. Ask the children in pairs to explore how many different ways they can find of putting numbers at all corners that total the number in the centre, within 5 minutes. Discuss and share.

For example:

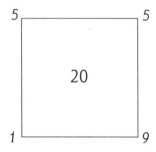 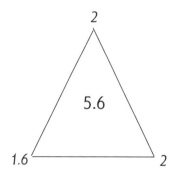

QUESTIONS

Can you make all the numbers the same?

Can you use only even/odd numbers?

How did you organise yourself to find different solutions?

Can you put numbers that multiply to make the centre number, rather than add?

VARIATIONS/EXTENSIONS

Look at different solutions for the same square and look at the total of or the difference between the two numbers along each side, e.g.

Totals   Differences

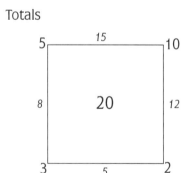 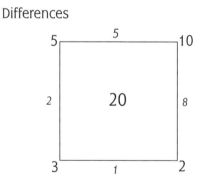

Look for patterns.

This can be extended into the main part of the lesson.

Links to:

'Corner Numbers Investigated', page 181

RESOURCES

paper

pencils

VOCABULARY

multiply

add

total

solution

difference

Around the class

AIM: Know by heart addition/subtraction/multiplication/division facts and use knowledge of number facts and place value to calculate.

ACTIVITY

Make up a set of question and answer cards, enough for at least one per child (spares can either be held by the teacher or given as extras to some of the children). Each card should have a number on one side and a calculation on the other and the children hold the cards with the number face up. The teacher has the start card and reads out the first calculation. Whichever child has the answer on their card calls it out then turns over their card and reads out the calculation. This process continues until reaching the person with the end card.

The same set of cards can be used on a number of separate occasions. For example:-

Prepare sets of question and answer cards for the multiplication tables you want the children to practice (see overleaf for examples). Organise the children into groups with a set of cards and time them. The first group to finish put up their hands. Repeat and compare times.

QUESTIONS

What helps you to remember certain facts?

What do you use to help you work out ones you can't recall?

How can you get quicker?

If you know 4 x 3 is 12, what else do you know?

VARIATIONS/EXTENSIONS

There are endless variations for this and it can be adapted for any age group and any particular aspect of calculating that you are focusing on. Possibilities include:-

Doubling and halving

Multiplication and division facts

Rounding

Addition and subtraction facts

Multi-step calculations

Negative numbers

Fractions and decimals

Children could do this in groups with cards appropriate to that group.

We have included some examples of cards on the next two pages (the first page contains two sets of cards).

Links to:

'What Number Am I Holding', page 112

RESOURCES

set of question and answer cards (see examples overleaf).

VOCABULARY

as appropriate to the cards

117

Question & Answer timetable cards (3&4xtable)

Start Card 3 **x** 3	9	15	36
21	27	24	18
12	6	33	30
39	45 Finish	Start Card 4 **x** 4	16
40	12	32	24
36	44	28	48
20	8	4	60 Finish

7 x 3	6 x 3	5 x 3	Start Card
9 x 3	2 x 3	10 x 3	11 x 3
8 x 3	4 x 3	12 x 3	13 x 3
10 x 4	Start Card	End Card	15 x 3
9 x 4	6 x 4	8 x 4	3 x 4
5 x 4	12 x 4	7 x 4	11 x 4
End Card	15 x 4	4 x 1	2 x 4

Doubling & Halving Cards

start double 9	18	30	24
20	50	11	26
16	14	34	12
32	22	36	100
52	19	60	40
15	90	55	150 end

Halve 40	Double 12	Double 15	Start Card
Double 8	Double 13	Halve 22	Double 25
Double 16	Halve 24	Double 17	Halve 28
Halve 80	Double 50	Double 18	Halve 44
Double 30	Halve 38	Double 26	Halve 30
End Card	Halve 300	Halve 110	Double 45

If I Know This I Also Know ....

AIM: Understand and use the relationship between addition and subtraction

ACTIVITY

Write up a fact such as:-

$$34 + 30 = 64$$

Tell the children that because you know this there are other things you know as well, such as:-

$$34 + 29 = 63$$
$$134 + 30 = 164$$
$$33 + 31 = 64$$
$$35 + 29 = 64$$
$$340 + 300 = 640$$

QUESTIONS

How do you think I used 34 + 30 = 64 to work these out?

Why do they work?

Can any of them be explained in a different way?

What about for another fact? Can you say other things you know because of it? Can you explain the connections?

VARIATIONS/EXTENSIONS

Ask the children to come out and demonstrate a number fact they know as a result of knowing another fact.

This could be extended into the main part of the lesson as an independent activity

Links to:

'What else do you know?', page 146

RESOURCES

VOCABULARY

add

subtract

explain

connections

Find the Function

AIM: Solve number problems, recognise simple patterns and relationships, understand the relationship between addition and subtraction

ACTIVITY

Draw some large function machines on the board:-

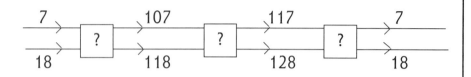

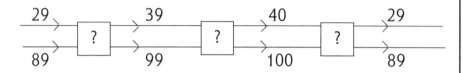

Tell the children that the machines have not shown the functions. Encourage them to discuss in pairs what the functions are doing to the numbers.

QUESTIONS

How are you working out the functions?

What patterns do you notice? How do these help?

What do you notice about the input and output numbers?

When you add or subtract a number what is a good way to check if your calculation is right?

VARIATIONS/EXTENSIONS

For younger or less able children, create a function machine using a table and a cloth. Cover the table and have someone sat inside it. Pass them in a bowl of cubes and they either add or subtract some cubes from it, obeying a given rule, and pass out the result. Can you see what has happened? Check by passing another number through the machine.

This can be extended into the main part of the lesson as an independent activity, giving children input and output numbers and asking them to create different function machines for these.

Links to:

'Think of a Number?', page 153

'More functions', page 154

RESOURCES
none

VOCABULARY
function
input
output
add
subtract
calculation

Grid Totals 3

AIM: Use knowledge of number facts and place value to add or subtract and multiply or divide two numbers mentally

ACTIVITY

1	2	3
4	5	6
7	8	9

Each child draws a three-by-three grid and puts the numbers one to nine in the corners of the boxes. The teacher either picks two number cards or throws two dice and calls out the numbers. The children must use these two numbers to make one of the numbers on their grid. They can use any of the four operations but can only make one number each time. They should record in the appropriate box how they made that number.

For example, two and three were called out by the teacher and this child decided to multiply them to make six. In the box for six, 2 x 3 has been recorded. Another child may have chosen to add them and recorded 2 + 3 in the box for five, or subtracted and recorded 3 - 2 in the box for one. The children are trying to fill in each box.

1	2	3
4	5	6 2 x 3
7	8	9

QUESTIONS

Which numbers can you make with five and two? How?
Can anyone make a different number?
How did you make the number 6? Did anyone make it a different way?
Are any numbers easier to make? Why?
Are any numbers harder to make? Why?

VARIATIONS/EXTENSIONS

Pick two numbers for example three and five. Can the children use these numbers alone to fill in their boxes?
For example 5 + 5 - 3 = 7.
Pick three numbers, for example four, one and two. Can they make all the numbers, using these numbers only once, for example 4 + 1 = 5, or having to use all the numbers in each calculation, for example
4 + 2 - 1 = 5?

Links to:

'Four fours', page 198

RESOURCES

paper
pencils
a set of number cards
or dice

VOCABULARY

single digit
two digit
total
multiple
tenths
hundredths

Dart Attack

AIM: Use knowledge of addition and multiplication facts and doubling and halving strategies to solve number problems

ACTIVITY

Draw a dartboard like the one below:

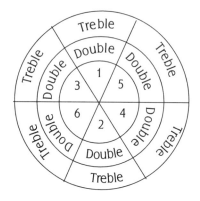

Ask children to double and treble a few numbers to check their understanding. Then ask them to imagine throwing 3 darts and set them a number of challenges, to solve in pairs:-

Where would the darts have to land to make the highest/lowest score?

How could you get a score of 30? 45?

What if you had 4 darts? What could be your highest score then?

Invite pairs out to the front to demonstrate their methods on the board.

QUESTIONS

How did you decide which was the highest/lowest score?

How did you check whether you were right?

Is there anyway you could score 35?

How many different ways do you think you could find?

What is trebling the same as?

Which facts do you know that help you work out others?

VARIATIONS/EXTENSIONS

Choose higher or lower numbers, change the layout of the board. This can be adapted for any age or ability and extended into the main activity by setting an investigation or playing a game in pairs.

Links to:

'Dartboards', page 192

"Dartboards 2", page 186

VOCABULARY
double
treble
score
total
highest
lowest
multiplication
addition

Multiplication Monsters

AIM: To be aware of patterns in the multiplication facts and the links between multiplication and repeated addition

ACTIVITY

Draw a large double headed, three fingered, five toed, triple footed monster on the board or use the one provided here (see next page). Ask the children how the monster is different to us and to work out how many eyes, fingers, toes, etc. it has.

Ask if two monsters arrived how we could work out the total number of eyes, fingers, etc.

Draw a chart and give the children copies. Ask them to record the totals for the monsters and to look for patterns:-

Monsters	Heads	Eyes	Hands	Fingers	Feet	Toes
1	2	4	2	6	3	15
2	4					
3					9	

QUESTIONS

What patterns can you see?
What is counting in fours the same as?
How are the number of feet and the number of toes related?
If there are 30 toes altogether, how many feet is that?
How can you use doubling to help work out the totals?
Can you think of a general rule to work out the total number of eyes for any number of monsters?
Can you predict how many feet 20 monsters would have? How did you do it?

VARIATIONS/EXTENSIONS

Give the children different monsters to investigate. Use to reinforce any multiplication tables and extend by asking children to come up with general rules to determine totals of eyes, hands etc. for any number of monsters.

Set problems such as there are cows and hens in a farmyard. You can see 10 heads and 32 legs. How many of each are there?

Links to:

'Body Multiples,' page 109

RESOURCES
photocopies of grids
picture of monster

VOCABULARY
repeated addition
multiplication
number patterns
general rule
prediction

Monster Multiplication

Beat the Calculator

AIM: To use and recall quickly multiplication facts

ACTIVITY

Give a calculator and a score sheet to the children in pairs. The teacher rolls the dice and one child in each pair uses the calculator to multiply the numbers and the other works it out in their head. Both must write down the answer - the first to do so each time scores a point. After 5 goes, swap over.

QUESTIONS

Which facts do you know?

How are you working out the ones you don't know?

What strategies could you use to become quicker at multiplying?

For which calculations did the calculator win?

Why is the calculator not always the best thing to use?

When is it more suitable to use the calculator?

If you know 2 x 6 what's a quick way of calculating 4 x 6?

VARIATIONS/EXTENSIONS

Practice addition/subtraction facts instead.

Extend by using dice with more sides.

RESOURCES

calculators

dice

VOCABULARY

multiplication facts

strategies

calculating

Doubling Patterns

AIM: To recognise and extend number sequences and use doubling to calculate other multiplication facts

ACTIVITY

Write on the board, in columns, part of the multiplication tables for 2, 4 and 8:-

Twos	Fours	Eights
2	4	8
4	8	16
6	12	24
8	16	32

Ask the children to count in twos from zero. Then ask if they don't know their four times table how they could work it out from knowing their twos. Put up some examples and show how they can use doubling to work out unknown facts.

For example 2 x 7 = 14 so 4 x 7 is double 2 x 7, that is double 14 which equals 28.

Look at the eight times table and ask how they could use their knowledge of the two times table and doubling to work out multiples of eight. Explain that by doubling the twos you get the fours and by doubling the fours you get the eights and explain why this works. Make it clear that this is the same as doubling the twos twice.

QUESTIONS

What patterns do you notice in the end digits? Why are they all even?
How many times in the sequence is it before the unit digits start repeating? Can you explain why?
If you know what three 4s are, how can you work out quickly three 8s? What about three 16s? Three 32s?
Where else could you use doubling? Can you think of some examples?
If doubling is the same as multiplying by two, what is halving the same as? How can you use this to check your multiplication facts?

VARIATIONS/EXTENSIONS

Explore the links between the five and ten times tables and the three, six and nine times tables.
Look at halving numbers and halving again and relate to division and fractions.

Links to:

'Dotty Doubles', page 102
'More Doubles', page 179

VOCABULARY

multiplication facts
double
halve
patterns
sequence
digits

How Many Boxes ?

AIM: To understand division, solving problems involving division

ACTIVITY

Give the children a word problem. For example a farmer's hen lay 35 eggs. The farmer wants to know how many half-dozen boxes she will need for the eggs. Ask the children to discuss in pairs, what kind of calculation it is and how they might solve it. Share their responses.

For example, one response might be "I know five 6's are thirty..." or "I don't know my tables but we can use counters and share into groups of six". Discuss how to use multiplication facts, e.g.
6 x 5 = 30 which is 5 boxes and 5 eggs left over. So she needs another box.

Ask why six boxes will be needed and not five.

QUESTIONS

How is division linked to multiplication?
Is a number line helpful? Why?
How could you use a number line to work out how many eggs the farmer had in total if she had 7 boxes? Where would we start on the number line? Why?

VARIATIONS/EXTENSIONS

Ask the children to make up their own word problems and give it to a friend.

RESOURCES
number lines

VOCABULARY
equal groups
division
how many groups of..?

Number Detectives

AIM: Count on or back in ones and tens; explain methods and reasoning about numbers

ACTIVITY

Use a large hundred square but arrange the numbers in a different format, for example:-

100	99	98	97	96	95	94	93	92	91
90	89	88	87	86	85	84	83	82	81
80	79	78	77	76	75	74	73	72	71
70	69	68	67	66	65	64	63	62	61
60	59	58	57	56	55	54	53	52	51
50	49	48	47	46	45	44	43	42	41
40	39	38	37	36	35	34	33	32	31
30	29	28	27	26	25	24	23	22	21
20	19	18	17	16	15	14	13	12	11
10	9	8	7	6	5	4	3	2	1

1	11	21	31	41	51	61	71	81	91
2	12	22	32	42	52	62	72	82	92
3	13	23	33	43	53	63	73	83	93
4	14	24	34	44	54	64	74	84	94
5	15	25	35	45	55	65	75	85	95
6	16	26	36	46	56	66	76	86	96
7	17	27	37	47	57	67	77	87	97
8	18	28	38	48	58	68	78	88	98
9	19	29	39	49	59	69	79	89	99
10	20	30	40	50	60	70	80	90	100

73	74	75	76	77	78	79	80	81	82
72	43	44	45	46	47	48	49	50	83
71	42	21	22	23	24	25	26	51	84
70	41	20	7	8	9	10	27	52	85
69	40	19	6	1	2	11	28	53	86
68	39	18	5	4	3	12	29	54	87
67	38	17	16	15	14	13	30	55	88
66	37	36	35	34	33	32	31	56	89
65	64	63	62	61	60	59	58	57	90
100	99	98	97	96	95	94	93	92	91

Turn over or cover all the numbers Invite a child to tell you a number they think they can turn over/uncover. All the children then have to look at what number is actually revealed and become number detectives - see if they can use this number to help them work out where other numbers will be. Invite another child to say a number they think they can turn over and repeat.

RESOURCES

hundred squares

VOCABULARY

between
left
right
above
below

QUESTIONS

Is that number you thought it would be?
How does that help you find another number?
What might be a good number to look for now?
Which squares are best to turn over first? Why?
What does that number tell you about the hidden hundred square?
What number do you think will be above/below/to the right/to the left of it? Why?
What do you think is on the end of that row? Why?

VARIATIONS/EXTENSIONS

Use the computer program 'Monty' from the SLIMWAM II disk (see appendix 5)

Links to:

'What's That Number 2?' page 101
'Guess the Number in my Pocket?' page 55

THINK MATHS!

Around the Hundred Square

AIM: Add or subtract 9,19, 29, ... or 11, 21, 31, ... by adding or subtracting 10, 20, 30, ... and adjusting by 1

ACTIVITY

Look at a hundred square. Start at a given number and then give directions for the children to follow. For example:-

Start at 25. Go down two squares and to the right one square. Which number am I on? What have I added to the 25?

Start at 17. Go left one square and down one square. Which number am I on? What have I added to 17?

Repeat for different numbers, initially restricting moves to one or two either both adding or both subtracting before mixing these. Draw direction movements on the board and discuss what happens on each move. Look at diagonal moves and how they relate to a combination of a vertical and a horizontal move. Practice diagonal moves and link to adding or subtracting 9 or 11.

QUESTIONS

What happens when we move diagonally to the right down the square?
Do the numbers get larger or smaller? Why?
What about if we move diagonally left and down?
What patterns can you see?
What's a quick way of adding or subtracting 9 or 11?

VARIATIONS/EXTENSIONS

Conceal the hundred square and ask the children to visualise the grid and follow the movements mentally.

Start at a number but instead of giving directions ask the children to add or subtract 1 or 10 or 9 or 11, etc. The children have to write down the directions as well as the answer, for example:-

33 + 19 = D2 L1

Use squares with larger numbers or decimals going up in different steps, for example 10 to 1000 in steps of 10

Links to:

'Add and Adjust', page 106

RESOURCES

hundred squares

VOCABULARY

vertical
horizontal
diagonal
add
subtract

Consecutive Numbers

AIM: Use knowledge of number facts and place value to add two numbers mentally

ACTIVITY

Discuss what it means for numbers to be consecutive. Focus on a hundred square, ask the children to choose two consecutive numbers and then add them together.

QUESTIONS

How did you add them together?

Can anyone explain another way of doing it?

What do you notice about your answer?

If the total is 21, what are the two consecutive numbers?

How did you work it out?

What are the first two numbers that have a total of more than 100?

Can we find two consecutive numbers to total any odd number?

Can you find two for 121, 243 etc.?

VARIATIONS/EXTENSIONS

Work with three digit numbers or consecutive numbers with tenths.

Links to:

'Consecutive Number Extended', page 195

RESOURCES

hundred square

VOCABULARY

consecutive

total

double

halve

Addition Chains

AIM: Add several small numbers, finding pairs totalling 10, and add several two and three digit numbers

ACTIVITY

Draw a four by four grid and fill it with single digit numbers. Each child will need paper and pencil for recording.

8	3	2	9
6	4	1	8
5	2	7	6
3	4	5	9

Ask the children to use it to make chains of three numbers, by linking squares either horizontally or vertically. For example, starting in the top left hand corner and moving right then down you get the chain 8, 3, 4.

For each chain the children add the three numbers.

QUESTIONS

How did you add the numbers? Which two did you add first? Why?

Can anyone find a chain that totals more than 18?

Can anyone find a different one?

Total less than 8?

What's the smallest/biggest total you can find? What other three numbers added together make the same total?

What about if you are allowed to link diagonally as well, can you make some different numbers?

Can you make all the numbers from 6 to 16?

What do you notice about the three numbers and the total each time?

Why does this happen? (Two odds and one even will give an even, etc.)

VARIATIONS/EXTENSIONS

Progress onto chains of four numbers.

Change the numbers to multiples of ten.

Use two or three digit numbers or numbers with one decimal place.

This can be extended into the main part of the lesson as an independent activity, exploring all the different totals possible.

Links to:

'Bridging Through Ten', page 107

RESOURCES

paper
pencils

VOCABULARY

horizontally
vertically
diagonally
add
total

Bridging Through Ten 2

AIM: Bridge though 10 or 20 then adjust as a mental calculation strategy for addition and subtraction, count up through the next multiple of 10, 100 or 1000.

ACTIVITY

Look at a calculation such as 428 + 45. Use a blank number line to model and ask:-

"What is the next multiple of ten after 428?"

"What does that leave you to add on?"

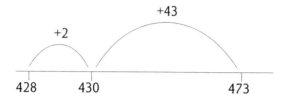

Use the same strategy for finding differences

For example 7000 - 2867

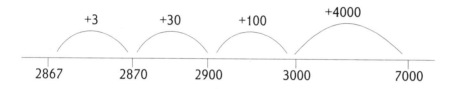

Difference is 4000 + 100 + 30 + 3 = 4133

QUESTIONS

Can you find the difference with fewer steps?

Can you visualise the number line in your head to do it?

Can you just jot down numbers to help you keep track?

Links to:

'Bridging Through Ten', page 107

Same Question, Different Solution

AIM: Choose an appropriate way of calculating

ACTIVITY

Write up a calculation, for example 27 + 35.

Ask the children to do the calculation in their heads and then share with a partner.

Ask children to come out to the front and demonstrate their method (or the teacher models using symbols whilst the child explains).

For example:-

I made the 27 into 25, added that to 35, which made 60 then added the 2, making 62.

27 - 2 = 25

25 + 35 = 60

60 + 2 = 62

I started with 35 then added the two tens making 55, then added the seven by splitting it into 5 and 2, making 62.

35 + 20 = 55

55 + 5 = 60

60 + 2 = 62

First I added the five by counting on in ones. This made 32. Then I added the 30, making 62.

27 + 5 = 32

32 + 30 = 62

I know that double 25 is 50. Then I added the 10 and the 2 making 62.

25 + 25 = 50

50 + 10 = 60

60 + 2 = 62

I started at 35 then counted on in ones until I had counted 25.

I made the 27 into 30 and added that to the 35 then took away 3, making 62.

27 + 3 = 30

30 + 35 = 65

65 - 3 = 62

QUESTIONS

Which of these methods is efficient? Why?

Which ones could we improve on? How?

Can you remember where you are when counting on in ones?

What's a quicker way of doing this?

VARIATIONS/EXTENSIONS

Look at different calculations and operations and emphasise that some methods are efficient for some calculations but not others.

Links to:

'Different Ways', page 185

RESOURCES

VOCABULARY

rounded

add

subtract

efficient

double

Add and Subtract

AIM: Recognise simple patterns and relationships

ACTIVITY

Sit in a circle or in lines. You are going to go around the class alternately adding two and subtracting one. You can start on any number you like. You may want to use a card to pass from child to child, with +2 on one side and -1 on the other and the children turn it as they pass it, or write the two operations on the board so that everyone remembers what you are doing.

If you start at 17 you will get:-
17, 19, 18, 20, 19, 21......
Record the numbers on the board.

QUESTIONS

If we start at 17 what number do you think we will get to?
Do you think it will be higher or lower than the number we would get if we just counted in ones? Why?
Will we say the number 27? Why?
Do you notice any pattern in the numbers?
Why does the pattern appear?
What if we added five and subtracted one?
Will we say all the numbers?
What pattern would we get then?

VARIATIONS/EXTENSIONS

This can be varied for all ages and abilities by changing the numbers added and subtracted. Choose numbers that focus the children on strategies you have been discussing, such as add nine and subtract five. Start at a larger number and ask them to subtract a larger number than you add, e.g. add two, subtract four - this will take you into negative numbers.
Add or subtract decimals or fractions for older classes.

RESOURCES

VOCABULARY

add
subtract
pattern
odd
even

Number Card Pairs

AIM: Use knowledge of number facts and place value to add/subtract a pair of numbers

ACTIVITY

Each child needs a partner and either a set of digit cards or an Eigen square (see appendix 4).

Ask the children to work with their partner to find two numbers each time that meet a given requirement, for example:-

Two numbers with a difference of one

Two numbers that total thirteen

Two even numbers that add up to make twenty-four

Two odd numbers that have a difference of four

Two numbers that are multiples of ten

Two numbers that are multiple of ten and have a difference of twenty

Two non-decade numbers (i.e. not multiples of ten) with a difference of forty

Two numbers whose product is twenty-four

Two numbers where one is double the other

The children could make one, two or three digit numbers using the cards or squares and hold up their pair of numbers once they have made them. The teacher keeps looking at the examples shown and invites the children to find other examples, changing the requirement after a minute or so. This can be quite fast and furious and involves all the children in making decisions about numbers and discussing numbers with a partner.

QUESTIONS

Can you find another pair?, and another?

How are you working out the answers?

Which type of questions have the most possible answers? Why?

Which did you find the easiest? Why?

VARIATIONS/EXTENSIONS

Include a decimal point so that you can ask them to find two numbers that total 5.5, have a difference of 0.3, etc.

Links to:

'Number Talk', page 99

RESOURCES

digit cards or
Eigen squares
(see appendix 4)

VOCABULARY

difference
total
add
multiple
product
decade
double
factor

Number Pyramids

AIM: Use knowledge of number facts and place value to add a pair of numbers mentally

ACTIVITY

Each child draws themselves a pyramid wall. Choose four numbers and tell the children to arrange these in any order they like at the bottom of the pyramid. For example:-

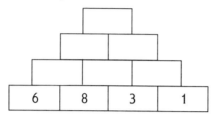

To fill the rest of the pyramid you build up from the bottom, adding two adjacent numbers together to make the number for the brick that sits on top of the them. So this pyramid would end up as:-

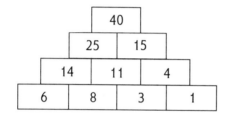

QUESTIONS

How did you work out 25 + 15?

Did everyone get the same number at the top? Why not?

Who got the biggest number? Why was that?

Who got the smallest number? Why was that?

Can you find a different way of working out what the top number will be?

VARIATIONS/EXTENSIONS

Start with larger numbers, two or three digit, or with decimals.

Find the difference rather than adding - the result for the numbers above is this pyramid.

Use pyramids with extra levels.

```
        0
      3   3
    2   5   2
  6   8   3   1
```

Links to:

'Number Pyramids 2, page 148

'Number Pyramids Investigated', page 196

RESOURCES

paper

pencils

VOCABULARY

adjacent

biggest

smallest

difference

Related Numbers

AIM: To recognise and use properties of numbers and use knowledge of number facts to add, subtract, multiply and divide

ACTIVITY

Write up a range of numbers including two and three digit numbers, fractions and decimals. The numbers chosen should be such that when different pairs are combined the answer is also on the board. For example:-

8	32	150	10	600	300	
$\frac{1}{3}$	75	0.5	16	3.2	64	50
2	$\frac{1}{2}$	450		$\frac{3}{4}$	9.6	25

Ask the children to choose a number and to write down a statement that links it to another number. For example:-

"The square root of 64 is eight"

"One hundred and fifty is divisible by fifty"

Share and discuss the numbers that were chosen. Next ask them to find a pair of numbers on the board, which when combined in some way have an answer which is also visible. For example:-

"3.2 plus 6.4 is 9.6"

"A third of 450 is 150"

Invite the children to write, on the board, the number sentence that matches their statement.

QUESTIONS

Which numbers are easiest to link? Why?

For which numbers is it harder to find number sentences? Why?

How do you know if your statement is true?

Which strategies did you use to help you find related numbers?

VARIATIONS/EXTENSIONS

One child chooses a number that is not on the board but that links to numbers that do appear on the board. The other children either have to work out which numbers on the board are connected with the given number (e.g. my number is 4) or have to work out what the number is when told the numbers it links with (e.g. my number connects with 300 and 10)

This can be adapted for different ages and abilities by varying the numbers chosen

Links to:

'Spotting Halves and Doubles', page 142

RESOURCES

VOCABULARY

properties
operations
relationship
connected

Spotting Halves and Doubles

AIM: To recognise and use halves and doubles

ACTIVITY

Write up between 10 and 15 numbers on the board such as 360, 1200, 250, etc. Tell the children that you are going to call out a number and ask them to 'Halve' or "Double'. The children have to find the answer on the board.

For example:-

Teacher calls out '125 double'

The answer on the board is 250

QUESTIONS

What is a quick way of working it out?

What facts do you know that help you?

What if I shouted "double, double" or "halve, halve"?

What would this be the same as?

What if I asked you to double then halve?

What does this tell you about multiplication and division?

VARIATIONS/EXTENSIONS

Children write their own numbers down and challenge each other. Extend to halving and doubling fractions, decimals and negative numbers.

Links to:

'Related Numbers, page 141

'Caterpillars', page 188

RESOURCES

VOCABULARY

double
halve
multiply
divide
fraction
inverse

Split Numbers

AIM: Know by heart addition and subtraction facts for all numbers to 20 and know multiplication facts up to 10 x 10.

ACTIVITY

Choose a number below 20 and ask for pairs of numbers that add to make that number. For each pair of numbers, ask for the product as well.

QUESTIONS

How many different pairs of numbers make 10? 11?

Can you see a pattern?

Which pair of numbers give the biggest product each time?

Can you generalise?

Can you say which pair of numbers that total to make 22 will have the biggest product?

This activity can be extended to the main part of the lesson as an independent activity.

Links to:

'First to One Hundred', page 184

RESOURCES

VOCABULARY

total

product

factors

Exploring Numbers

AIM: Know by heart addition and subtraction facts for all numbers to 20 and know multiplication facts up to 10 x 10.

ACTIVITY

Put a number on the board and ask the children how many ways they can make that number, using different operations. Invite children out to demonstrate how they have made it and ask questions as they are recording their methods on the board.

QUESTIONS

What's the biggest number you have used?

Could you use a bigger number? How?

What's the smallest number you can use?

Can you use negative numbers?

Did anyone else use a number ending in 9 - what do you notice?

Sarah has written 42 on the board, what do you think she is going to write next? Could it be anything else?

VARIATIONS/EXTENSIONS

Give the children parameters to work within, for example you must find subtractions as well as additions, or you must only use numbers with one decimal place.

This can be extended to the main part of the lesson as an independent activity.

Links to:

'First to One Hundred', page 184

RESOURCES

paper
pencils

VOCABULARY

total
difference
product
multiply
divide
negative
addition
subtraction

Which Pair ?

AIM: Use knowledge of number facts, place value and properties of numbers to add/subtract numbers and solve number problems, explaining methods and reasoning.

ACTIVITY

Draw a six-by-six grid filled with numbers, and two boxes with numbers in, which are covered to begin with. Explain that the numbers on the grid have been produced by adding together pairs of three digit numbers, one from each of the covered boxes.

928	504	1244	707	940	1703
862	1023	376	1056	755	1196
1258	1385	1520	365	1060	699
859	1129	549	1491	1667	457
781	412	1177	811	836	1770
1115	1009	284	1121	811	641

164	292
348	300
429	874
903	245

764	212
896	407
511	829
120	617

Choose one of the numbers (for example, 781) and ask questions about the numbers that will have added together to make that number.

RESOURCES

grid on the board

VOCABULARY

odd
even
total
three digit

QUESTIONS

What do we know about the two numbers?

Could either of the numbers be odd?

What might the two numbers end with? If one ends with a two, what will the other one end with?

If you just added together the hundreds, what would they have to equal?

Then look at another number, a large one, for example 1703. Ask the same questions but also ask:-

If the numbers are both three digit numbers what's the smallest that one of them can be? How do you know?

Look at a small number, for example 504 and ask:-

If the numbers are both three digit numbers what's the biggest that one of the numbers can be? How do you know?

Now reveal the two sets of numbers and use the strategies for working out pairs to total given numbers. Try to get four in a row.

VARIATIONS/EXTENSIONS

Subtract instead of adding, or multiply or divide. Use different size numbers including decimals.

Links to:

'Four in a Row', page 200

What Else Do You Know ?

AIM: Know and use a range of number facts; make links between the operations.

ACTIVITY

Write on the board a multiplication fact such as 12 x 5 = 60. Ask the children if we know this, what else do we know? Share some suggestions then ask the children to brainstorm in pairs, recording on paper. One pair could work on the board. Discuss, highlighting the links between doubling and halving, multiplying and dividing by 10 etc.

For example :-

$$10 \times 5 = 50$$

$$3 \times 5 = 15$$

$$11 \times 5 = 55$$

$$6 \times 5 = 30$$

$$60 \div 5 = 12$$

$$12 \times 5 = 60$$

$$24 \times 5 = 120 \qquad 12 \times 100 = 1200 \qquad 12 \times 10 = 120$$

$$48 \times 5 = 240 \qquad\qquad 12 \times 20 = 240$$

$$96 \times 5 = 480$$

QUESTIONS

What strategies are you using?

Which ones are the easiest? Why?

How can you check if you're right?

How many different facts can you find?

If you double and then multiply by 10 what is this the same as?

What do you know about division and multiplication?

What patterns can you find?

VARIATIONS/EXTENSIONS

This can be extended to the main part of the lesson as an independent activity.

Give the children a number of related facts and ask them to explain the relationships.

Ask the children to start from their own known facts.

Start with an addition/subtraction fact.

Links to:

'If I Know This I Also Know...', page 123

RESOURCES

VOCABULARY

number facts

connections

relationships

patterns

operations

multiply

divide

halve

double

Two Digit Multiplication

AIM: Develop mental calculation strategies for multiplying by two-digit numbers.

ACTIVITY

Write up some one digit by two digit multiplications. Choose an example such as 7 x 10 and ask what could be drawn to illustrate it. Draw a rectangular array on the board showing the multiplication.

e.g.

10 'lots' of 7 is 70
7 has become ten times bigger

Then ask what 7 x 14 might look like and model in a similar way. Partition 7 x 14 into 7 x 10 and 7 x 4 and ask the children how this is helpful. Show that since we know 7 x 10 is 70 and 7 x 4 is 28
(maybe by doubling and doubling again) then 7 x 14 = 70 + 28. Explain that this strategy can be used for any two digit number.

Ask the children to work in pairs, choosing a multiplication from the board, and be prepared to explain how they did it. Encourage them to sketch a rectangular array (not necessarily to scale) to reinforce this image of multiplication. Share and work through specific examples to highlight efficient strategies.
For example:-
15 x 9 = (10 + 5) x 9
10 x 9 = 90 so 5 x 9 = 45 therefore 15 x 9 = 90 + 45

QUESTIONS

Why is multiplying by ten easy?
What happens to the size of the number when you multiply by ten?
What do you know about 7 x 10 and 10 x 7? How is this helpful?
What can you do if you don't know all your multiplication facts by heart?
Is partitioning into tens and units always the best method?
When would another method be more appropriate?

VARIATIONS/EXTENSIONS

Multiply two digit numbers by two digit numbers by partitioning in the same way.
Multiply a number with one decimal place by partitioning into units and tenths.

Links to:

'Four in a Row', page 200
'Dotty Rectangles', page 152

RESOURCES

squared paper
(not essential for all children)

VOCABULARY

partition
tens
units
multiply
rectangular array
strategies
efficient
halving
doubling

Number Pyramids 2

AIM: Use knowledge of number facts and place value to add or subtract a pair of numbers mentally and to multiply a pair of numbers mentally.

ACTIVITY

Variation on Number Pyramids. Draw a wall in the same way. This time there is a different operation for each row - multiply to create the next row, then add then find the difference. For example:

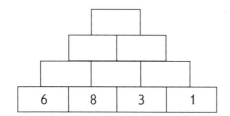

becomes:-

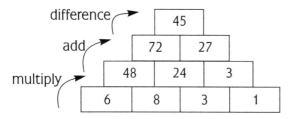

QUESTIONS

How did you work out 48 + 24?

Did everyone get the same number at the top? Why not?

Who got the biggest number? Why was that?

Who got the smallest number? Why was that?

Can you find a different way of working out what the top number will be?

VARIATIONS/EXTENSIONS

Change the order of the operations so that you add first, multiply and then find the difference.

Start with larger numbers, two or three digit, or with decimals.

Links to:

'Number Pyramids', page 140

'Number Pyramids Investigated', page 196

RESOURCES

paper

pencils

VOCABULARY

adjacent

biggest

smallest

difference

multiply

Target

AIM: Choose appropriate number operations to solve a number problem and use knowledge of number facts and place value to mentally calculate.

ACTIVITY

Either have a set of cards for the children to choose from randomly or select the numbers yourself. Choose one or two multiples of one hundred and four or five numbers between 1 and 10.

Write up any three digit number (there is absolutely no need to make sure the number can be made, in fact it is more beneficial if you don't know whether or not it can be made).

Set a time limit (five minutes or less) and tell the children they are to use the numbers to try and make the three digit number or get as close as they can. They must not use the given numbers more than once, but don't have to use all of them.

For example, the chosen numbers are:-

100, 3, 10, 9, 6 and 8

and the target number is

364

After the time is up ask children how close they have got and to explain how they did it. Invite the children to come out to the board to demonstrate.

For example, 100 x 3 = 300

9 x 8 = 72

300 + 72 = 372

372 - 6 = 366 (only two away).

QUESTIONS

Which operations did you use?

Has anybody got to the same number but in a different way?

What's the connection between the two methods?

Where did you begin? Why?

What was the first thing you noticed about the numbers when looking at the target number?

How might working backwards help?

VARIATIONS/EXTENSIONS

Introduce possibilities such as square and square root.

Try to identify strategies that work well for different targets.

Change the numbers that you might pick to include 25, 50 and 75.

Change the numbers to decimals.

Links to:

'Four fours', page 198

RESOURCES

number cards

paper

pencils

VOCABULARY

add

subtract

multiply

divide

total

difference

operations

square

square root

Fraction Cards

AIM: Use fraction notation, recognise fractions that are several parts of a whole, recognise the equivalence between simple fractions and between decimals and fractions.

ACTIVITY

Give each child a set of digit cards. Show how fractions can be made by holding one card above another. Tell them you are going to ask a number of questions that may involve fractions as answers. They are to make the answer with their cards and then all to show their answers on a given word.

QUESTIONS

What's the largest fraction you can make? Smallest fraction?

Can you show me three-quarters? five-sevenths?

Can you show me a fraction equivalent to one whole?, two wholes?

What's the connection between these two fractions?

Can you show me a half? Again, but using different numbers?

What would the numerator be if the denominator is 100 and you want it to be equivalent to a half?

What do you add to three-quarters to make 1? To four-fifths to make 2?

What fraction is the same as 0.5? 0.25?

VARIATIONS/EXTENSIONS

Use the digit cards with a decimal point to work this in reverse.

RESOURCES

digit cards

VOCABULARY

fraction
denominator
numerator
whole
equivalent fraction
half, quarter, ...
decimal

Negatives

AIM: Find the difference between a positive and negative number or two negative numbers, in a context such as temperature.

ACTIVITY

Introduce a number line to represent the money in your piggy bank or bank account. Use this to model money going in and out.

Record on the board the calculations completed each time.

QUESTIONS

If I have £5 and I need to pay £7, how much will my balance be?

Can you write this as a calculation?

If I have a balance of ⁻£4 (I owe or am overdrawn by £4) and I then receive £2 which I add to my account, what will my balance be?

What if I have a balance of ⁻£4 then £2 of what I owe is paid for by someone else and so is taken off my balance. What will my balance be now?

What's the connection between these two situations

⁻£4 + £2 and ⁻£4 - ⁻£2 ?

Can you generalise about subtracting a negative number? Are you sure it always works? Why?

If I owe £5, giving me a balance of ⁻£5 and then I owe another £3 (⁻£5 + ⁻£3) what is my balance now?

What do you notice about adding a negative number? Can you generalise? Why does it always work?

VARIATIONS/EXTENSIONS

Temperature rather than money.

RESOURCES

number line
negative numbers

VOCABULARY

negative number
positive number
add
subtract
balance
owe
generalise

Dotty Rectangles

AIM: Develop mental strategies for multiplication and mental imagery of numbers.

ACTIVITY

Put up an overhead or large sheet of paper showing several rectangular arrays of dots or hand out photocopies to the children in pairs. Select one example and ask the children how many dots they think are there. Next ask if they can find a way to calculate the total number of dots without having to count them all. Discuss rows of dots, columns and any rectangular shapes the children 'see'; within the whole array. Ask the children to find at least three different ways and to record their methods. Share and model on the board. For example:-

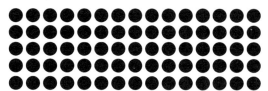

5 rows of 15 dots

15 columns of 5 dots

5 rows of 10 and 5 rows of 5

QUESTIONS

Which method is the easiest/hardest to follow? Why?

Which method is the quickest? Why?

Which known facts were you using?

How can you check your answer?

VARIATIONS/EXTENSIONS

Give the children numbers and ask them to investigate different ways of displaying the numbers as rectangular arrays. Link to finding factors of numbers.

Links to:

'Two Digit Multiplication', page 147

RESOURCES

OHT of dots

squared paper

VOCABULARY

columns

rows

estimate

strategies

multiplication

Think of a Number

AIM: Know how to combine operations in calculations; use knowledge of inverse operations; begin to use formulae.

ACTIVITY

(It would be useful to have experienced 'More Functions' prior to this activity)

Ask a child to think of a number between 1 and 10. Double it, add 4, multiply by 5 and say the answer. By performing the reverse calculation in your head you can tell them the number they started with.

Write up the instructions and ask the children to record each step numerically. Once they've got an answer, ask them if they can work backwards to the number they first thought of and record their working. Can they find a general rule that enables them to work out their friend's starting number?

Discuss as a class. Ask the children to imagine the unknown number as a thought bubble and model how to devise a formula. For example:-

Starting number = ☁

$$(2☁ + 4)5 = N \text{ (end total)}$$
$$10☁ + 20 = N$$
$$10☁ = N - 20$$

Therefore, $$☁ = \frac{N - 20}{10}$$

Alternatively, $$☁ = \frac{N}{10} - 2$$

QUESTIONS

What do you know about the relationships between the operations that could help us get back to our starting number?

Why do we need to put brackets around the numbers?

Which order should we do the operations in?

Will this formula always work?

How could we prove it?

VARIATIONS/EXTENSIONS

This can be extended into the main part of the lesson as an independent activity with children making up their own 'Think of a number' puzzles and challenging each other.

Links to:

'More Functions', page 154
'Find the Function', page 124

RESOURCES

VOCABULARY

inverse
reverse
operation
multistep
algebra
formula
general rule
brackets

More Functions

AIM: To combine operations to solve number problems and use knowledge of the relationship between multiplication and division.

ACTIVITY

Draw up some large function machines, like the ones below, which involve combinations of operations. Encourage the children to work in pairs to fill in the missing numbers and functions and to explain the patterns. For example:-

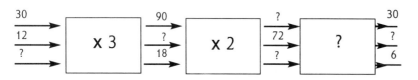

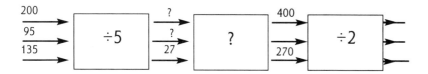

QUESTIONS

How are you working out the functions?

What patterns do you notice? How do these help?

What do you notice about the input and output numbers? Why is this?

When you multiply or divide a number what is a good way to check if your calculation is correct?

VARIATIONS/EXTENSIONS

Use multi-step function machines where the input and output are different.

Explore ways of finding input numbers if you only have the output and the functions.

The children could make up their own function machine for others to work out.

Links to:

'Think of a Number', page 153

'Find the Function', page 124

RESOURCES

VOCABULARY

function

multiply

divide

inverse

input

output

Long Division

AIM: Develop a range of paper and pencil methods for division, use knowledge of place value, known facts and the relationship between multiplication and division.

ACTIVITY

Write up a range of three digit numbers divided by two digit numbers, some of which can easily be solved mentally and others which cannot. For example:-

375 ÷ 25   800 ÷ 4   300 ÷ 15   453 ÷ 24   396 ÷ 32
210 ÷ 15   256 ÷ 12   650 ÷ 37   299 ÷ 14   496 ÷ 33

Ask the children to choose one they can do in their heads and discuss how they did it and why some of the calculations were not chosen. Ask the children to give an approximate answer to one that is difficult to do in their heads and also to think about what they might write down to help work it out accurately.

For example 800 ÷ 40 is easy to calculate mentally because 80 divided by 40 is 2 so 800 divided by 40 is 20.

496 ÷ 33 is hard to calculate because 33 is not a factor of 496. An approximate answer is 15 (450 divided by 30) but to keep track of the numbers there is a need to jot something down.

QUESTIONS

How are you estimating an answer?
What facts do you know that are helpful?
What strategies are you using?
Would you always use the same strategy? Why?

VARIATIONS/EXTENSIONS

Ask the children to jot down their methods in detail and exchange with one another to see if they can be understood.

RESOURCES

VOCABULARY

multiplication
division
estimate
approximate

Shape and Space

Mental/oral mathematics sessions do not have to focus on number. They can involve activities relating to measures, shape and space and data handling. We have indicated that many of the number activities in this book could be undertaken in the context of different measures. Data handling needs to be relevant to the children. Parts of the data handling process, in particular making decisions about what data to collect, how to collect it, how to present it, interpretation and comparison of data and raising further questions, can occur during the beginning part of a lesson.

The activities that follow explore some ideas specifically focused on shape and space. They deal, primarily, with developing vocabulary and use of language in shape and space. Many can be adapted for different ages by changing the vocabulary.

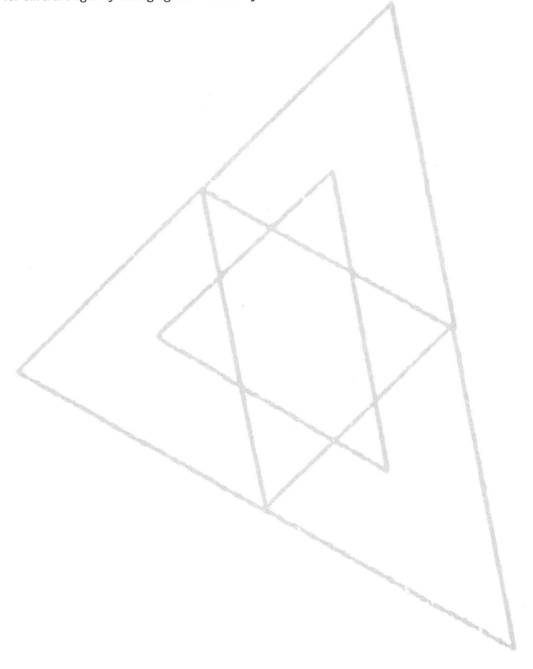

Unfold a Shape

AIM: Recognise, name and describe a square, triangle, rectangle and circle.

ACTIVITY

Fold a tablecloth or sheet of fabric many times so that each time you unfold a part a different shape is revealed. Sit the children in a circle and put the folded tablecloth in the middle.

QUESTIONS

What shape do you think will be next?

How do you know what shape this is?

Can you describe what it looks like from where you are sitting?

Does it look different if you are sitting somewhere else?

VARIATIONS/EXTENSIONS

Stand up and move around the shape, stopping to look from different view points and reinforcing that it is still the same shape.

RESOURCES

tablecloth

VOCABULARY

square

triangle

rectangle

circle

sides

Imagine a Shape

AIM: Visualise and describe 2D and 3D shapes.

ACTIVITY

Imagine a shape. For example a circle. Draw it in the air. Think about how you would describe the way your finger moves. Now choose a different shape and do the same thing. Think about what's different and what's the same about the way your finger moved for the two shapes. Or imagine the shape in your head and move a toy car along the sides of the shape.

QUESTIONS

How did your finger move?

What was different about the way it moved for the two shapes?

What was the same about the way it moved?

Can you think of another shape for which your finger would move in straight lines?

ACTIVITY - KS2

Imagine a square. Now imagine a diagonal line drawn in. Look at the shapes you can see now. Imagine a triangle. Cut off one of the corners and imagine what the shape would look like now. Imagine a hexagon and imagine folding it in half.

QUESTIONS

What shape can you see now?

Does anyone see a different shape?

How has the shape changed?

Can you draw what you can see?

Is the shape symmetrical?

VARIATIONS/EXTENSIONS

These are just suggestions - you can ask the children to imagine any shapes they are familiar with in different ways such as by cutting them, folding them or tracing round them and turning them.

RESOURCES

VOCABULARY

circle

triangle

square

rectangle

hexagon

pentagon

diagonal

corner

folded

half

straight

curved

sides

symmetrical

Guess My Shape?

AIM: Recognise, name and describe 3D and 2D shapes.

ACTIVITY

Give each child a set of shape cards with pictures of appropriate 2D and 3D shapes on them. The teacher or a child holds a shape (3D or 2D) where no-one else can see it. They then describe the shape and the others must decide which it is. They then show the card with the shape they think has been described.

QUESTIONS

What made you decide it was that shape?

Could any of the information have been about another shape?

How is this shape special?

VARIATIONS/EXTENSIONS

Rather than pictures of shapes have names of shapes to select from.

Instead of describing the shape, the other children ask yes/no questions to ascertain which shape it is - 'Does it have six faces?' etc.

Use shapes that the child can't see, inside a feely bag. They must describe what they can feel and see if together they can name the shape.

RESOURCES

shapes

shape cards

VOCABULARY

flat

curved

straight

corner

vertex

face

edge

side

circle

triangle

square

rectangle

pentagon

hexagon

cube

cuboid

pyramid

sphere

cylinder

cone

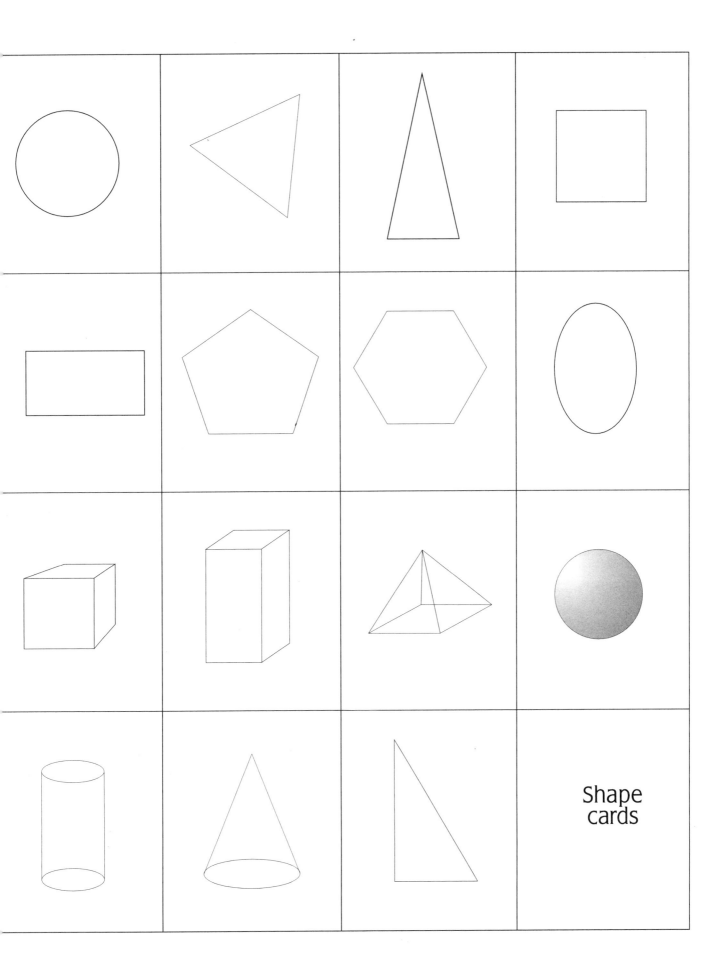

Shape cards

SQUARE	ISOSCELES TRIANGLE	EQUILATERAL TRIANGLE	CIRCLE
OVAL	HEXAGON	PENTAGON	RECTANGLE or OBLONG
SPHERE	SQUARE - BASED PYRAMID	CUBOID	CUBE
	RIGHT-ANGLED TRIANGLE	CONE	CYLINDER

Build A Shape

AIM: Recognise, understand and use vocabulary for position and direction and symmetry.

ACTIVITY

Give each child a small pile of multilink. Give instructions about how to build a shape. Compare the models at the end.

For example:-

Start with one cube. Put two on top of it and one underneath. Add two onto the right hand side of the top cube.

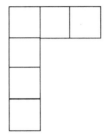

QUESTIONS

Are all the models the same?

Is your model symmetrical?

What would you need to do to your model to make it symmetrical?

What colour is the cube I started with? How do you know?

Which instruction was hardest to follow? Why?

If you turned your model over could you describe how to make it? What would change about the instructions?

VARIATIONS/EXTENSIONS

Children working in pairs, back to back, one giving the instructions, the other making the model.

Give the children some appropriate words and ask them to make a model, the instructions for which would need to use these words. Then get them to give the instructions to the class and compare the different models produced by using these words.

RESOURCES

multilink

VOCABULARY

underneath

above

below

top

bottom

side

beside

next to

left

right

symmetrical

match

Hidden Treasure

AIM: Describe and locate the position of a square on a grid with the rows and columns labelled.

ACTIVITY

Each child needs to draw a grid on paper to match one on which treasure is hidden. Treasure is hidden under some of the squares and each item takes up two squares, so the treasure is in blocks. Let the children suggest squares that the treasure might be under - they keep track on their grids of those that have been offered and those which have treasure under them.

QUESTIONS

If the treasure is partly under B3, where could the other part be?
Which squares are good ones to start with? Why?

Links to:

'Jellyfish Hunt', page 170

RESOURCES

paper
pencils

VOCABULARY

position
rows
column
direction

Fractions of Shapes

AIM: Recognise fractions of shapes and recognise and name 2D shapes.

ACTIVITY

Use pieces of paper or fabric of different shapes, e.g. square, circle, etc. Start by folding in half, then progress to folding in half again and discussing the shape and fraction, unfolding to demonstrate where needed.

QUESTIONS

What shape will it be when folded in half?

Could we fold it in half and get another shape? How?

How do you know it is folded in half?

If we fold again, what fraction of the original sheet will we have? How do you know?

How many quarters make one half? How do you know?

What fraction will we have if we fold a third time? A fourth time?

What is the pattern? Why does it happen?

VARIATIONS/EXTENSIONS

Look at patterns in shapes generated by dividing the shape up by a simple rule. For example, with a square, divide it into four smaller squares. Then each of those squares into four smaller squares and so on. Discuss the fraction of the original square represented by one small square in each case.

Cut sandwiches into different fractions and discuss how much of the original sandwich is being eaten, has been eaten, is about to be eaten, as well as the shapes of the pieces.

 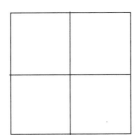 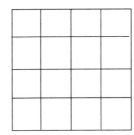

RESOURCES

paper or fabric shapes

VOCABULARY

half
quarter
fraction
square
rectangle
triangle
circle
semi-circle
right-angle

Drawing Shapes

AIM: Recognise and describe properties of shapes, understand names of parts and properties of shapes.

ACTIVITY

Choose a child and give them a card on which is a picture created from shapes. For example

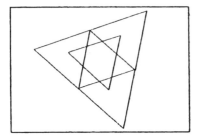 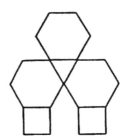

The child must describe the picture and the other children must draw the picture as it is described. Allow the children to ask questions to clarify what has been said. All children show their picture at the end and compare it with the original (which could also be on OHT so that all the children can see it clearly).

QUESTIONS

Which bits of information were most useful? Why?

What was unclear?

Why did you need to ask that question?

What else could have been said to make it clearer?

VARIATIONS/EXTENSIONS

This can be used to focus on particular language. Put on the card specific vocabulary that you want the child to use when describing and tell them they must use all the words.

Let the children ask questions and the child describing must answer them.

Aim to get the size of the picture correct as well as the detail of the shapes.

RESOURCES

shape pictures

paper

pencils

VOCABULARY

names of shapes

symmetrical

rotational

reflective

regular

irregular

equilateral

same

identical

congruent

Name the Shape

AIM: Recognise, name and describe properties of 2D shapes; measure and calculate perimeter and area of shapes.

ACTIVITY

Describe a shape that could be drawn in more than one way.

For example:-

I'm thinking of a shape, it has four right angles and sides, opposite sides are equal and the perimeter is 12cm.

Ask the children to sketch a shape that fits the description and write the name beside it and the length of the sides along the sides.

Invite children out to draw their shape for the class to see.

QUESTIONS

Does this shape fit the description?

What is it?

Does anyone have a different shape that also fits the description?

Does anyone have different lengths for their sides?

Are there any other possibilities?

How did you decide on the lengths of the sides?

VARIATIONS/EXTENSIONS

This can be used to focus on particular vocabulary and allow misunderstandings about words to be discussed.

paper
pencils

VOCABULARY

opposite
adjacent
right-angle
obtuse
acute
angles
regular
irregular
perimeter
area
sides

That Looks Like

AIM: To recognise and name 2D and 3D shapes.

ACTIVITY

Using an OHP, with the children unable to see the 3D shape placed on the projector. Look at the shape in different positions and try to deduce which shape you are using.

QUESTIONS

Which shapes could this be? How do you know?

Can you name a shape that is definitely not the one on the projector? How do you know?

Have you changed your mind about it now you have seen it from another direction? Why?

What could it be now?

Are there any other shapes it could be?

What would you expect to see if I turned it to stand it on its end?

VARIATIONS/EXTENSIONS

With 2D shapes, reveal only part of the shape from behind a piece of card or on an OHP. Again discuss all the possibilities, what it couldn't be as well as what it could be.

RESOURCES

OHP

collection of shapes

VOCABULARY

cube
cuboid
sphere
pyramid
cone
cylinder
prism
hemi-sphere
tetrahedron
square-based pyramid
square
circle
triangle
rectangle
pentagon
hexagon
demi-circle
octagon
heptagon
parallelogram
rhombus
trapezium
kite
equilateral
isoscele
scalene
right-angled
regular
irregular
faces
edges
vertices
sides

Elastic Shapes

AIM: Recognise, name and describe 2D shapes, use the language of angle.

ACTIVITY

Use a large loop of elastic and ask children to stand inside it and move out until the elastic is pulled tight.

QUESTIONS

What shape would we make if three people stand inside the elastic?

How would you make it an equilateral triangle? an isosceles triangle

What happens if one person moves further out? How will that change the shape?

What happens if two people move further apart but stay the same distance from the third?

What shapes could we make if four people stand inside the elastic?

How do we change from a square to an oblong?

VARIATIONS/EXTENSIONS

Children work in pairs doing the same with elastic bands and fingers.

Give each child an elastic band and ask them all to use their fingers to make a shape, for example a square, and then to 'show me'.

Explore on pegboards.

RESOURCES

elastic loop
pegboards

VOCABULARY

triangle
square
rectangle
parallelogram
trapezium
rhombus
equilateral
isosceles
right-angled

Jellyfish Hunt

AIM: Explain reasoning, solve number problems and puzzles, predict, locate the position of a square on a grid with columns and rows labelled.

ACTIVITY

Draw an 8 x 8 grid and hide 10 jelly fish in it. Draw the grid on the board or OHT. The children have to try and locate the jellyfish, without stepping on them. They are given clues. For each square they choose that does not have a jelly fish in it they are told how many squares with jellyfish in it is touching, either with a side or a corner. The maximum number of squares one square is touching is 8.

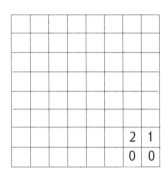

For example this shows the eight squares touching the centre square. As the centre square has a three in it, three of these eight squares must contain a jellyfish.

Let the children record on their own sheets to help thinking.
Give the children a starting square. For example:-

On this grid neither of the squares to the left of the 0 and the 2 can contain a jellyfish as they both touch the square with the zero in it. Only one of the squares above the 2 and the 1 can contain a jellyfish as they both touch the square with one in it. This means the square that touches the top lefthand corner of the square with 2 in it must contain a jellyfish.

The children choose squares to step on, revealing a number, or name a square as having a jellyfish in it.
"I wish to step onto C5"
"I think D8 has a jellyfish in it"

Some sample squares are included on the next page.

QUESTIONS

How do you know there is not a jellyfish in that square?
Why do you think there is a jellyfish in that square?

Links to:

'Hidden Treasure', page 164

RESOURCES

blank grids
(see page 171)

VOCABULARY

above
below
diagonal
position

●	2	1	2	1	2	1	1
1	2	●	2	●	2	●	1
0	1	1	2	2	3	3	2
0	0	0	0	1	●	2	●
1	1	1	0	1	3	4	2
1	●	1	0	1	●	●	1
1	1	1	0	1	2	2	1
0	0	0	1	●	1	0	0

0	1	●	1	0	0	0	0
0	1	2	2	1	0	0	0
1	1	2	●	3	1	0	0
●	1	3	●	●	1	0	0
1	2	2	●	3	2	1	1
0	1	●	3	2	2	●	1
0	1	1	2	●	3	2	2
0	0	0	1	1	2	●	1

0	0	0	0	0	1	●	●
0	1	1	1	1	2	3	2
0	1	●	1	2	●	2	0
1	2	2	2	3	●	3	0
●	1	1	●	4	●	2	0
1	2	2	2	●	2	1	0
0	1	●	2	1	1	0	0
0	1	1	1	0	0	0	0

●	1	0	0	0	1	1	1
1	2	1	2	1	2	●	1
0	1	●	3	●	2	1	1
0	2	3	●	2	1	1	1
1	2	●	2	2	1	1	●
●	3	2	3	●	1	1	1
1	2	●	2	1	1	0	0
0	1	1	1	0	0	0	0

●	1	0	0	1	●	1	0
1	1	1	1	2	1	2	1
1	1	1	●	1	0	1	●
●	1	1	1	2	1	2	1
1	1	1	1	2	●	1	0
1	1	1	●	2	1	1	0
●	1	1	1	2	1	1	0
1	1	0	0	1	●	1	0

1	●	2	●	2	●	1	0
1	2	3	3	3	3	2	1
0	1	●	2	●	2	●	1
1	2	2	3	2	3	2	2
1	●	1	1	●	1	1	●
1	1	1	2	2	2	1	1
0	0	0	1	●	1	0	0
0	0	0	1	1	1	0	0

MAIN ACTIVITY AND PLENARY

Interactive whole class teaching

This is not so much 'chalk and talk' as 'thought and talk'. It means being proactive and not intervening simply when a child is stuck but exploring and extending children's thinking in a lively and engaging way through questioning, demonstrating, explaining and illustrating. It also involves children sharing, discussing, demonstrating and explaining their own methods and solutions to each other and to the teacher during the lesson. Good interaction is as important in group and paired work as it is in whole class work. Talk is the window to the mind and through encouraging children to engage in mathematical discussion children will not only learn from each other but also teachers will learn more about their children as mathematicians and how best to teach them.

Main teaching activity

This part of the lesson can be used to introduce a new topic, to extend previous work, use and apply skills and concepts and to develop language. During this time the teacher may directly teach the whole class, one or two groups of children, targeted pairs or individuals. When working with the whole class it is important to seat them facing the front so that they are all able to see the teacher and other children demonstrating and explaining on the board. A horse shoe shape or two 'U' rings one inside the other (with the least able closest to the teacher) can work well. For some activities a circle may be appropriate. At the start of the lesson it is important that the children are told the aim of the lesson and what they are expected to bring back to the plenary.

To maximise interaction and provoke thinking it is useful to plan at least some of the questions that could be asked during the lesson. These should include both closed and open questions which both support and extend the children (see appendix one). It is also important to identify misconceptions as they arise and use mistakes as positive teaching points. This approach helps to allay children's fears of embarrassment and humiliation at being 'wrong' while valuing everyone's contributions.

When working with the children in groups it is best to have no more than four groups, providing activities on the same theme, differentiated at three levels. The teacher should focus on teaching and questioning one or two groups in this time, not flitting between them all, so that by the end of the week all the groups have received direct teacher input at least once. By working this way the teacher is able to provide intensive support for the less able and directly challenge and extend the more able. As one more able Y5 child remarked 'We all get time now to spend with our teacher'!

When working with groups of children, pairs or individuals it is important that the teacher is not interrupted by other pupils. In order to achieve this the children need to be trained to work independently. This does not necessarily mean sitting still filling in a worksheet. Being independent is about being able to make decisions for oneself, being able to choose and use appropriate resources and being in control of one's own learning. For example, laying the table for 'tea' in the role play corner is an independent activity.

Care should be taken to ensure that these activities, for children working independently, are meaningful, motivating and absorbing and not just 'holding' tasks.

Tips for developing independence during the main teaching activity

Developing independence takes time, especially if it hasn't been encouraged from an early age. Children may need time to adapt to changes in classroom organisation and management and teachers will need time to try out and develop strategies that encourage an independent way of working. The following list contains examples of strategies that teachers have found useful:-

1) Name the groups and put up a timetable so that pupils can see clearly when the teacher will and won't be working with them during the week. With very young children wear a hat or scarf when you don't want to be interrupted.

2) Teach them this mnemonic, and display it, as a guide for what to do of they get stuck. For
   example:-   **Think TALL**
                        Take a risk
                        Ask a friend
                        Look at similar examples
                        Look at the answer and work back

3) Encourage the children to work together and help each other. Sometimes pair up across ability groups; whilst your less able child will obviously benefit from the experience so will the more able child since being able to explain something so that another person can understand demands an even higher level of understanding.

4) Make the resources that the children need accessible and organise monitors within the groups to give out equipment and tidy it away.

5) Provide an 'activity' box of puzzles and games that the children can help themselves to if they finish early or if they are unable to progress without the teacher's help.

6) Choose activities that require few instructions and are easy to administer. For example, set an open-ended investigation such as 'How many different ways can you find to make 50?', give them a puzzle to solve in pairs or a game that has simple rules and requires minimum equipment, such as 'Four in a Row'. (see page)

7) Make the aims of the lesson clear to the children and give them a task to do for the plenary and a dead-line for its completion. It may be helpful to write up the questions for the plenary to help focus their attention during the main teaching activity.

8) With very young children set up a circus of activities around a similar theme so that their interest is maintained.

The Plenary

The plenary can be used for a variety of different things but in order for it to be successful it must be planned for and regular time allocated to it. It can be a powerful tool for assessment, not only of what pupils have learned during the lesson but also how they have learnt it. In order to achieve this teachers need to have a clear focus and make the aims of the plenary clear to the children before the main teaching activity begins, so that they know what they are expected to feedback. Writing up some key questions for the children to consider will also encourage them to remain on task when not working with the teacher.

The plenary demands a lot of prompting, modelling and encouragement from the teacher, to prevent it from being a 'show and tell all' session. Managing and facilitating the discussion can be difficult as, initially, children may be reluctant to share their methods and their thinking through fear of being 'wrong' or 'different'. They may also lack the vocabulary needed to articulate their thoughts. Initially the teacher will need to model suitable responses either by reflecting back what a child has said, describing what they observed a child doing or by offering alternative answers.

What is planned for the plenary will very much depend on the main teaching activity.

Examples include:-
- helping the children to reflect on what was important and needs to be remembered;
- informally assessing individuals or groups and giving feedback to disseminate good ideas and practice;
- asking pupils to present, explain and demonstrate their work so that others can ask questions about it;
- sharing, discussing and comparing different methods of calculating to help pupils develop more efficient strategies;
- encouraging children to generalise a rule from examples;
- clarifying and correcting misconceptions and misunderstandings;
- marking and rectifying written work together;
- setting 'follow up' activities for pupils to do at home.

Remember:-
- be clear about the aims of the plenary and what the children are expected to contribute;
- plan questions for the plenary;
- summarise important key facts, concepts and vocabulary;
- inform pupils of what they will be doing next;
- bring the lesson to a sharply defined end and evaluate its success.

The following are examples of activities that children can work on independently. Each includes examples of questions for the plenary.

Ladybird Spots

AIM: Solve number problems, recognise simple patterns, generalise and predict.

ACTIVITY

A ladybird has spots on its back. The spots can be on either side of its body. If it has two spots there are three ways of arranging the spots, two on the left, two on the right and one on each side. Explore for three spots, four spots, etc. using the large ladybird and counters and recording on the small ladybirds (see following two pages).

QUESTIONS FOR PLENARY

Did you find an easy way to make sure you had found all the ways of arranging the spots?

Can you give addition sentences to go with each ladybird? What do you notice about the numbers?

How many ways did you find for three spots? Four spots? Five spots? Can you see a pattern? Can you say how many you think there would be for six spots and why?

For which numbers could you put the same number of spots on each side? Why can't you do it for the other numbers?

Links to:

'Hidden Numbers', page 89
'Line Jumps', page 90
'Countdown', page 96
'Grid Toals 2', page 114

RESOURCES

ladybird sheet
counters

VOCABULARY

arranging
addition sentences
pattern
odd
even

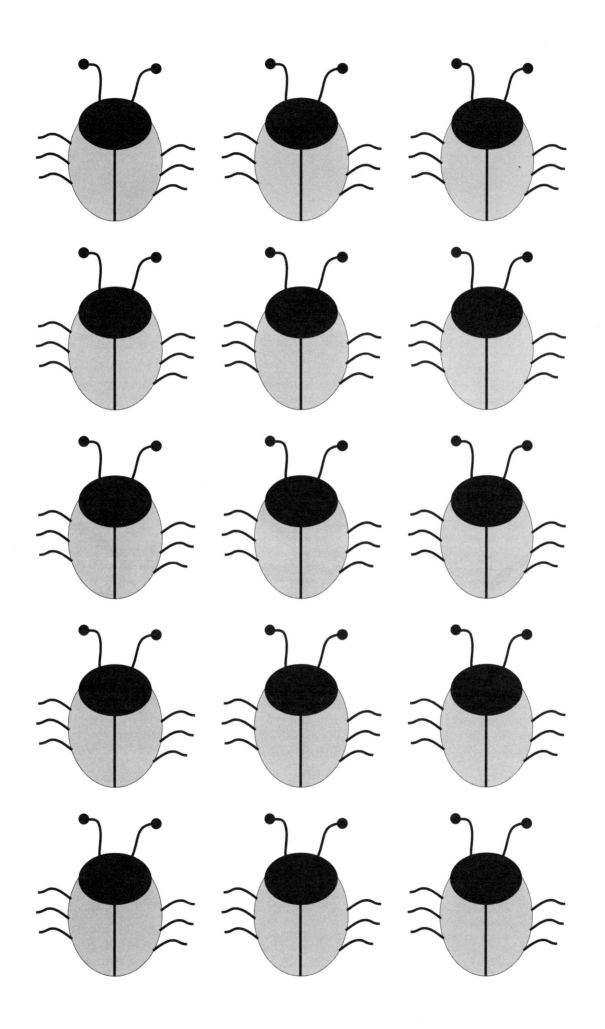

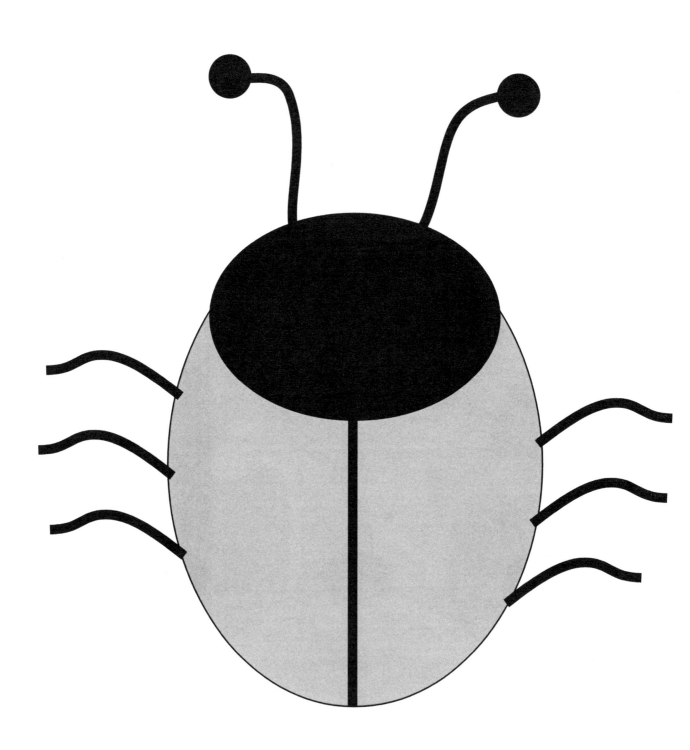

More Doubles

AIM: To know and use double facts to 20.

ACTIVITY

Give the children a blank 6 x 6 grid and a die marked 7 to 12, (you can buy blank dice which you can write on). The children throw the die, double the score and write the total on the grid. Once it is filled, the children take it in turns to roll the die again, doubling the score and covering the number with a counter. The first to get four in a line is the winner.

QUESTIONS FOR PLENARY

What doubles do you know off by heart?
How do you work out the harder ones?
What is the highest double you can make? Why?
What strategies did you use to help you to win?
Can you make 10? How do you know?

VARIATIONS/EXTENSIONS

Children could continue playing until the whole board is covered in counters. The child who has the most counters on the board is the winner.
Make the game easier or harder by using lower or higher numbers, for example use two dice to generate two digit numbers.

Links to:

'Dotty Doubles' page 102
'Doubling Patterns' page 130

RESOURCES

blank 6 x 6 grids
(see next page)
blank dice
counters

VOCABULARY

doubles
doubling
digits
multiply

Corner Numbers Investigated

AIM: Add several small numbers, solve number problems and puzzles, use knowledge of multiplication and division facts.

ACTIVITY

Set up as for the mental/oral session. Possible questions to explore:-

a) How many different ways can you find for the same number inside the same shape?

b) What happens if you change the number of sides the shape has but keep the number the same?

c) What happens if you change the centre number but keep the shapethe same?

d) What if I do or don't use 0?

e) What if I only put 1 at each corner, what happens with different shapes?

f) Does it make a difference if all the numbers have to be different?

g) Do even numbers have more ways when inside shapes with an even number of sides?

QUESTIONS FOR PLENARY

How did you organise yourself?

How did you record what you found?

Did you need any equipment to help you?

Can you make a general statement about what is happening?

Did your investigation raise more questions? - what else do you want to know?

Links to:

'Corner Numbers', page 116

RESOURCES

sheets of shapes
(see next page)
counters

VOCABULARY

shape
multiply
add
total

Corner Numbers

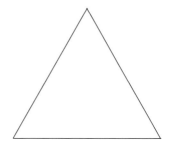 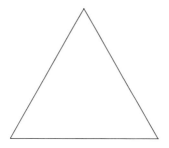 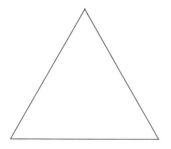

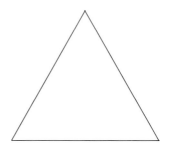 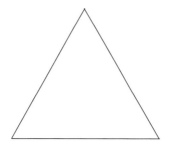 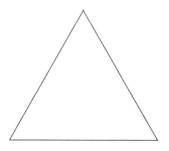

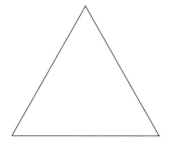 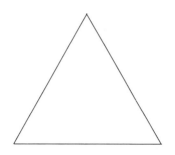 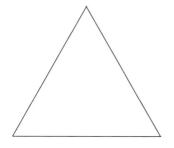

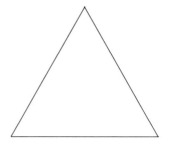 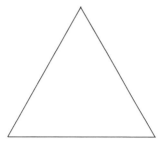 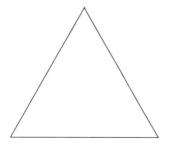

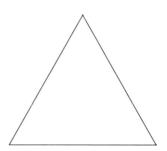 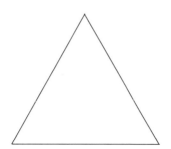 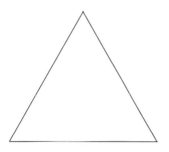

Corner Numbers

First to One Hundred

AIM: To combine operations and develop quick recall of number facts.

ACTIVITY

Give pairs of children a 0 to 100 number line or a hundred square, and two dice. Take it in turns to throw the dice and find the product and the sum of the two numbers. Then find the difference between the product and the sum - this is the score. Record the original numbers, the product, the sum and the score each time. Move forwards the number of places represented by the score.

For example if they throw a 5 and a 6, the product is 30, the sum is 11, the difference is 19 so move forwards 19.

The first to reach a hundred is the winner.

QUESTIONS FOR PLENARY

What quick ways did you use to work things out?

What combinations give the worst score? Which give the best score? Why?

What scores can't you make? Why?

What do you notice about all the scores?

VARIATIONS/EXTENSIONS

The children could start at a hundred and move backwards.

Work without a number line, recording the running total.

Start with a higher target number such as 300 and use digit cards or dice with larger numbers.

Links to:

'Split Numbers', page 143

'Exploring Numbers', page 144

RESOURCES

number lines

hundred squares

dice

VOCABULARY

product

multiply

sum

addition

difference

total

score

How Close Can You Get?

AIM: Read, write and order three digit numbers, partition into hundreds, tens and units, use estimation skills.

ACTIVITY

Organise the children into groups of two or three pairs and give each group a bag of counters, a set of digit cards, two dice and a baseboard for each pair.

The rules are that one child turns over three digit cards to make a three digit number. This becomes the target for the group. In pairs, they then throw two dice, add the score and collect that number of counters. The aim is to get as close as they can to their target number by arranging their counters on the baseboard.

For example:-

The target number is 135. A child throws a 5 and a 3 and collects 8 counters. To get as close as they can the pair lay their counters out like this:-

H	T	U
●	● ● ●	● ● ● ●
1	3	4

Each pair records the target number and the number they manage to make. After each pair has had a go they compare their numbers and the closest pair wins a point. The first pair to ten is the winner.

QUESTIONS FOR PLENARY

How did you decide where to place your counters?
Which was the most important digit to try and make? Why?
How did you work out how close you were to the target number?
How could you find the difference between each of your numbers and the target number?
If you threw two sixes what's the largest number you could make?

VARIATIONS/EXTENSIONS

When the digit cards are turned over, make the target number as high or as low as possible.
Extend to numbers in the thousands

Links to:

'What's is it's Value?', page 52

RESOURCES

counters
dice
HTU baseboards
digit cards

VOCABULARY

order
estimate
digit
numbers
hundreds
tens
units

Dartboards 2

AIM: To solve whole number problems using addition and multiplication, explain orally methods and reasoning about numbers.

ACTIVITY

Give each pair of children a copy of a dartboard and set them a number of challenges. For example:-

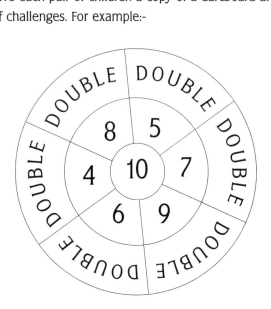

Using three darts how many different scores can you make where:-

1) You throw no doubles;
2) You throw one double;
3) You throw two doubles;
4) You throw three doubles?

QUESTIONS FOR PLENARY

What strategies helped you to work them out?

How did you check your scores?

How do you know you have found them all?

Did you work systematically?

What was your highest score? What was your lowest score?

What facts did you know?

How did you work out ones you didn't know?

VARIATIONS/EXTENSIONS

Add a fourth dart.

Give the children target scores to investigate how many different ways they can be made?

As well as doubles, add another ring for trebles (as in 'Dart Attack')

You could also add a ring for squaring the number.

The children design their own dartboards to investigate.

Links to:

'Dart Attack', page 126

'Dartboards', page 192

RESOURCES

dartboard
(blank on the next page)

VOCABULARY

double

fact

investigate

score

total

highest

lowest

method

strategy

pattern

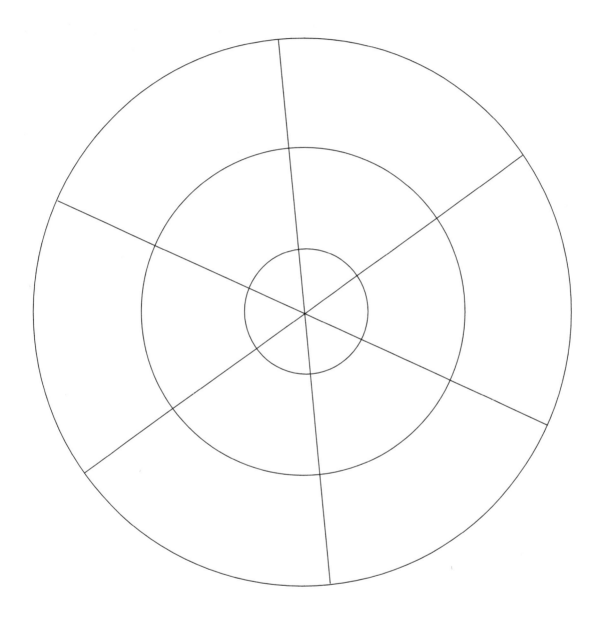

Caterpillars

AIM: Know by heart halves of numbers to 100 and add or subtract 1 to any number; recognise and explain patterns and relationships, generalise and predict.

ACTIVITY

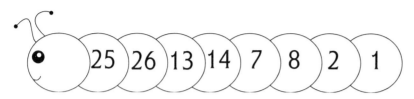

You make the pattern in the caterpillar's segments by adding 1 when the number is odd and halving the number when it is even. This caterpillar, starting with 25, has 9 segments.

Find the length of caterpillars for other numbers up to 20 and beyond.

QUESTIONS FOR PLENARY

What did you notice about the numbers in the caterpillars? Why does this happen?

Can you find a quick way of working out the lengths of caterpillars for the bigger numbers?

Which numbers have short caterpillars? Why?
Which have long caterpillars? Why?

Can you find the number between 1 and 100 that forms the longest caterpillar? How did you do it? Can you use this method to quickly find the number with the longest caterpillar between 1 and 1000?

What do you think would happen if you subtracted 1 instead of adding 1? How would this change the longest and shortest caterpillars?

VARIATIONS/EXTENSIONS

Graph the lengths of the caterpillars to aid pattern seeking.
Change the rule, to halve and add 5 for example.

Links to:

'Spotting Halves and Doubles', page 142

RESOURCES

VOCABULARY

odd

even

add

subtracr

halve

double

pattern

graph

Different Ways

AIM: Choose an appropriate way of calculating.

ACTIVITY

Give the children, in pairs, some calculations and ask them to find different ways for doing each one, starting with the ways they would use.

For example:-

147 + 296

59 x 5

Find a way to record each method and decide which ones are appropriate and efficient.

QUESTIONS FOR PLENARY

Can you explain and demonstrate the methods you found for one calculation?

Which ones did you think were appropriate and efficient? Why?

What is 'wrong' with the other methods? Can you think of calculations when these would be good methods ?

Links to:

'Same Question, Different Solution', page 137

RESOURCES

VOCABULARY

methods

appropriate

efficient

Are they the same?

AIM: To recognise equivalent fractions, decimals and percentages.

ACTIVITY

Hand out a set of fraction cards to each pair of children. The children place the cards face down on the table and take turns to turn two over and decide whether they match. If they do, they keep the pair. If not, they turn them back over.

QUESTIONS FOR PLENARY

How did you decide if they matched or not?

What does the top part of the fraction, the numerator, tell you?

What do you understand by the bottom number, the denominator?

What did you use to help you?

What equivalent fractions do you know?

Why are some harder to work out than others?

VARIATIONS/EXTENSIONS

Cut up sets of squares or circles into halves, thirds, etc. Children can overlay them to try and work out equivalence.

Play pairs with decimal fractions and or percentages or extend to finding equivalence between combinations of them.

RESOURCES

fraction cards

(see opposite page)

calculators

VOCABULARY

fraction

equivalent

numerator

denominator

half, quarter, third, etc.

$\dfrac{1}{2}$	$\dfrac{1}{4}$	$\dfrac{4}{4}$	1
$\dfrac{2}{2}$	$\dfrac{8}{8}$	$\dfrac{6}{8}$	$\dfrac{16}{16}$
$\dfrac{2}{2}$	$\dfrac{3}{8}$	$\dfrac{6}{16}$	$\dfrac{12}{32}$
$\dfrac{12}{16}$	$\dfrac{3}{4}$	$\dfrac{24}{32}$	$\dfrac{10}{16}$
$\dfrac{5}{8}$	$\dfrac{20}{32}$	$\dfrac{16}{32}$	$\dfrac{8}{16}$
$\dfrac{4}{8}$	$\dfrac{5}{8}$	$\dfrac{2}{4}$	$\dfrac{3}{6}$
$\dfrac{2}{8}$	$\dfrac{4}{16}$	$\dfrac{8}{32}$	$\dfrac{7}{8}$
$\dfrac{6}{16}$	$\dfrac{14}{16}$	$\dfrac{28}{32}$	$\dfrac{7}{8}$

Dartboards

AIM: Use knowledge of number facts and a range of strategies to solve number problems.

ACTIVITY

In small groups, containing two or three pairs, give each pair a dartboard, three counters, a blank die coloured to match the rings on the dart board, two ordinary dice and a score sheet The children throw the two dice to generate a target number for the group. The aim of the game is to get a total score which is as close to the target number as possible. Players take turns to throw the coloured die and place a counter on one of the matching regions of the dartboard.

Each time they enter a score on their sheet. After the third counter has been placed the players add up their scores and see how close they are to the target number. The winner is the pair that is closest.
Repeat for a new target number.

QUESTIONS

How did you decide where to place your counters?
What strategies did you use to calculate the totals?
How did you check your answers?
What known facts helped you work out other answers?

VARIATIONS/EXTENSIONS

Use higher numbers, change the layout of the dartboard.
Set an investigation to find different ways to make a particular score or investigate how many different scores can be made.
For example, imagine throwing three darts at this board. How many different scores could you make? Can you work systematically?

Links to:

'Dart Attack', page 126
'Dartboards 2', page 186

RESOURCES

die with two faces white, two grey and two black.
dartboards & score sheets (see next pages)
counters
two numbered dice

VOCABULARY

strategies
addition
score
total
sum
multiplication
double
treble

Dartboards

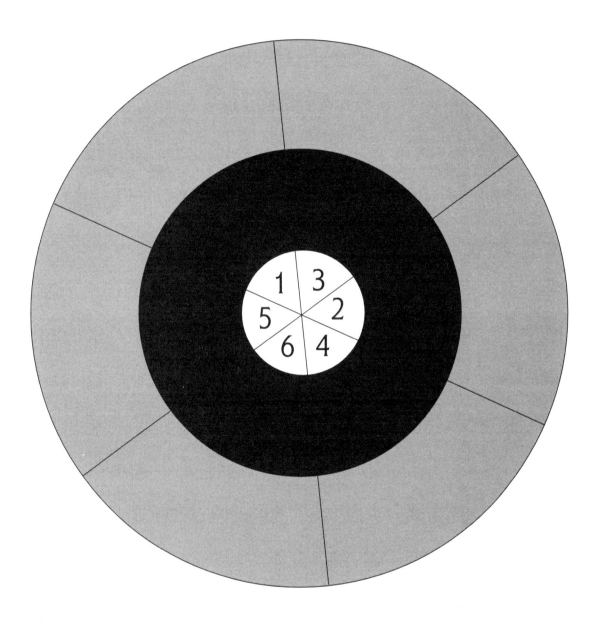

BLACK   =   Double
GREY   =   Treble
WHITE   =   Single Digits

Dartboards Score Sheet

1st Throw	2nd Throw	3rd Throw	TOTAL

Consecutive Numbers Extended

AIM: Use knowledge of number facts and place value to calculate mentally.

ACTIVITY

Consecutive numbers lead to a variety of activities:-

1) Make numbers by adding consecutive numbers
2) Consider three consecutive numbers, multiply the first and last, square the middle number and compare answers.
3) Consider four consecutive numbers, multiply the first and last, multiply the middle pair and then compare answers.
4) Consider running totals of consecutive odd numbers:-

   1
   1 + 3
   1 + 3 + 5
   1 + 3 + 5 + 7
   etc.
   and look for patterns in answers.

QUESTIONS FOR PLENARY

(the numbers alongside these questions relate to the activities above)

1) Which numbers can't you make between 1 and 30? What do you think will be the next number you won't be able to make?
   Which numbers can be made by adding three consecutive numbers?

2) What do you notice about the difference between the product of the first and last numbers and the square of the middle number? Can you explain why it works? What if you did the same with three consecutive odd numbers? What happens then?

3) What do you notice about the difference between the products of the first and last numbers and the middle pair? Can you explain why this happens? Can you generalise?

4) What did you notice about the totals? Could you generalise for any number of odd numbers? Can you explain why it happens?

VARIATIONS/EXTENSIONS

Let the children develop their own investigations about consecutive numbers.

Links to:

'Consecutive Numbers', page 134

RESOURCES
none

VOCABULARY
consecutive
multiply
square
product
total
odd
even
generalise

Number Pyramids Investigated

AIM: Explain methods and reason about numbers, solve number problems, recognise and explain patterns and relationships, generalise and predict, calculate mentally.

ACTIVITY

This is an extension of the mental/oral activity 'Number Pyramids'. The children can be enouraged to investigate different aspects of the activity and the questions below all start from the basic four layer pyramid.

QUESTIONS FOR PLENARY

How many different ways are there of organising the four numbers at the bottom of the wall? How did you work this out? What if it were a five layer wall, how many ways would there be then?

Can you give a general rule for how to arrange numbers so that you always get the highest or lowest top number? How does the rule need to change for a five layer pyramid?

Can you see a connection between the numbers at the bottom and the number at the top? Can you explain that connection?
What about if the wall now had five layers? What would the connection be now?

What do you notice about the pyramid if you start with four even numbers? Four odd numbers? Why is this? How would this change for a five layer pyramid?

If I give you the top number for the pyramid, rather than the bottom number, what is the easiest way to fill in the rest of the pyramid? How else could you do it? Can you create a pyramid with 20 at the top that has negative numbers in it?

If you are finding the difference instead of adding, can you give a general rule for how to arrange the numbers so that you always get the highest or lowest top number? What is the connection between this number and the numbers on the bottom layer?

If you use the operations add, subtract and multiply, which order gives you the biggest top number? Why do you think that is? Does it work for all numbers on the bottom?

Links to:

'Number Pyramids', page 140
'Number Pyramids 2', page 148

RESOURCES

number pyramid sheets
(see page opposite)

VOCABULARY

organising
general rule
explain
connection
even
odd
negative
add
subtract
difference
multiply

Fours Fours

AIM: Use all four operations to solve problems, recognise and explain patterns and relationships, use knowledge of number facts and place value for calculating.

ACTIVITY

Try to make all the numbers from 1 to 100 using any operations and exactly four fours each time. For example,

$4 + 4 + 4 - 4 = 8$

QUESTIONS FOR PLENARY

Which numbers have been easiest to find, odd or even? Why do you think that is?

How have you organised this activity? Are you using any particular method to help you find as many numbers as possible?

How many different ways have we found for making the number one using four fours?

Which numbers do you think will be hardest to find? Why? Are there any other things we know about, as well as adding, subtracting, multiplying and dividing, that will help us make new numbers?

VARIATIONS/EXTENSIONS

This can be undertaken by the whole class with children working independently on it. To complete the activity will take a number of sessions. You can use this as an opportunity for introducing and revisiting concepts such as square roots, squaring, brackets and factorials, so that the children have the tools to help them.

Use a hundred square to keep track of the numbers found (as a class) and have a book to show different ways found for the same number. For example,

$(4 \div 4) \div (4 \div 4) = 1$

$4 \div 4 + 4 - 4 = 1$

$(4 \div 4) \times (4 \div 4) = 1$

$4 - 4 + (4 \div 4) = 1$

$((4 \div 4) \div 4) \times 4 = 1$

An example of how one Y5 child did this is shown on the opposite page. This is not the definitive answer but it gives you an example for each number (with only one correction!).

Links to:

'Grid Totals 3', page 125

'Target', page 149

RESOURCES

hundred square

VOCABULARY

add
subtract
multiply
divide
square
cube
power
square root
multiple
odd
even
brackets
factorial

1 $(4 + 4 - \frac{4}{4}) = 4$ 26 $4^2 + 4 + 4 + \sqrt{4}$ 51 $4^3 - 4^2 + 4 - 4$ 76 $(4^3 + 4^2 - 4) \div 4^0$

2 $(4^2 - 4 - 4) \div 4$ 27 $4^2 + 4^2 - 4 - 4^0$ 52 $4^2 + 4^2 + 4^2 + 4$ 77 $4^3 + 4^2 - 4 + 4^0$

3 $(4^2 - 4) \div 4) \div 4$ 28 $4^2 + 4 + 4 + 4$ 53 $4^3 - 4^2 + 4 + 4^0$ 78 $4^3 + 4^2 - 4^0 - 4^0$

4 $4^2 - 4 - 4 - 4$ 29 $4^2 + 4^2 - \sqrt{4} - 4$ 54 $4^3 - 4^2 + 4 + \sqrt{4}$ 79 $4^3 + 4^2 - \sqrt{4} + 4^0$

5 $(4^2 + 4) \div 4) \div 4$ 30 $4^2 + 4^2 - 4^0 - 4^0$ 55 $4^2 - 4 - 4 - 4^0$ 80 $4^3 - 4^3 + 4^3 \frac{4}{4}$

6 $4^2 - 4 - 4 - \sqrt{4}$ 31 $(4^2 + 4^2 - 4^0) \div 4$ 56 $4^3 - 4^2 + 4 + 4$ 81 $(4^3 + 4^2 + 4^0) \div 4$

7 $(4^2 - 4) \div 4) + 4$ 32 $4^2 + 4^2 - 4^2 + 4^2$ 57 $4^3 - 4 - \sqrt{4} - 4^0$ 82 $(4^3 + 4^2 + \sqrt{4}) \div 4$

8 $4^2 - 4 - 4 = 4$ 33 $(4 \times 4) + 4^2 + 4^0$ 58 $4^3 - 4 - 4 + \sqrt{4}$ 83 $4^3 + 4^2 + 4 - 4^0$

9 $4^2 - 4 - 4 + 4^0$ 34 $(4 \times 4) + 4^2 + \sqrt{4}$ 59 $4^3 - 4 - \sqrt{4} + 4^0$ 84 $(4^3 + 4^2 + 4) \div 4$

10 $4^2 - \sqrt{4} - \sqrt{4} - \sqrt{4}$ 35 $4^2 + 4^2 + \sqrt{4} + 4^0$ 60 $4^3 - 4^3 + 4^3 - 4$ 85 $4^3 + 4^2 + 4 + 4^0$

11 $4^2 - \sqrt{4} - \sqrt{4} - 4^0$ 36 $(4 \times 4) + 4^2 + 4$ 61 $4^3 - 4 + \sqrt{4} - 4^0$ 86 $4^3 + 4^2 + 4 + \sqrt{4}$

12 $(4 + 4 \times 4) \div 4^0$ 37 $4^2 + 4^2 + 4 + 4^0$ 62 $4^3 - 4 - 4^0 + 4$ 87 $4^3 \sqrt{4} + 4^2 + 4^0$

13 $4^2 - 4^0 - 4^0 - 4^0$ 38 $4^2 + 4^2 + 4 + \sqrt{4}$ 63 $4^3 - 4 + \sqrt{4} + 4^0$ 88 $4^3 + 4^2 + 4 - 4$

14 $4^2 - 4 + 4 - \sqrt{4}$ 39 $(4^3 + 4^2 - \sqrt{4}) \div \sqrt{4}$ 64 $4^4 - 4^3 - 4^3 - 4$ 89 $4^3 + \sqrt{4^3} + 4^2 + 4^0$

15 $4^2 - 4 + 4 - 4^0$ 40 $4^2 + 4^2 + 4 + 4$ 65 $4^3 + 4 - \sqrt{4} - 4$ 90 $(4^2 - 4^0) \times (4 + \sqrt{4})$

16 $4 + 4 + 4 + 4$ 41 $(4^3 + 4^2 \sqrt{4}) \div \sqrt{4}$ 66 $4^3 + 4 - 4^0 - 4$ 91 $4^3 + \sqrt{4^3} - 4 - 4^0$

17 $(4 \times 4) + 4^0 - 4^0$ 42 $4^3 - 4^2 - 4 - \sqrt{4}$ 67 $4^3 + 4 - \sqrt{4} + 4^0$ 92 $4^3 + 4^2 + 4^2 - 4$

18 $4^2 - 4 + 4 + \sqrt{4}$ 43 $4^3 - 4^2 - 4 - 4^0$ 68 $4^3 + 4 - 4 + 4^0$ 93 $4^3 + \sqrt{4^3} - 4 + 4^0$

19 $4^2 + 4^0 + 4^0 + 4^0$ 44 $(4^3 - 4^2 - 4) \div \frac{4}{4}$ 69 $(4^3 + 4) + (4 \div 4)$ 94 $4^3 + 4^2 + 4^2 - \sqrt{4}$

20 $4^2 + 4 + 4 - 4$ 45 $4^3 - 4^2 - 4 + 4^0$ 70 $4^3 + 4 + 4 - \sqrt{4}$ 95 $4^3 + 4^2 + 4^2 - 4^0$

21 $4^2 + \sqrt{4} + \sqrt{4} + 4^0$ 46 $4^3 + 4^2 + 4^2 - \sqrt{4}$ 71 $4^3 + 4 + \sqrt{4} + 4^0$ 96 $(4^3 + 4^3 + 4^2) \div 4^2$

22 $4^2 + \sqrt{4} + \sqrt{4} + \sqrt{4}$ 47 $4^2 + 4^2 + 4^2 - 4^0$ 72 $(4^3 + 4 + 4) \div 4^0$ 97 $4^3 + 4^3 + 4^2 + 4^0$

23 $4^2 + 4 + \sqrt{4} + 4^0$ 48 $(4^3 + 4^2 + 4^2) \div 4$ 73 $4^3 + 4 + 4 + 4^0$ 98 $4^3 + 4^2 + 4^2 - \sqrt{4}$

24 $(4^2 + 4 + 4) \div 4$ 49 $4^3 + 4^2 + 4^2 + 4^2$ 74 $4^3 + 4^2 - 4 - \sqrt{4}$ 99 $4^3 \sqrt{4^3} + 4 - 4^0$

25 $4^2 + 4 + \sqrt{4} + 4^0$ 50 $4^2 + 4^2 + 4^2 + \sqrt{4}$ 75 $4^3 + 4^2 - 4 - 4^0$ 100 $4^3 + 4^2 + 4^2 + 4$

Four in a Row

AIM: Know and use number facts, multiply 2 two digit numbers mentally, identify and use factors.

ACTIVITY

Give each pair of children a set of digit cards from 1 to 20 and a blank 8 x 8 grid. Ask them to randomly select two cards, multiply the numbers together and write the answer on the grid. Encourage them to check their answers by performing the calculations in different ways, by using estimation and division. For example:-

12 x 15 = (10 x 15) + (2 x 15)

12 x 15 is approximately 150

12 x 15 = (12 x 10) + half of (12 x 10)

Ask the children to continue until they have filled in the 8 x 8 grid

Once they have filled in the grid the children take turns turning over two cards, multiplying the numbers and finding the answer on the grid. They cover the answer each time with a counter or cube and the first to get four in a row in any direction is the winner.

For example:-

180	72	26	48	18	24	65	70
77	90	76	132	80	135	228	80
165	20	30	88	216	42	28	51
72	52	105	36	15	(90)	32	144
50	63	21	20	99	33	100	98
24	120	44	64	40	160	45	150
56	36	216	54	105	65	110	180
198	64	112	380	120	165	240	84

15 x 6 = 90, so cover up the square with 90 on.

QUESTIONS FOR PLENARY

What strategies did you use to work out the answers?

Can you explain how you would calculate 15 x 17?

Which method is quickest?

How did you check your answers?

Why is it important to know how to use a range of strategies?

VARIATIONS/EXTENSIONS

Give children a ready-filled in grid and a collection of numbers that are factors of the numbers in the grid. They choose a number on the grid and have to identify its factors to gain the square.

Links to:

'Which Pair?', page 145

'Two Digit Multiplication', page 147

RESOURCES

number cards 1 to 20

blank 8 x 8 grids

(see opposite)

counters or cubes

VOCABULARY

estimation

number facts

multiply

divide

halving

doubling

partitioning

product

factor

How Many Minutes Have You Lived?

AIM: Make and justify estimates of large numbers, use all four operations to solve word problems involving length, mass, capacity, money and time.

ACTIVITY

Give the children a particular problem to solve such as:-

"How many minutes have you lived?"

"How many loaves of bread does this class eat in a year?"

"How much thicker is sugar paper than tissue paper?"

"Which breakfast cereal is the best value?"

"How much money would you need to make a pile of pound coins as tall as Nelson's column (56.5m)?"

"How many raindrops fall on the playground in an hour?"

"Would you rather have your weight in chocolate bars or two hundred 250g bars?"

"Would you rather receive a present every day of your life or a present every second for ten hours?"

"How many sheets of A4 paper would there be in a pile 10m high?"

"How many litres of water does the average family use in a week?"

"How many people could stand on the school playground?"

"How many hours of television do you watch in a year?"

The question can be as topical as you like and focus on any measure.

QUESTIONS FOR PLENARY

What did you need to measure? Why?

Did you do any rounding? Why?

What calculations did you decide you needed to do? Why?

What did you estimate the calculation to be? Why?

Can you explain what you discovered?

Links to:

'How Many?' page 75

'This Container Holds ....', page 70

RESOURCES

calculator

measuring equipment as necessary

VOCABULARY

how many?

average

round

estimate

measure

calculation

Grains of Rice

AIM: Use all four operations to solve word problems involving length, mass, capacity and money, justify estimates of large numbers; read and write any whole number.

ACTIVITY

This activity is built around a story which can be told in many forms (and could be left to the children to write). It originates from a story about the invention of chess but another version is told opposite; vary it as you choose. This could spread over a number of sessions beginning with calculating and number analysis, then later solving the problems about volume, weight and money. The results are astounding and children will be fascinated by the amount of rice involved.

QUESTIONS FOR PLENARY

How did you start to work out the total number of grains of rice? How did you double the larger numbers? What did you have to write down to help you?

How many digits do you think the final number will have? Why?

What do you notice about the numbers? Why are they all even after the first number? Why do the last digits have a pattern?

How many grains of rice are there in total on the first three squares? Four squares? Five squares? Do you see a pattern? Can you find a quick way to total the number of grains of rice on the whole chessboard?

What will all this rice look like? How much space do you think it will take up? How many times would it fill your classroom? How could we work out the approximate volume?

How much do you think the rice would weigh? Why? How can we check this?

How much would it cost? How could we work this out?

Links to:

'Jar of Mung Beans', page 76

RESOURCES

'Grains of Rice' story
(see next page)
rice
scales
squared paper

VOCABULARY

square
cube
power
approximate
estimate
double
pattern
space
volume
weigh
cost

Grains of Rice

There was once a Chinese Emperor whose country was threatened by a fierce and powerful dragon. The Emperor was desperate to be rid of the dragon and offered a reward for anyone who found a way to free China from its tyranny. A young warrior came to the palace and said he had the solution.

"And what do you seek as your reward?" asked the Emperor.

"Only the hand of your daughter in marriage" replied the warrior.

"Never!" said the Emperor.

"Then you and your country shall be ruined by this dragon."

But as the warrior left the palace he passed an old man dressed in rags and walking with the aid of a stick. The man approached on shaking legs and whispered to the guards that he needed to see the Emperor.

"I can rid you of the dragon" said the old man.

"And what do you seek as your reward?" asked the Emperor.

"I am but a poor man with little to eat. I ask only that you give me rice. Take a simple chess board, give me one grain of rice for the first square, two for the second, four for the third and continue to double the grains until all the squares are accounted for. That is all I ask."

The Emperor smiled to himself.

"This seems like a very fair request" he thought. So he agreed.

The man kept his word and the dragon was a problem no more. The Emperor gave orders for the man to be rewarded as he had requested. But, before long, the chief servant returned to the Emperor's side with a grave and worried look upon his face.

SAMPLE LESSON PLANS

We have included six examples of lesson plans following the 'Numeracy Hour' structure. These explore the different ways to organise a class especially during the main teaching activity. In some of the lessons the mental/oral activities lead directly to the main part of the lesson; in the others the two parts are separate. The main activities include games, solving word problems and investigations. There is differentiation by both outcome and task and the examples include grouping by ability, working in pairs and working as a whole class. The plans are written in great detail to give a clear indication of the intention of each part of the lesson; teachers would not need to write such detailed plans. The most important elements are clear objectives and provocative questions.

Fraction - Halves & Quarters

AIM: Begin to recognise one half and a quarter and use them to find halves and quarters of shapes and numbers of objects (eg half a piece of string, half of 8 bricks, a quarter of a square).

Resources

A range of Christmas cards chopped into 4 parts, some in quarters, both as triangles and as rectangles. Various lengths of string, lumps of plasticine, plastic knives, box of small sorting animals and cardboard fields, rectangular and square sheets of paper and coloured pencils, bead tray and strings, rulers, multilink cubes, apples, sweets and flipchart.

Mental/Oral Introductory Sessions: 10 minutes

(whole class on carpet; apples, multilink cubes, sweets, flipchart).
Ask the children what is meant by half of something and use the apple, sweets and multilink cubes to demonstrate.

Questions:

How can an apple be cut in half?
How do we know where half is?
If I cut it here would that be half? Why not?
What should each half of the apple be?
How many pieces will we have?
What do we mean by a quarter?
How many pieces would we have if we cut it into quarters?
How many quarters make a half?
If we shared this apple equally between four of you how much would you get each?
What if I cut 3 apples into halves, how many people could get a half each?
What if I cut 2 apples into quarters, how many people could have a quarter?
How are you working it out?

Write the words whole, half and quarter on the board and illustrate with pictures. Invite children to the board to complete the pictures by drawing in the fraction lines. Draw on the symbols for 1/2 and 1/4 and discuss the vocabulary of fractions.
Repeat using the sweets or multilink cubes, but encourage the children to make the links between fractions and division and to apply their knowledge of number bonds to larger numbers.

For example:
I have 6 sweets, I'm going to eat half of them. How many will I have left?
How do you know?
If I shared 8 sweets equally between two of you, how many would you have each?
What do you notice about sharing into 2 equal groups and halving?
If I had 8 sweets and shared them equally between 4 of you, how many would you get each?
What's a quarter of 8 ?
If I eat a quarter of them, how many will be left?
What's half of 2? Half of 4 ? Half of 200 ? 400 ?
What other facts like this do you know?

Main Teaching Activity: 20 minutes

(4 Groups - a circus of 4 activities, 6 minutes to be spent on each one. Organise each activity table with resources and a question card before hand).

Group 1: Investigate how to find a half and a quarter of a sheet of paper.

Group 2: Investigate how to find a half and a quarter of a piece of string.

Group 3: Find out which Christmas card puzzles consist of 4 quarters

Group 4: Investigate how to find half of a string of beads.

Extension Activity (if needed):

Choose a number of farm animals and try to share equally between 2 fields.

Inform the children that you want them to be able to explain how they found a half and a quarter of the different objects at the end of the lesson. Prepare the children for the plenary session by saying something like "While you are working, think about these questions - we will talk about these at the end". (At this point share the plenary questions with the children - you may wish to write them on the board).

Focus on one activity so that you see each group as they visit it.

Some suggested questions for activities 1 and 4
Activity 1

What do you know about the shape of this piece of paper?

How can we check its pairs of sides are the same length?

How can you be sure when you fold the paper that you are folding it in half?

Is there another way you could fold it in half? What do you notice when you fold it in half one way and then another?

What do 2 quarters make then?

Is there another way you could find to divide it into quarters without folding it?

What if we folded each quarter of the paper into half, how many parts would the paper be in then?

Activity 4

How are you going to find the half-way mark on the string of beads?

Is there a different way you could check you are right?

Is the number of beads odd or even? How do you know?

If the beads were different sizes would folding the string in half mean each half would have the same number of beads? Why?

If a string has an odd number of beads can you find half of them?

Show me half of ten beads. What would half of 12 be? 20?

What can you use to help you work it out?

If a necklace has 8 beads, how many beads would be in a quarter of the necklace?

What if it had 12?

Plenary: 15 minutes
Questions

Can you explain how you found a half or a quarter of the paper, string and beads?

What do 2 quarters make? If something is cut into 4 parts, is each one always a quarter? How do you know?

What do you know about the numbers of beads or animals that can be divided in half?

Can you find half of an odd number? How?

Ask the children which objects they found the easiest to find half and then a quarter of and why. Discuss the various ways they solved the problems. Ask a couple of children to demonstrate how they found half of the string or paper.

Re-emphasise that for 2 parts to be halves they have to be the same size. Hold up an example of the Christmas card puzzle where the 4 pieces are of unequal size and one where the pieces are quarters. Reiterate that when finding half of a set of objects it's the same as sharing into 2 equal groups. Finally hold up 2 multilink towers, one an even number of cubes, the other of an odd number and discuss what happens when you try to break it in half.

Addition of 3 single digit numbers.

AIM: Be able to add 3 single digit numbers together mentally. Put the larger number first. Understand vocabulary associated with addition. Solve problems involving money

Resources:

Shop items with prices ranging from 3p to 10p. Dice, cubes, number lines 0-20. Digit cards, sets of number cards 3-40. Coins, calculator.

Mental/Oral Introductory Session: 15 minutes

(whole class on carpet facing display of shop items)

Recap on what finding the total cost or price means and then tell the children that you are going to buy some items from the shop, and you want them to show the answers on their fingers. Where the answer is greater than 10 they combine with a partner to show the result.

Questions:

What is the total cost of the rubber and pencil?

What change would I get from 20p if I spend 14p?

What do 3 rubbers cost if one costs 10p?

What could I buy exactly for 15p?

What 3 items could I buy for 20p? Are there any other possibilities?

Can you choose 4 of the same item that cost an exact amount eg 12p?

Then hand out a number card to each child from a pack of cards numbered 3 to 40. Tell the children that the card represents the amount of money they have to spend and that you want them to choose a way to spend all of their money in the 'shop'. Give them a few minutes to share and discuss with a friend and then ask for some examples and model their methods on the board. Ask what coins they might have paid for the items with and what are quick ways of adding up to find the total cost.

Main Teaching Activity: 20 minutes
(4 differentiated groups)

Less able group

Children take turns being shopkeeper and customer and buying 3 items. Prepare a set of money stamp cards up to 20p, which children shuffle and select one from each time. This represents the money they have to spend. They then collect this money from the 'bank' and decide what to buy. Limit them to using 5p, 2p and 1p coins.

2 Middle ability groups (in pairs, each with 3 dice, a number grid and some counters))

The children take turns to throw 3 dice, add up the score and cover the answer on the grid with a counter. Each child has a different coloured set of counters. The winner is the one with the most counters on the board at the end.

More able group (in pairs, each with a three 9 sided dice, number line 0-30 and some cubes)

The children take turns throwing the three dice and finding the total. They place a cube on the number line at their answer. At each go the child that makes the highest total scores a point. The first to score 20 points wins. The children also have to investigate which numbers get visited least and most often on the number line.

Before introducing these activities explain to the whole class the aims of the lesson and the purpose of the tasks. Prepare them for the plenary session by saying something like, "While you are working together, think about these questions - we will talk about these at the end of the lesson". (At this point share with the children the plenary questions - you may wish to write them up on the board). When the groups begin work, aim to work with one for ten minutes and then another.

Questions to ask pairs / group
More able / Middle ability (as appropriate):
How are you working it out in your head?

What facts can you use?

How are you checking your answers?

When you throw a 'double' or a 'treble', is there a quick way of working out the score?

What if the dice were marked in tens and you throw a double 20 and a 30, how would you work out the score?

What's the quick way of calculating three 8s or 9s?

Will all the numbers from 0-30 on the number line end up being covered? Why do you think this is?

Why do you think some numbers are coming up more often than others?

Are you just as likely to score 15 as 20? Why do you think that?

Less able:
How do you know if you've collected the right amount of money?

Can you count it out again in a different way?

Is it quicker paying for something in pennies or 2p's? Why?

How are you deciding which three items to buy with your money?

Will you spend exactly all your money? How do you know?

How are you adding up the cost of the items? What could you use to help you?

How can you work out the change you're going to get?

Is it easier counting on or counting back?

What coins would you use to pay for a rubber and 2 pencils?

Plenary: 10 minutes
Questions:
Can you explain how you added the numbers together?

What do you think is the quickest way to add 3 or more digits? Why?

What's the best way to check your answers?

Why do you think some numbers are easier to score than others?

Which numbers came up the most? the least? Why?

As children give their responses model their methods on a number line on the board with specific examples. Discuss the different ways the numbers could be added and which way is the most efficient. Highlight why knowing number bonds to 10 is so important.

e.g. Adding 1, 6 and 9 may be tackled in a number of ways:-

(i) Counting on in 1s

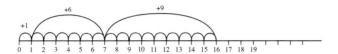

(ii) Noticing that 9 and 1 is 10 and then counting on 10 from 6

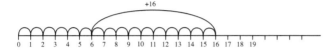

.... and, the most efficient,

(iii) use knowledge of bonds to 10 to pair up 9 and 1 first and then know 10 + 6 = 16 as a number fact.

Pick another example and ask a more confident child to show their method on the board. Encourage the child to start from the largest number and count on. (See Mental/Oral activity: 'Starting Big' page 91)

Discuss why some numbers can be made more easily than others by referring to specific examples, eg 27 is hard to score because you can only make it by throwing 3 'nines' 12 is easy to score because there are lots of ways you can make it 5 + 5 + 2, 5 + 4 + 3, 5 + 6 + 1, 4 + 4 + 4, 1 + 2 + 9, 1 + 3 + 8, 1 + 4 + 7, etc.

Link with the shopping group by asking which amounts they found easy to buy 3 items with and which they found more difficult. Recap on the vocabulary of addition, and ask the children to make up some money problems involving buying 3 or more things for homework.

Rectangular Numbers

AIM: To use multiplication facts and search for patterns. Develop awareness of rectangular and square numbers. Begin to understand the term factor.

Resources:
Pegboard, pegs, cubes.

Mental/Oral Introductory Session: 5 minutes
(Whole class, seated at tables)
Hand out pegboards or multilink cubes to pairs of children and ask if they can arrange 12 pegs or cubes in a rectangle. Give them a few minutes and then ask children to describe the dimensions of their rectangle and to draw on the board. Discuss the number of rows and columns.

Questions:
How long is your rectangle? How wide?

Are there any other ways we could arrange the pegs or cubes as a rectangle?

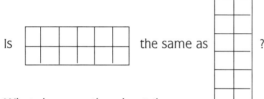

Is [ ] the same as [ ] ?

What do we notice about the number of rows, the number of columns?

What multiplication facts have 12 as an answer?

Do you think 11 can be arranged as a rectangle?

Why do you think that?

Main Teaching Activity: (25 minutes)
(Three groups)

Tell the children that some numbers of pegs or cubes can be arranged in several different rectangular shapes, whilst for others only one can be found, and that you would like them to explore the numbers between 10 and 40. Organise the whole class so that one group works on the numbers 10 to 20, another group works on those from 20 to 30 and the third group works on the numbers from 30 to 40.

Ask the children to keep a record of the sizes of the different rectangles they can find for each number and to look for patterns and anything else interesting. Tell them that you will want groups to feedback to the rest of the class later during the plenary session. Draw a table on the board so that as children investigate they can display their results.

e.g.

Number	Size of rectangle
10	2 by 5, 10 by 1
11	11 by 1
12	2 by 6, 4 by 3, 12 by 1

Questions to ask a focused group:

How are you organising yourselves?

Has everyone got a task?

What are you using to help you?

How do you know if you've found all the rectangles?

How long is that rectangle? How wide?

What if the rectangle was twice as big, what would its length be then? Why?

Do you spot any patterns?

Is there anything you know that helps you find the size of rectangle quickly?

Plenary: (15 minutes)
Questions

What patterns did you notice?

Which numbers made the most rectangles?

Why do you think some numbers are called square numbers?

Why do you think you could find lots of rectangles for some numbers and not others?

Can you predict what other numbers greater than 40 will be rectangular numbers? How?

Ask each group to feedback to the class and discuss the results with reference to the plenary questions. If the children find them all, write down part of the sequence of square numbers. Ask them to predict what the next square number might be. Also link the class results to the multiplication tables and demonstrate with an example. You can make several rectangles from 16 pegs because 16 appears in a number of times-tables x2, x4, x8. Tell the children that 16 is a multiple of these numbers and can be thought of as a friendly number because it can be linked to several other numbers. Whereas a number like 13 is a less friendly number because it doesn't appear in many times-tables and we therefore don't know many facts about it. Use the term 'factors' by saying, for example, "All the different numbers that make up the sides of the rectangles for certain numbers are called factors. How many factors did we find for 16? Let's check again and see".

Ask the children to be on the look out throughout the week for numbers that have a lot of factors and other that don't have very many.

Decimals

AIM: Begin to use decimal notation for tenths and hundredths. Recognise the equivalence between some decimal and fraction forms. Read, write and order decimals and fractions.

Resources:

Large class number line 0-3 divided into tenths

Set of tenth and hundredth cards and other equivalent fractions

'Ladder' game boards, sets of decimal cards 0.1 - 3.0

Mental/Oral Introductory Session: 15 minutes

Write up a range of lengths, weights and amounts of money on the board to one decimal place and ask the children to choose 2 and find the total. Give them a minute or so and then ask them to share with a partner how they worked out the answer. Discuss as a class the different strategies used and model the children's responses on the board. Encourage a few children to demonstrate their methods to the others.

Recap on what the decimal point means and how a half and a tenth are expressed in decimal form.

Questions:

What do you estimate the answer to be?

Which 2 numbers did you choose? Why?

How did you work the answer out?

How did you check you were right?

Which method is the quickest?

Is there another way you could have worked out the answer?

What's a tenth of a pound? £1000? £5500?

How many grams are in a tenth of a kilogram?

Do you know how a quarter could be expressed as a decimal?

Main teaching activity: 35 minutes

(Y3/4 in pairs, Y5/6 as a class)

The aim of this part of the lesson is to introduce Y5/6 children to hundredths, whilst giving Y3/4 time to become familiar with and practice using tenths as expressed in decimal form.

Briefly explain the 'Ladder Game'. Each pair has a ladder board and a set of decimal tenth cards from 0.1 - 3.0. They take it in turns to turn over a card and place it on one of the rungs of the ladder in order. Each card once placed can't be moved. When they can't place a card in the correct order they miss a turn. The winner is the one who places the most cards on the board. Play the best of 5. Ask the children to think about the strategies they are using as they play the game and to feedback to the class at the end of the lesson. Provide tenth number lines for the less able / younger children to refer to.

2.5
2.1
1.9
1.7
0.5

Extension Activity for early finishers

In pairs fill in an empty number square with 'decimal tenths' (see below) Then with a die marked as follows, 0.1, 0.2, 0.3, 0.4, 0.5, 1.0, play 'First to 10'. with a partner.

To play, 'First to Ten', roll the die and place a counter on the square containing that decimal. On subsequent throws of the die, add the number rolled to your current position and move to a new decimal number. The winner is the first to reach 10.

0.1	0.2	0.3	0.4	0.5	0.6	0.7	0.8	0.9	1.0
1.1	1.2	1.3	1.4	1.5	1.6	1.7	1.8	1.9	2.0
2.1	2.2	2.3	2.4	2.5	2.6	2.7	2.8	2.9	3.0
3.1	3.2	3.3	3.4	3.5	3.6	3.7	3.8	3.9	4.0
4.1	4.2	4.3	4.4	4.5	4.6	4.7	4.8	4.9	5.0
5.1	5.2	5.3	5.4	5.5	5.6	5.7	5.8	5.9	6.0
6.1	6.2	6.3	6.4	6.5	6.6	6.7	6.8	6.9	7.0
7.1	7.2	7.3	7.4	7.5	7.6	7.7	7.8	7.9	8.0
8.1	8.2	8.3	8.4	8.5	8.6	8.7	8.8	8.9	9.0
9.1	9.2	9.3	9.4	9.5	9.6	9.7	9.8	9.9	10.0

While the Y3/4 children play the Ladder game, organise the Y5/6 group into a 'U'-shape facing the large 0-3 number line marked in tenths. Focus on a tenth section, such as 0.5 - 0.6, and ask them what we could label the half-way point between the tenths. Ask them to imagine magnifying this section and splitting it into ten smaller divisions. How many divisions would there be if we did this for every tenth, between 0 and 1. Link to centimetres on a metre ruler. Ask several children to mark in the divisions on the larger number line and discuss how a hundredth is shown as a decimal.

Hand out a series of decimal and fraction cards, including some equivalents, which the children hold up. Ask the children to arrange themselves in order.

Questions:

How do you know if you're standing in the right place?

What fraction comes before you? after you?

What's another way we could refer to that position?

What's a quarter expressed as a decimal? How do you know?

How many hundredths are there in $2\frac{1}{2}$?

What is 0.15 expressed as a fraction?

What's 0.75 expressed as a fraction?

Do you know any other equivalent fractions?

Why can't a third be expressed in hundredths?

What might a third look like as a decimal on a calculator?

Next give out calculators to pairs of children and ask them to explore how a few different fractions such as $\frac{1}{2}, \frac{1}{3}, \frac{1}{4}, \frac{1}{5}, \frac{1}{6}$, etc are displayed on the calculator and to record them. Ask them to try and explain why for some numbers the decimal part keeps recurring.

Plenary: 10 minutes

Questions:

Y3/Y4   What strategies did you use in order to win?

Which cards were easiest / hardest to place? Why?

Y5/Y6   Which fractions are easy to express as decimals? Why?

What is the value of the digit in the third decimal place? Fourth?

Can you explain what is happening?

Recap on how a tenth and a hundredth are expressed as decimals and link back to money and the measures by writing up some examples and asking children the relative values of each digit.

eg   1.25m What's the value of the '5'?

£10.56 What's the value of the '5'?

Decimals and Fractions

AIM: To introduce decimal notation; know what each digit in a decimal number represents and order a set of decimal fractions, understand that $\frac{1}{10}$ is the same as 0.1 and be able to count forwards and backwards in tenths.

Resources:

Digit card sets 0-9,

class number line 0-3 with tenth divisions,

Place value boards for less able

e.g.

UNITS	TENTHS
●	

Mental/Oral Introductory Session: 5 minutes

This brisk whole class introduction is designed to encourage a quick recall of fraction bonds to 1 and to become familiar with same equivalent fractions.

Give each pair of children a set of 0-9 digit cards, which they layout face up in front of them. Tell them that you will hold up a fraction card and you want them to find its partner to make 1. For example "What do you need to add to a $\frac{1}{4}$ to make a whole?" Hold up a range of fractions - halves, quarters, thirds, fifths, sixths, eighths, etc. The children show the answer by holding up the relevant cards one above the other eg

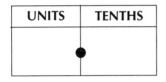

Questions:

How are you working it out?

What does the top number mean?

What does the bottom number mean?

What different ways can you show a half? a quarter?

Can you show a whole as a fraction with your cards?

What's a half and a quarter? Show me?

What's two thirds take away a sixth? Show me?

Main Teaching Activity: 35 minutes

(Whole class in pairs)

Tell the children the aims of the lesson, point to the number line and ask them how many intervals or divisions there are between zero and one, and what they are called.

Ask how they think we write a half as a decimal and what the decimal point means. Ask them how you could write a tenth as a decimal and then mark up the line in decimal fractions. Count on and back in 0.1's on the line bridging the units. Extend past either side of the number line, i.e. above 3 and below zero.

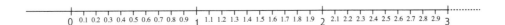

Discuss the unit and decimal part and ask questions about place value. For example, "How many units are in 2.3? How many tenths?"

Then split the class into 3 different groups, working in pairs.
Explain that you want them to investigate how many decimal numbers to one decimal place, ie units and tenths, they can make with a given number of digits and then to order them. They can use the same digit twice to make a number.

Refer to questions written up for the plenary and tell the children that you will want their feedback at the end of the investigation.

Differentiate by giving the groups of pairs of children fewer or more digits.
For example Group A   0,1,2,3, and place value boards
             Group B   0,1,2,3,4,
             Group C   4,5,6,7,8,9,
Ask the children to keep a record of all the numbers they find.

Questions to ask identified groups:
How are you going to make sure you find all the numbers?
What can you use to help you?
Can you read and say that number?
What if it was a tenth smaller?
Where will you place that number on the number line?
What does that number represent?
Can you explain how you are working?

Plenary: 10 minutes
Questions
How many different decimal numbers have you found?
What strategies did you use to ensure you found all the numbers? Explain.
What is the largest / smallest number you can make? Why?
If you had been given one more digit how many decimal numbers do you think you could have made?
Where do we see decimals?
What is the smallest number?
Can you say these decimals as fractions?
How are fractions and decimals linked?

Run through the questions asking several pairs to demonstrate their method on the board. Draw out the need to work systematically. Show the pattern, for example:

0.0	1.0	2.0	3.0
0.1	1.1	2.1	3.1
0.2	1.2	2.2	3.2
0.3	1.3	2.3	3.3

Recap on the links between fractions, decimals and division and ask them how we might show a number smaller that a tenth as a decimal. Ask them what they think the smallest fraction is and discuss their concept of infinity. Finally ask them to collect examples of decimal numbers for homework (e.g. from newspapers, magazines, food packets, etc.).

Multiplication and Division

AIM: Develop mental strategies for adding two digit numbers. Use closely related known facts to derive new ones. Use doubling and halving. Choose appropriate number operations to solve a calculation and an appropriate way of calculating. Develop pencil and paper methods of recording.

Resources:

A3 size number square 0-99

highlighter pen

photocopies of 'Cola' activity sheets

Mental/Oral Introductory Session: 10 minutes

This activity has been used regularly throughout the year to encourage children's mental imagery and to develop mental strategies. It involves a large 0-99 number square which the children are asked to 'picture', in their heads. They are then asked to start at a particular number on their 'mental' number square and follow a series of instruction for moving around the grid. As the class has become familiar with it, so the numbers and the steps between them on the grids have been extended. (For a detailed description of this activity see 'Around the Hundred Square', page 113).

Remind children of previous vertical, horizontal and diagonal moves on the number square and recap on the mental strategies involved, eg How does a number change when you move diagonally down to the right? left? How does it change as you move diagonally up to the right or left? For example, as you move diagonally up to the left so the number decreases by 11. As you move diagonally down to the right so the number increases by 11.

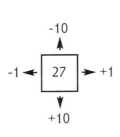

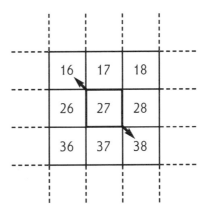

Now introduce a 0-990 square (see appendix 4). Hold up the square and allow children to look at it for 15 seconds. Then turn the square to face you and give the class a series of directions to follow. The pupils have to work out where you end up. The child that gives the correct answer takes over. Emphasise the need for a slow, steady pace.

Ask the class to describe what happens to the numbers on each move and how they are following the moves. Who sees a mental picture of the number square in their heads and who actually calculates the moves? What is the easiest way of working out the diagonals? Why? Model childrens' responses on the board and illustrate the patterns with an extract from the number square. Discuss the strategies and quick ways of adding or subtracting 90 or 110.

e.g.

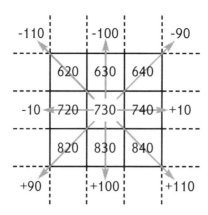

Main Teaching Activity: 30 minutes

(Whole class in pairs)

Recap on the different strategies for multiplying and dividing including halving and doubling and inform the class of the objectives for the lesson. Hand out one 'Cola' activity sheet (see page 222) for each pair. Briefly explain task and run through the questions on the board which you want pupils to focus on for the plenary. Explain that you want them to try to find the most efficient methods of calculating and to be prepared to explain their methods to the rest of the class. Ask them to think about how they can use the facts they know to work out ones they don't know during the activity. Encourage them to check their answers by performing the calculations in different ways, or using the inverse operation.

Identify 2 or 3 pairs of children to work with.

Questions to ask focused groups:

What information will you use?
What do you estimate the answer to be?
Is your answer reasonable?
What facts do you know that you can use?
How else could you check your method?
Is your way the easiest / quickest way?
How are you recording your work?

Plenary: 10 minutes

Questions

How did you solve the initial problem?
Did you use the initial answer to help you? If so, how did you use it?
Did you find any other 'tricks' or strategies to make the calculation easier?
Was there any need to do a long multiplication sum? Why?

Ask one of the pairs you worked with to come out to the board and explain how they calculated the initial cost of the bottles of lemonade. Ask them too, to demonstrate their method on the board.

Discuss whether or not it is the most efficient way and ask if another pair tackled it differently. Share methods and record on the board. If it isn't mentioned by the children then model the most efficient method shown below:

"100 bottles will cost £72. Therefore 50 bottles will cost £36 by halving and if you halve again then you can work out that 25 bottles will cost £18. Now it's easy to work out the cost of 24 bottles as you simply subtract 72p from £18, which gives you £17.28"

Run through the other plenary questions and summarise the children's strategies on the board. Which problems were easiest / hardest to work out and why? Which facts were easiest to remember? Why are doubling and halving strategies so effective? When is the written method of long multiplication the most appropriate?

End the lesson by giving them a range of calculations for homework and asking them to choose the most efficient and appropriate methods of calculation.

Cola

Angus has to buy 24 bottles of cola for his party and they cost 72p each. How much will he have to spend? Record how you calculated this.

Now that you know this can you answer the following questions and explain how you did each one?

What is the cost of 25 bottles of cola?

    I know that.....

    So the sum I will do is....

What is the cost of 48 bottles of cola?

What is the cost of 24 bottles if they cost 36p each?

What is the cost of 24 bottles if they cost 144p each?

What is the cost of 24 bottles if they cost 73p each?

What is the cost of 48 bottles of cola at 144p each?

What is the cost of 10 bottles of cola at 72p each?

What is the cost of 100 bottles of cola at 72p each?

What is the cost of a packet of crisps if 72 packets cost £17.28?

Can you answer any other questions using this information?

Write your question and how you would work out the answers.

THINK MATHS!

APPENDICES

APPENDIX 1 - QUESTIONS

WHAT QUESTIONS COULD I ASK?

At the beginning of an activity:

What could we find out?

What might you need to help you?

What could you use to help you?

What would you like to find out?

Can you estimate?

What do you already know that might help?

What apparatus would you like to use?

How could you.....?

What do think might happen?

While the children are working:

Can you tell me what you have done so far?

What do you notice about....?

How are the numbers growing or changing?

What do you think will come next?

Can you see a pattern?

Can you explain it?

Will that always work?

Does that always happen?

Could there be a different answer?

Is there a rule?

Does your rule always work? Why do you think that happens?

Does this make sense?

Are there any similarities or differences?

Is there a connection between this and the work we did last week?

Can you find a way to check your answer?

Is it what you expected?

Is that the answer you thought you would get?

Is that a good answer?

How could you record that?

Is your answer going to be bigger or smaller?

How could you check?

Can you prove it?

When have you seen this before?

When children are stuck:

Can you tell me what you've done so far?

How did you get to where you are stuck?

Would it help to draw a table, picture, diagram or graph?

Could you try smaller numbers?

Would putting them in some sort of order help?

Would a number line, cubes, etc. help?

Have you seen this before?

Tell me what's going on in your head?

What is it that you're trying to find out?

What can you tell me about...?

What do you know about...?

Can you find out how someone else did it?

Do you understand the question?

To help develop other lines of enquiry:

What would happen if...?

What are you going to do next?

What is the quickest way of doing it?

Can you think of another question?

What if you change...?

How many different ways...?

What about odd numbers, even numbers, etc?

What if...?

At the end:

How did you do that?

How did you work that out?

How did you get that answer?

Can you tell us about it?

Has anyone found a different way?

Show me another way to do it.

How do you feel about the result?

What subject have you been studying?

What have you found out?

What questions would you ask next?

The questions can be used and adapted to suit the children and the activity you are working with.

For many of the above the all important question **WHY?** can follow the initial answer and is perhaps one of the most useful questions in the whole of mathematics.

Keep in mind that it is important for the teacher to model the use of mathematical language in their questioning.

APPENDIX 2 - MENTAL STRATEGIES

IDEAS FOR MENTAL STRATEGIES:

It is vital that, from the earliest stage, children are aware of the connections between operations when calculating. They need to be aware that if they have calculated an addition, then there is a related subtraction fact that can now be stated. Similarly, multiplication problems give rise to division and vice-versa. So all the time, try to link operations together in this way. If children have worked out a calculation, whether using a number line, a number square, a calculator or in their head, ask them how they might reverse the process and get back to where they started.

Children will inevitably use a wide range of strategies when calculating mentally. There will also be a number of useful strategies which you will want to actively introduce to children in order to help them become efficient in mental calculations.

What follows are examples of strategies which you may want to be on the look out for and develop:

PUTTING THE LARGE NUMBER FIRST -

Rearrange 2 + 7 as 7 + 2, 8 + 129 as 129 + 8

COUNTING ON OR BACK IN REPEATED STEPS -

Do 7 + 4 by starting at 7 and counting on in ones, 12 - 5 by starting at 12 and counting back in ones, 60 + 30 starting at 60 and counting on in tens, 80 - 20 starting at 80 and counting back in 10's, 43 + 20 starting at 43 and counting on in 10's, 87 - 30 starting at 87 and counting back with 10's, 64 - 8 by starting at 64 and counting back in 2's, 760 + 800 by starting at 760 and counting on in 100's.

IDENTIFYING NEAR DOUBLES USING DOUBLES ALREADY KNOWN -

Work out mentally 5 + 6 by using double 5 and then add 1 or double 6 and then subtract 1.
Other examples where this strategy is useful include 80 + 81, 60 + 70, 55 + 56, 89 + 90, etc.

PARTITIONING INTO 5 AND A BIT WHEN ADDING 6, 7, 8 OR 9 THEN RECOMBINING

8 + 6 is (5 + 3) and (5 + 1) = 10 + 4
18 + 6 is (15 + 3) plus (5 + 1) = 20 + 4

USING PATTERNS OF SIMILAR CALCULATIONS -

10 - 0 = 10, 10 - 1 = 9, 10 - 2 = 8, or 10 - 0 = 10, 11 - 0 = 11, 12 - 0 = 12
3 + 5 = 8, 13 + 5 = 18, 23 + 5 = 28
4 - 3 = 1, 14 - 3 = 11, 24 - 3 = 21
4 + 3 = 7, 40 + 30 = 70, 400 + 300 = 700, 4000 + 3000 = 7000

USING THE RELATIONSHIP BETWEEN ADDITION AND SUBTRACTION -

Knowing one of these facts -
2 + 4 = 6, 4 + 2 = 6, 6 - 2 = 4, 6 - 4 = 2
means you know all of them.

PARTITIONING INTO HUNDREDS, TENS AND UNITS AND RECOMBINING

16 + 13 is 10 + 10 and 6 + 3
13 + 8 is 10 + 3 + 8 = 18 + 3
98 - 43 = 98 - 40 - 3, etc.

COUNTING UP THROUGH THE NEXT MULTIPLE OF 10, 100 OR 1000 -

428 + 45 = 430 + 43

ADDING OR SUBTRACTING 9, 19, ... OR 11, 21, .. BY ADDING OR SUBTRACTING 10, 20,... AND ADJUSTING BY 1 -

15 + 9 is the same as 15 + 10 - 1

30 - 11 is the same as 30 - 10 - 1

58 + 11 is the same as 58 + 10 + 1

BRIDGING THROUGH 10 OR 20 AND ADJUSTING

6 + 7 by doing 6 + 4 = 10, 10 + 3 = 13

15 - 8 do 15 - 5 =10, 10 - 3 = 7

68 + 7 = 70 + 5

N.B. This strategy is often associated with some movements on a number line where you try to get to a convenient decade number first.

ADDING OR SUBTRACTING THE NEAREST MULTIPLE OF 10, THEN ADJUSTING

24 + 58 = 82 because it is 24 + 60 - 2

4005 - 1997 = 2008 because it is 4005 - 2000 + 3

FINDING A SMALL DIFFERENCE BY COUNTING UP FROM THE SMALLER TO THE LARGER NUMBER -

20 - 17 by starting at 17 and counting up to 20

5003 - 4996 by starting at 4996 and counting up to 5003

ADDING SEVERAL NUMBERS BY PUTTING THE LARGEST FIRST AND / OR FIND A PAIR TOTALLING 9, 10,11 OR MULTIPLES OF 10 -

2, 7, 8 by doing 2 + 8 =10 and 10 + 7 = 17

2, 3, 12 by starting with 12 and adding on 3 and 2

27 + 36 + 13 by doing 27 + 13 = 40 first, then 40 + 36 = 76

USING KNOWLEDGE OF NUMBER FACTS AND PLACE VALUE TO ADD OR SUBTRACT A PAIR OF NUMBERS MENTALLY -

Adding or subtracting multiple of 10

Adding a single digit to any number

USING THE RELATIONSHIP BETWEEN MULTIPLICATION AND DIVISION AND OTHER OPERATIONS -

Recognise and use that $4 + 4 + 4 = 4 \times 3$

Recognise that knowing one of the facts

$9 \times 7 = 63$ $7 \times 9 = 63$

$63 \div 9 = 7$ $63 \div 7 = 9$

means you know all of them

USING KNOWLEDGE OF NUMBER FACTS AND PLACE VALUE TO MULTIPLY OR DIVIDE -

Dividing by 10 or 100

DOUBLING BY DOUBLING THE MOST SIGNIFICANT DIGIT FIRST -

Double 34 is double 30 add double 4   i.e 60 add 8

Double 78 is double 70 and double 8   i.e. 140 add 16

USING CLOSELY RELATED FACTS -

To multiply by 9 or 11, multiply by 10 and add or subtract the number

eg $13 \times 11 = 130 + 13$

Work out 12 times table by adding the two times table facts to ten times table facts.

PARTITIONING AND USING THE DISTRIBUTIVE LAW -
Multiply a two digit number by a single digit by doing the tens first
eg 47 x 5 = (40 x 5) + (7 x 5)

USING FACTORS -
To calculate 15 x 6 do 15 x 3 = 45 then 45 x 2 = 90 because 2 x 3 = 6
To calculate 90 ÷ 6 do 90 ÷ 3 = 30 then 30 ÷ 2 = 15 because 2 x 3 = 6

USING DOUBLING OR HALVING, STARTING FROM KNOWN FACTS -
4 x 8 is double 4 x 4
Halve 160 by halving 16 then multiplying by 10

It is also important that children make sense of their answers and check results of calculations are reasonable. Strategies for this include:

CHECKING WITH INVERSE OPERATION -
Check 3 + 1 = 4 by doing 4 - 1, check 15 - 6 = 9 by doing 9 + 6
100 ÷ 5 = 20 by doing 20 x 5 = 100 or 20 + 20 + 20 + 20 + 20 = 100

REPEATING ADDITION / MULTIPLICATION IN DIFFERENT ORDER -
Check 2 + 7 by doing 7 + 2
Check 11 + 19 by doing 19 + 11
2 x 5 x 10 by doing 10 x 5 x 2

CHECKING WITH AN EQUIVALENT CALCULATION -
31 - 7, check 31 - 1 - 6

CHECK THE EFFECT OF AN OPERATION -
When working with positive numbers recognise that adding increases the size of the number and subtracting reduces the size of the number, for example
7 + 8 is more than 8, 15 - 7 is less than 15
Multiplying one whole number by another the product is greater
Dividing one whole number by another the quotient is less
eg 26 x 2 > 26, 26 ÷ 2 < 26

APPROXIMATING BY ROUNDING -
9 + 19 must be close to 30 because 9 is close to 10 and 19 is close to 20 and 10 + 20 = 30

USING TESTS OF DIVISIBILITY -
Know and use the knowledge that exact multiples of 100 end in 00
Multiples of 5 end in 0 or 5
Multiples of 2 end in a 0, 2, 4, 6 or 8
The number formed by the last two digits of a multiple of 4 is itself a multiple of 4
e.g. 21048 is a multiple of 4 because 48 is a multiple of 4.

USING KNOWLEDGE OF SUMS, DIFFERENCES OR PRODUCTS OF ODD AND EVEN NUMBERS -
Recognise that the sum of two even numbers is even, etc.

It is vital that children see connections between facts, that they do not just learn facts in isolation but realise that by knowing one thing they know many others. It is the link between facts and using strategies to derived facts that need to be fostered.

APPENDIX 3 - WRITING FRAMES

WRITING FRAMES FOR MATHEMATICS

Writing Frames are a way of helping children to structure their written work by providing key words and a skeleton sentence structure as a 'scaffold' for their writing. If you have not used writing frames before it is important not to just present them to the children cold , as sheets to fill in. We strongly recommend reading the book "Writing Frames: Photocopiable sheets to help scaffold children's non-fiction writing in a range of genres" (see appendix 5 - useful addresses) before embarking on using them.

In the book it says
"Use of the frame should always begin with discussion and teacher modelling before moving onto joint construction (Teacher + children) and then to the child undertaking the writing supported by the frame."

Once children become familiar with the format and language of writing explanations, reports, procedures, proofs, etc., they will be able to record without the use of the frame. It is not intended to be a straight jacket, rather a starting point, to be adapted as the child sees fit.

Writing frames can be used to help children communicate their ideas, to structure their thoughts and understanding about a particular concept and to help them work through a problem in a systematic way. This means they may be used alongside an activity, or after an activity has taken place.

We have included a small sample of types of frames; they are very easy to construct and need to be made to suit the purpose and area you want the children to write about. It is important that the children understand the reason for using them.

Here is an example of a writing frame which was completed and adapted by a Y5 child:-

I wanted to calculate 17 x 4

I estimated that the answer would be around 60 because 20 x 4 = 80 and you will have to take some off.

First I rounded 17 to 20 because it is easier to multiply and this made 80 because 20 x 4 = 80

Then I took away 12 because 3 x 4 = 12 and I added 3 to make 20, and this came to 68

I checked this with a calculator. I got 68

REPORT

Although a   and a   are both   they are different
in many ways.

                    has   whilst   has
They are also different in that

Another way they are unlike is

Finally

PROOF

I want to prove that

First

From this I can argue

Therefore

I have now proved

PROCEDURE

This is how to

For this you will need

First

Then

Next

Finally

REASONING

There is more than one reason why

First

Also

As well as this

Therefore

APPENDIX 4 Photocopiable Resources

10 11 12

20 21 22

30 31 32

40 41 42

50 51 52

60 61 62

70 71 72

0 - 99 square

0	1	2	3	4	5	6	7	8	9
10	11	12	13	14	15	16	17	18	19
20	21	22	23	24	25	26	27	28	29
30	31	32	33	34	35	36	37	38	39
40	41	42	43	44	45	46	47	48	49
50	51	52	53	54	55	56	57	58	59
60	61	62	63	64	65	66	67	68	69
70	71	72	73	74	75	76	77	78	79
80	81	82	83	84	85	86	87	88	89
90	91	92	93	94	95	96	97	98	99

1 - 100 square

1	2	3	4	5	6	7	8	9	10
11	12	13	14	15	16	17	18	19	20
21	22	23	24	25	26	27	28	29	30
31	32	33	34	35	36	37	38	39	40
41	42	43	44	45	46	47	48	49	50
51	52	53	54	55	56	57	58	59	60
61	62	63	64	65	66	67	68	69	70
71	72	73	74	75	76	77	78	79	80
81	82	83	84	85	86	87	88	89	90
91	92	93	94	95	96	97	98	99	100

Blank 100 square

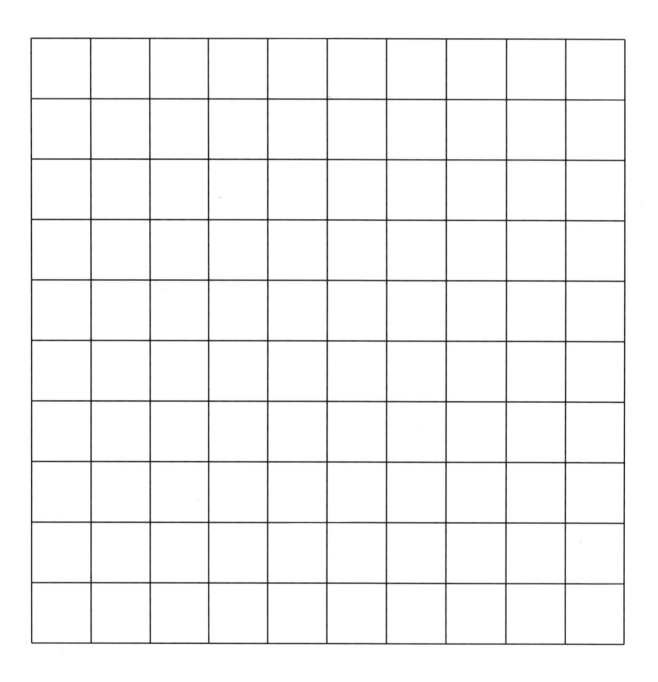

12 x 12 number square

1	2	3	4	5	6	7	8	9	10	11	12
13	14	15	16	17	18	19	20	21	22	23	24
25	26	27	28	29	30	31	32	33	34	35	36
37	38	39	40	41	42	43	44	45	46	47	48
49	50	51	52	53	54	55	56	57	58	59	60
61	62	63	64	65	66	67	68	69	70	71	72
73	74	75	76	77	78	79	80	81	82	83	84
85	86	87	88	89	90	91	92	93	94	95	96
97	98	99	100	101	102	103	104	105	106	107	108
109	110	111	112	113	114	115	116	117	118	119	120
121	122	123	124	125	126	127	128	129	130	131	132
133	134	135	136	137	138	139	140	141	142	143	144

0 - 990 square

0	10	20	30	40	50	60	70	80	90
100	110	120	130	140	150	160	170	180	190
200	210	220	230	240	250	260	270	280	290
300	310	320	330	340	350	360	370	380	390
400	410	420	430	440	450	460	470	480	490
500	510	520	530	540	550	560	570	580	590
600	610	620	630	640	650	660	670	680	690
700	710	720	730	740	750	760	770	780	790
800	810	820	830	840	850	860	870	880	890
900	910	920	930	940	950	960	970	980	990

Blank Number Lines

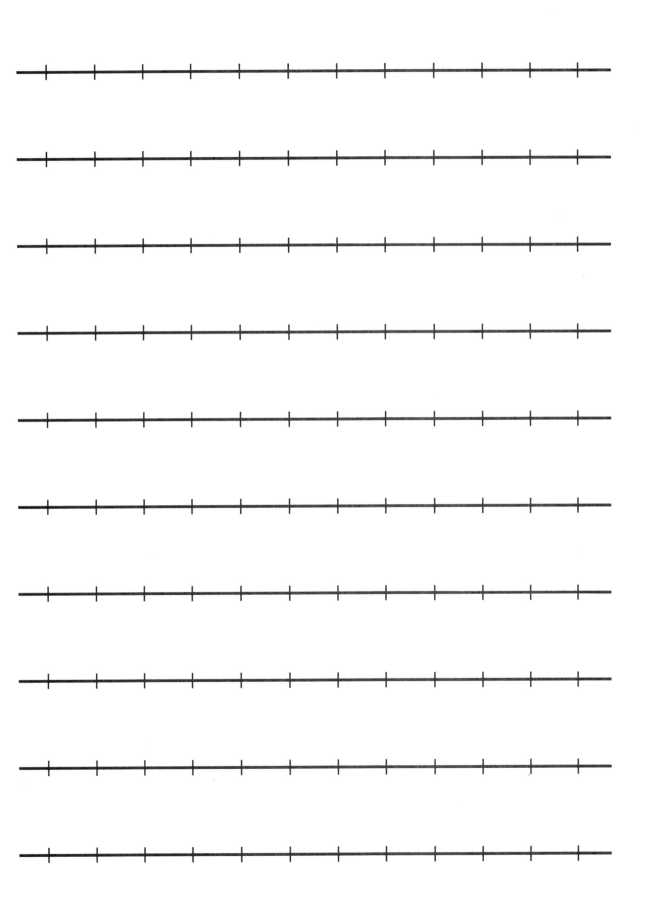

Place Value Chart

1	2	3	4	5	6	7	8	9
10	20	30	40	50	60	70	80	90
100	200	300	400	500	600	700	800	900
1 000	2 000	3 000	4 000	5 000	6 000	7 000	8 000	9 000
10 000	20 000	30 000	40 000	50 000	60 000	70 000	80 000	90 000
100 000	200 000	300 000	400 000	500 000	600 000	700 000	800 000	900 000

Digit Cards

1	2	3
4	5	6
7	8	9
0	10	

Digit Cards for Young Children

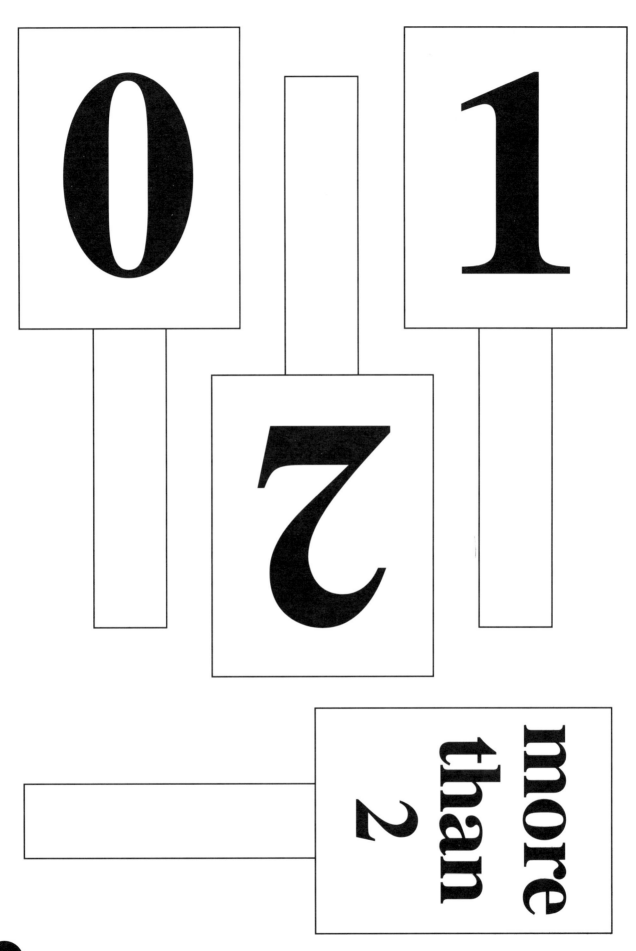

Arrow Cards

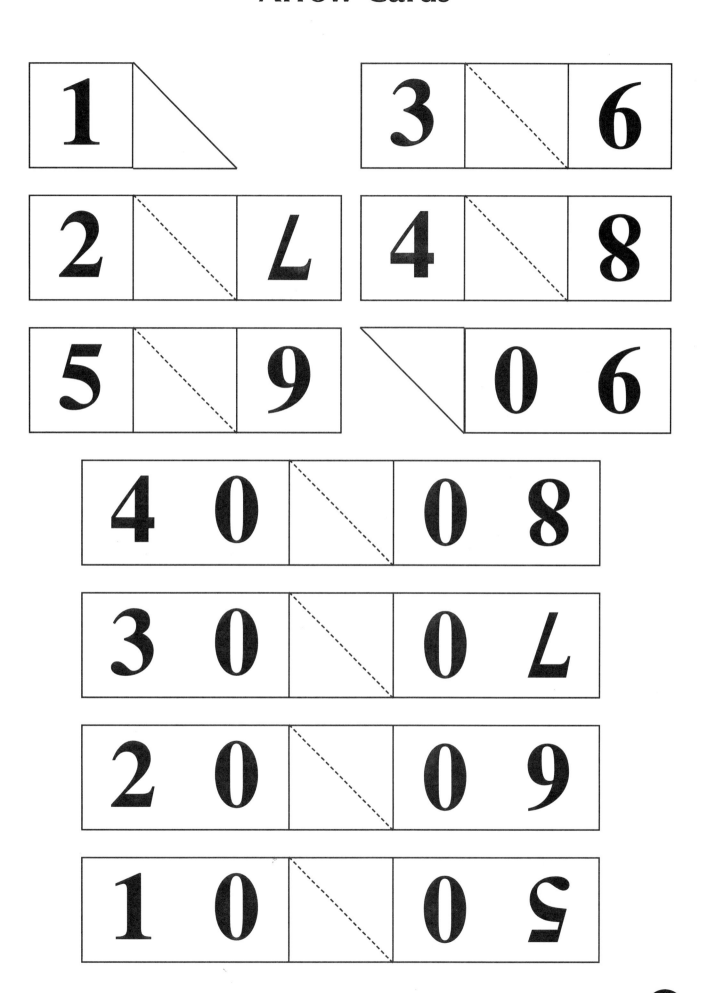

Arrow Cards (cont'd)

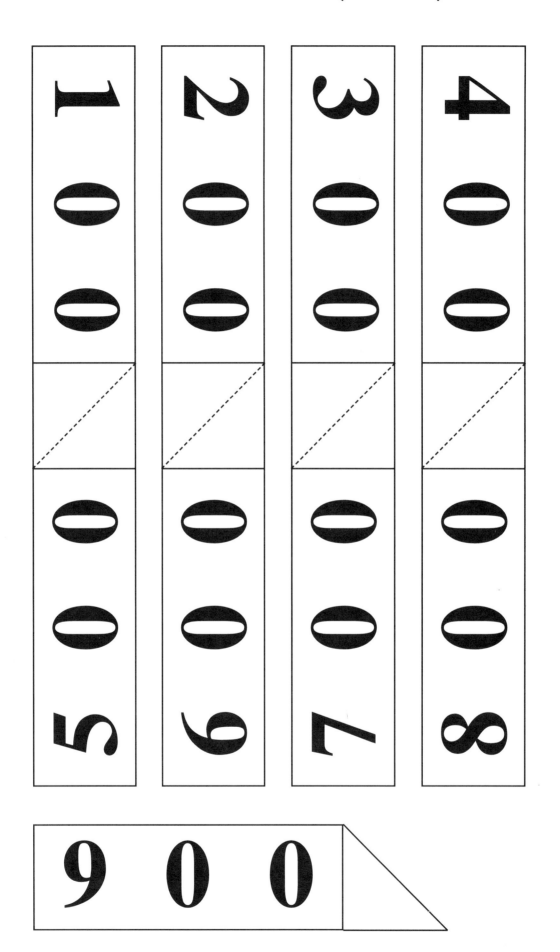

Decimal Arrow Cards

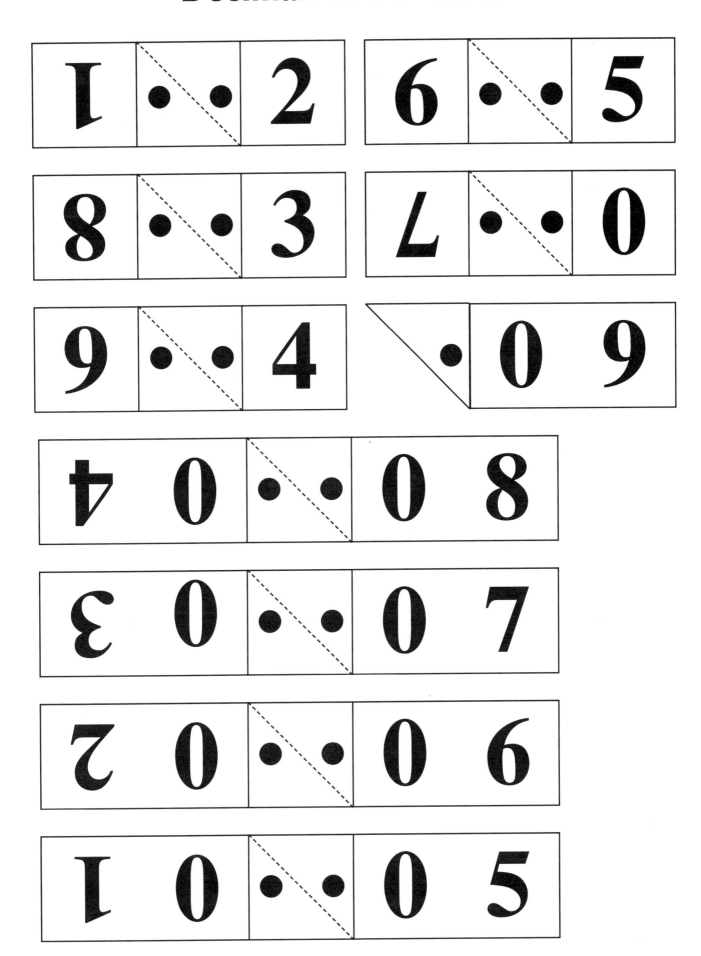

Decimal Arrow Cards (cont'd)

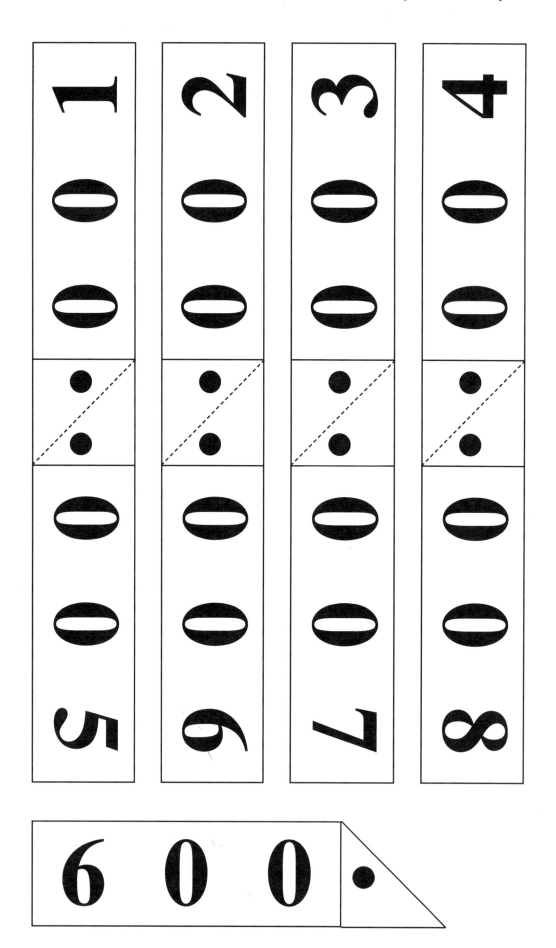

Eigen Square Front

Each number needs to be on an individual piece of card with the appropriate number on the back (see next page). In true 'Blue Peter' style, lay the cards out with gaps in between and seal between two pieces of 'sticky backed plastic'. You will then be able to fold these to produce different numbers.

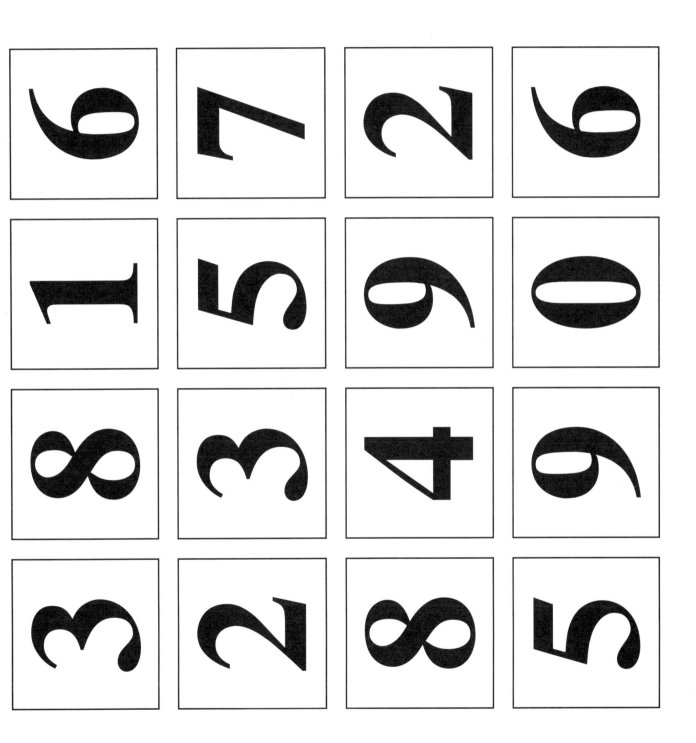

Eigen Square Back

(Top left is reverse of top right on the previous page)

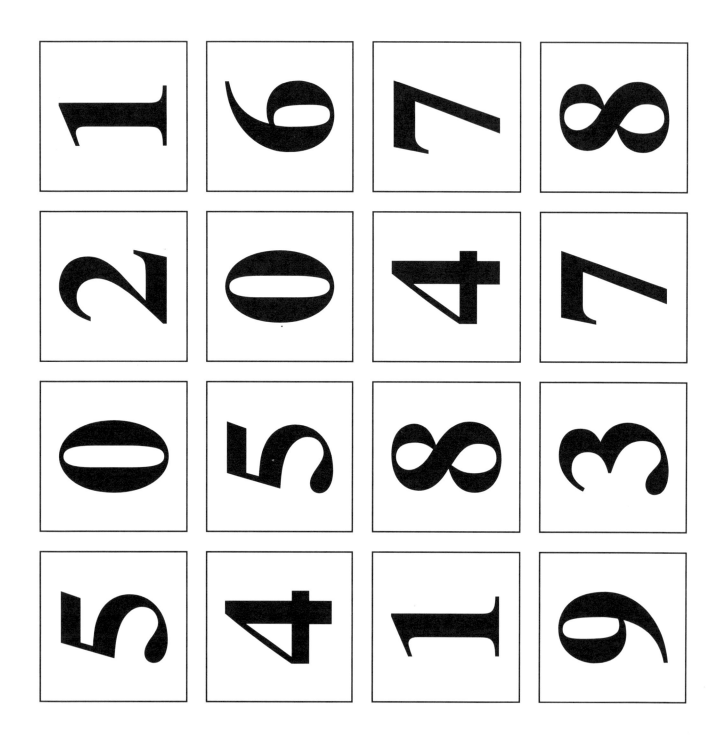

Subitizing and Estimating Sheets

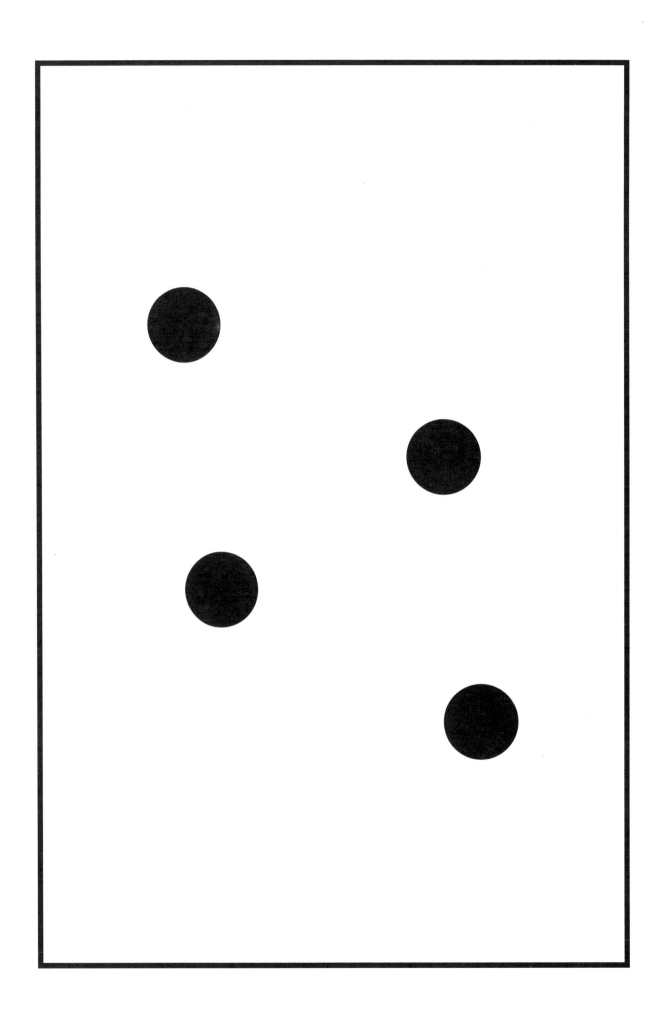

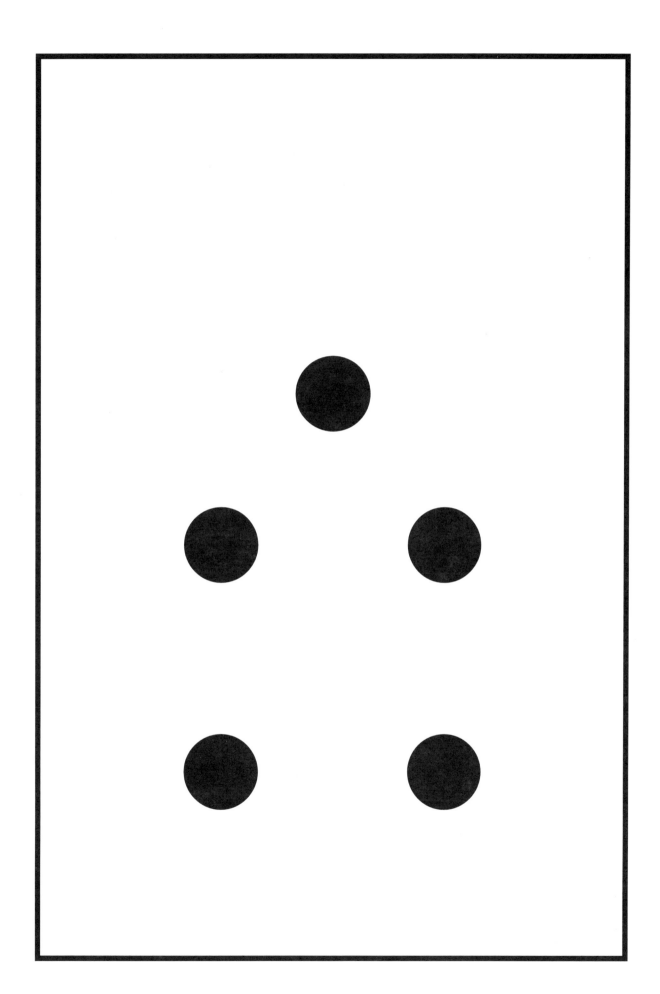

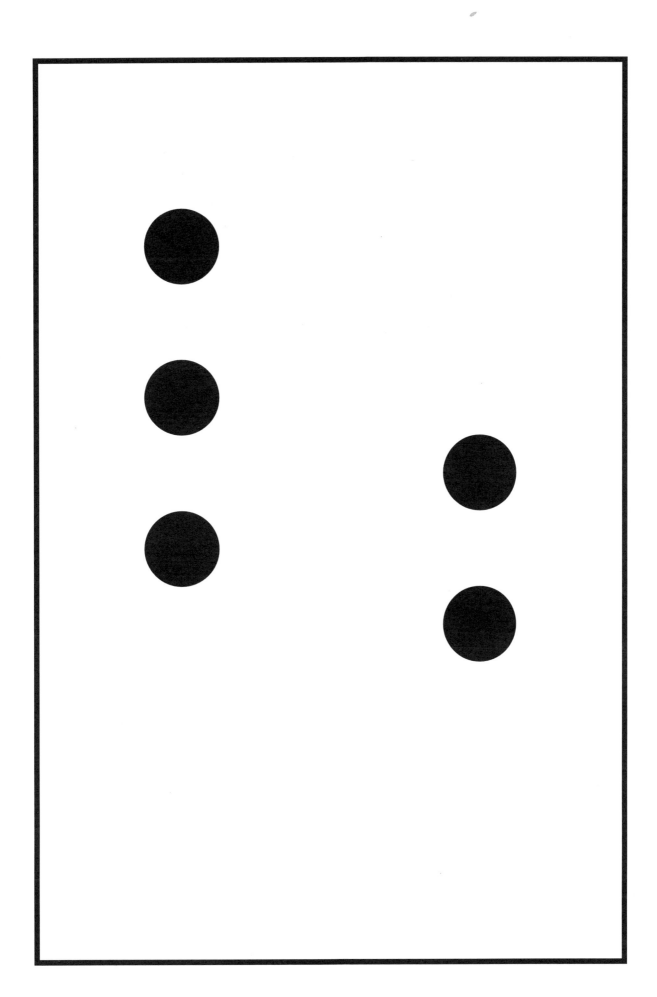

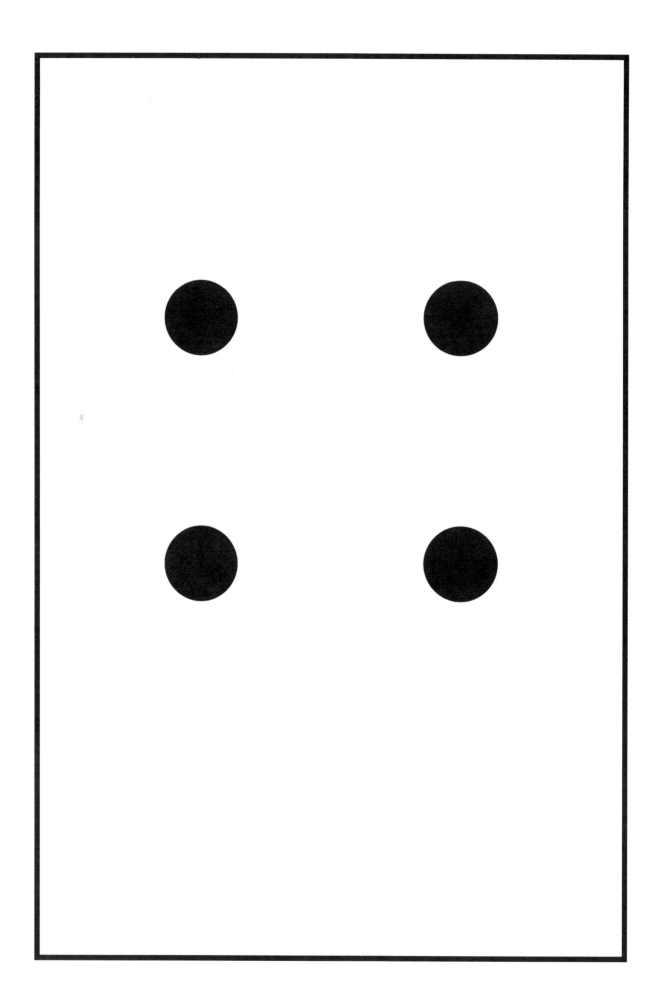

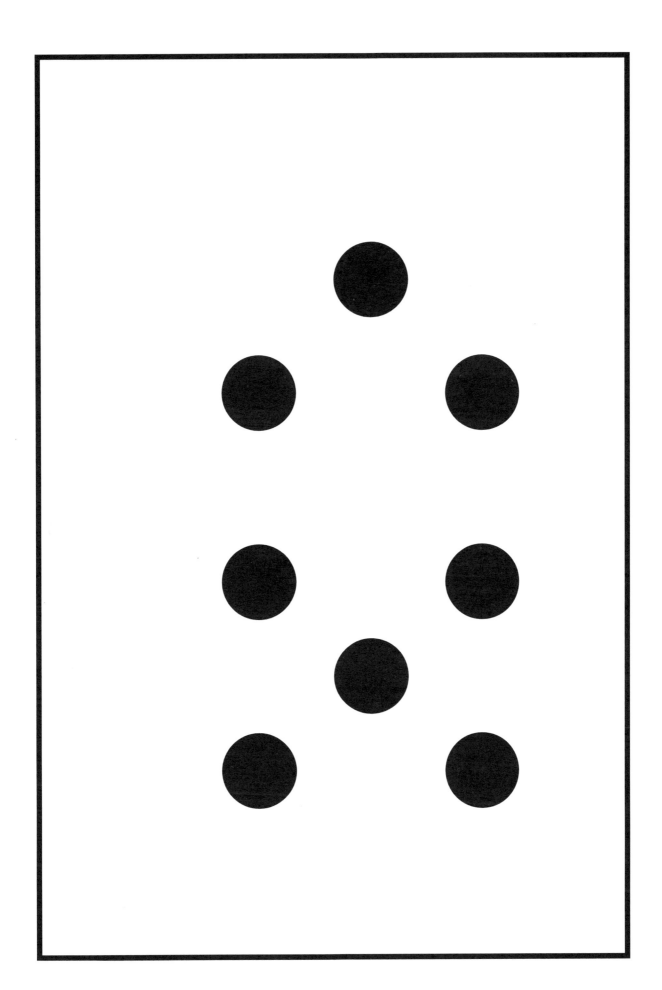

THINK MATHS!

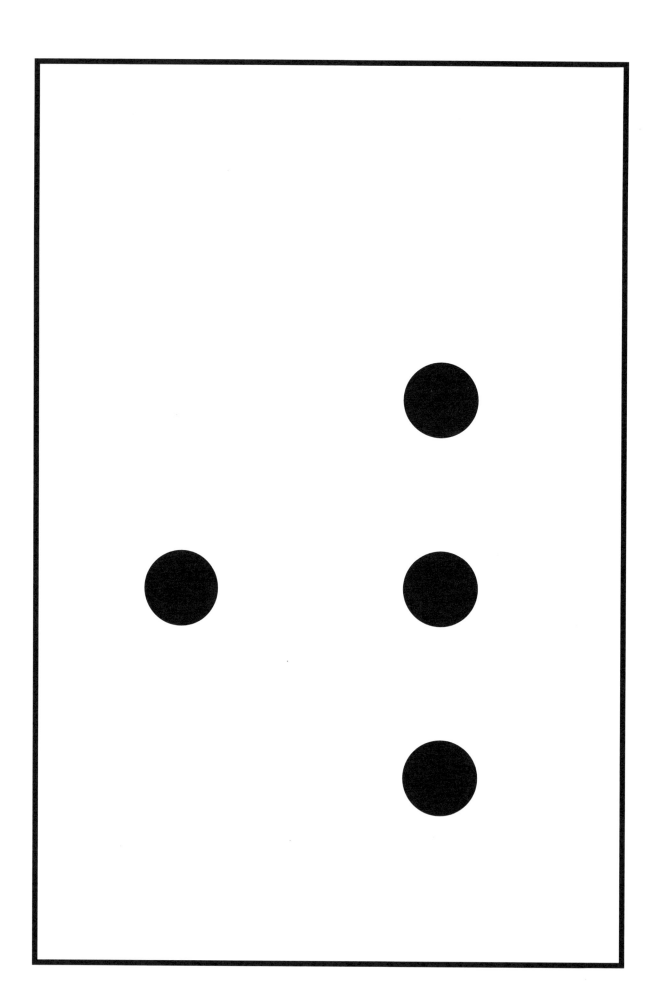

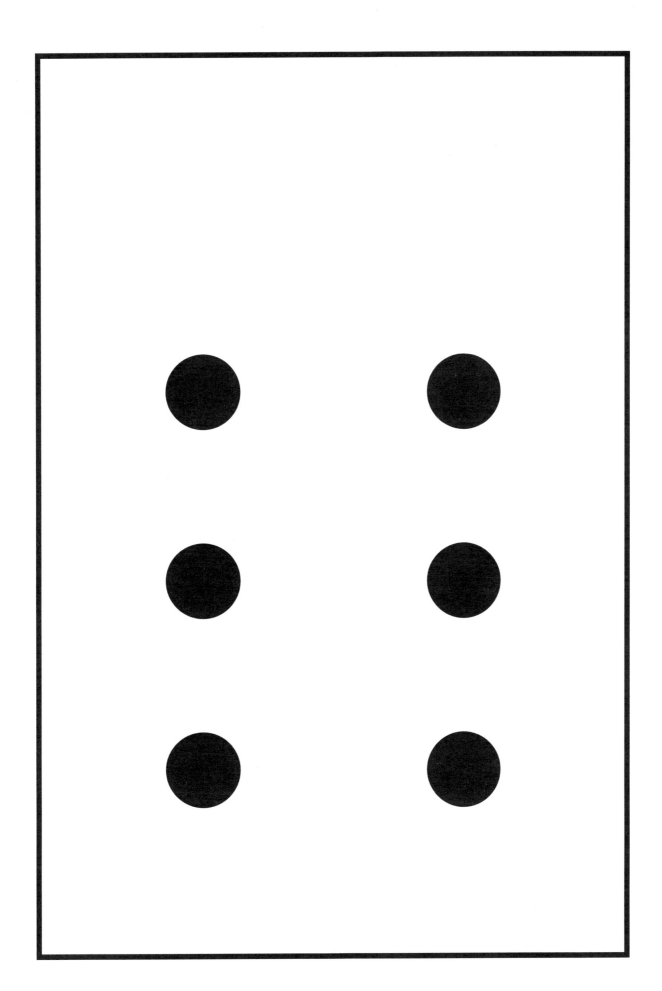

THINK MATHS!

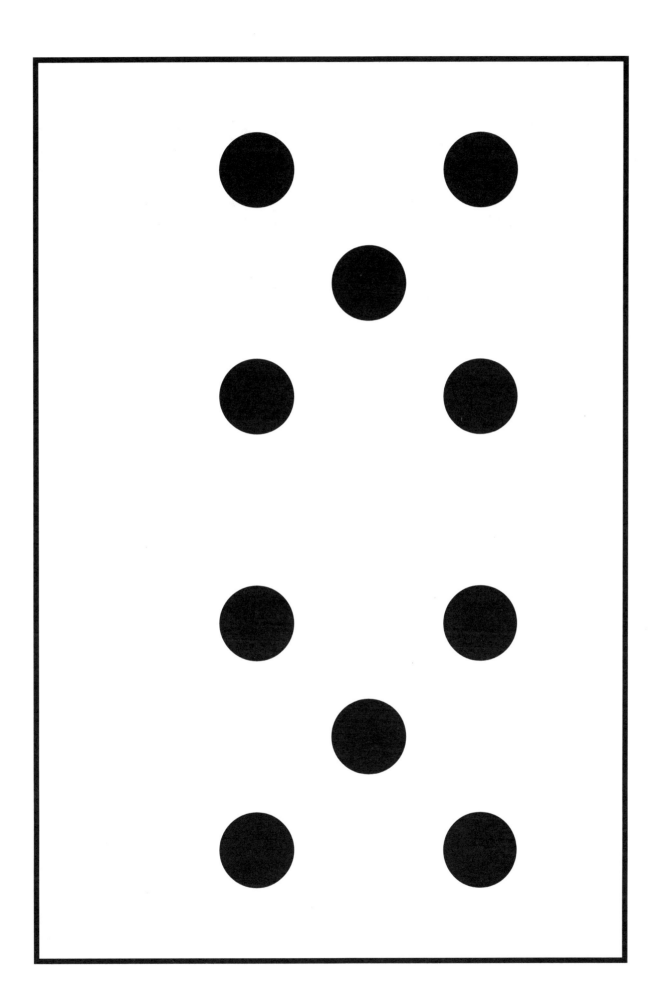

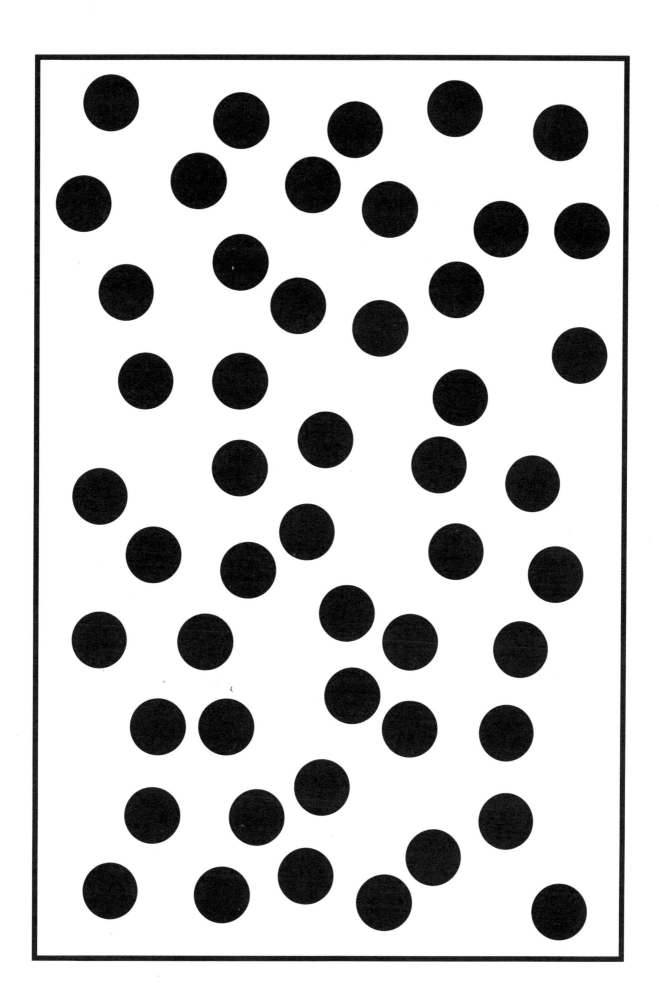

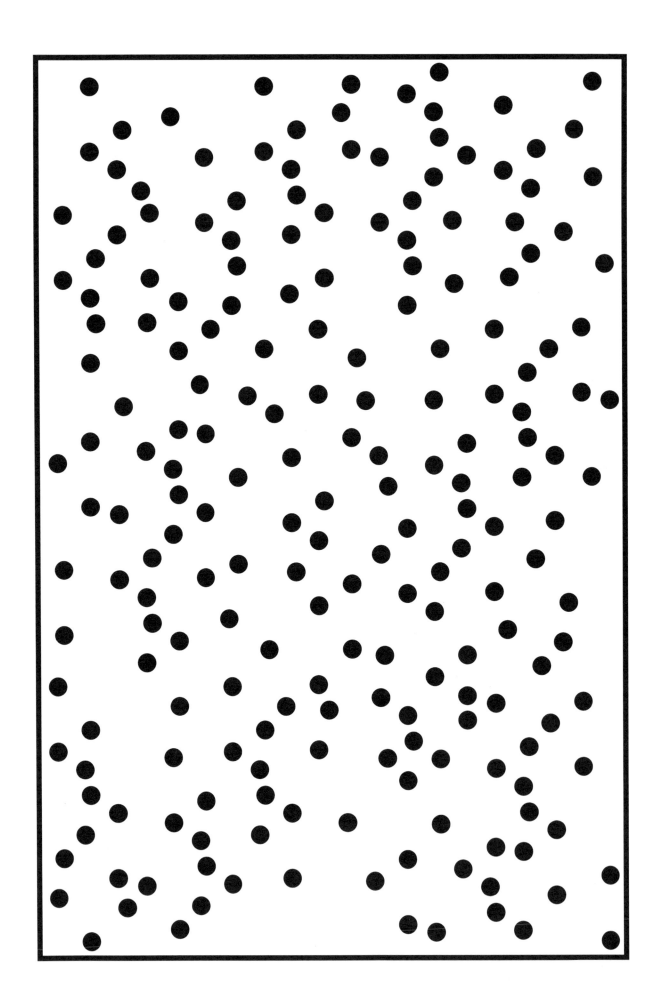

Dots - 1 to 100,000

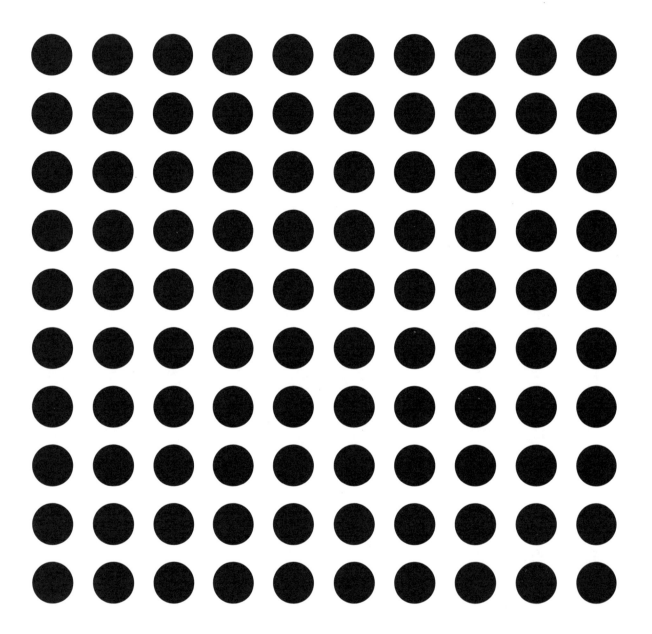

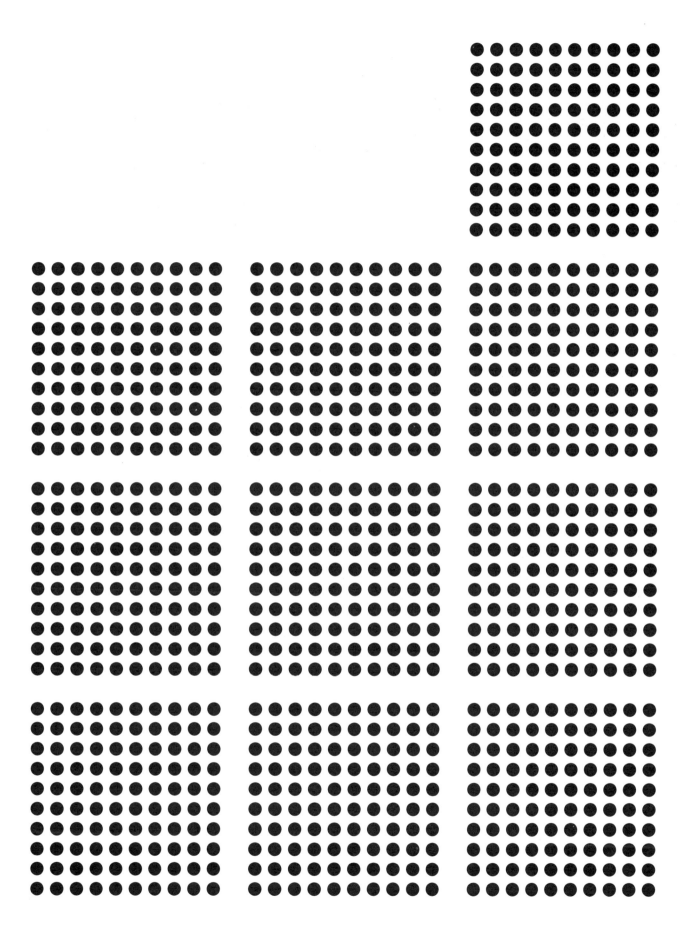

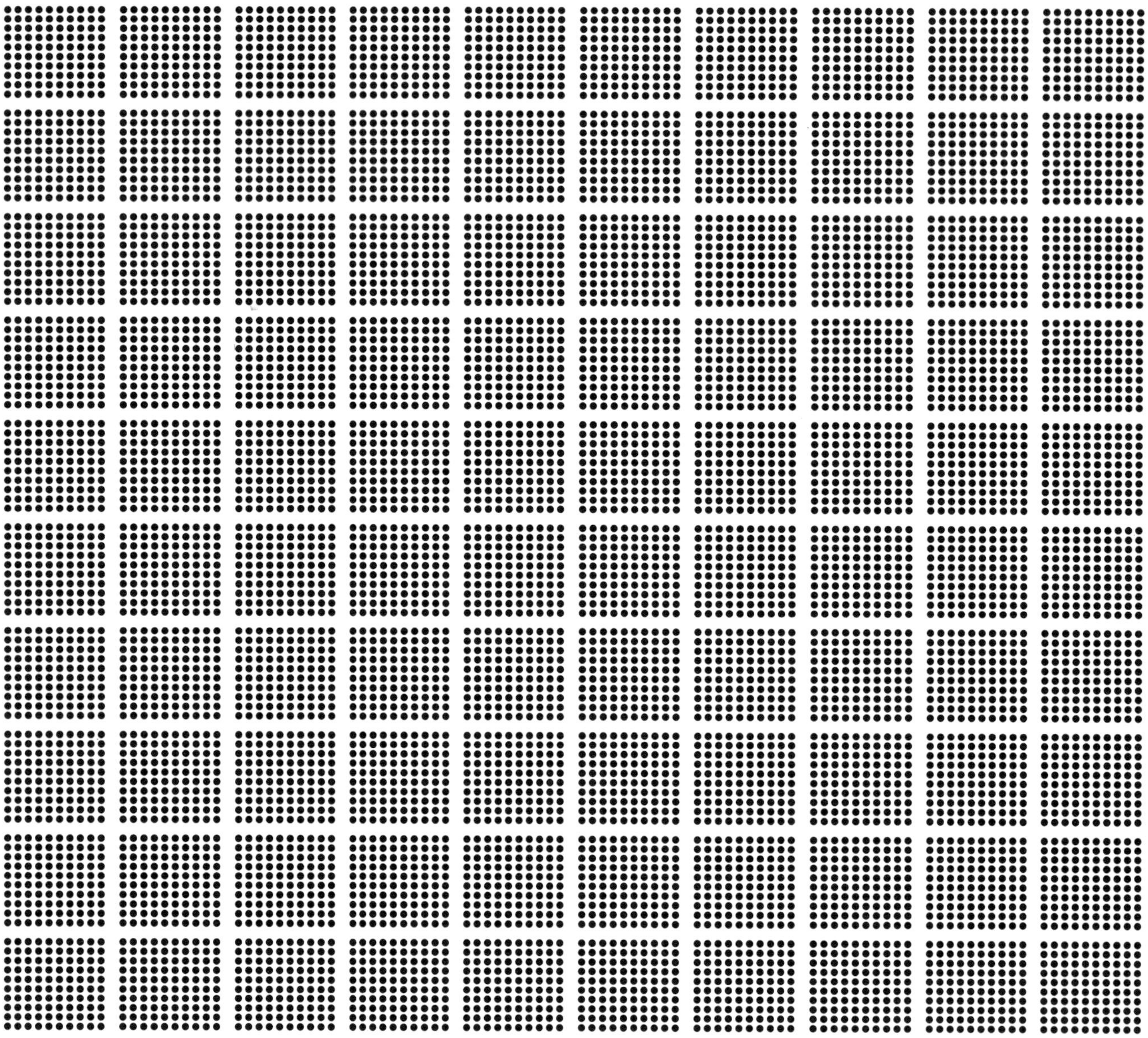

APPENDIX 5 -
USEFUL ADDRESSES & RESOURCES

TARQUIN MATHEMATICS   Tel: 01379 384218 Fax: 01379 384289
Stadbroke   email: orders@tarquin-books.demon.co.uk
Diss
Norfolk IP21 5JP
Suppliers of a wide variety of dice, playing cards and excellent posters and books primarily relating to shape and space.

SYNERGY LEARNING PRODUCTS LTD   Tel: 01243 779967   Fax: 01243 53247
PO Box 202
Chichester
West Sussex PO19 2WF
Suppliers of digit cards, number lines, place value cards and hundred square boards.

CLAIRE PUBLICATIONS & JONATHON PRESS   Tel: 01206 212755
Unit 8
Tey Brook Craft Centre
Great Tey
Colchester   Essex CO6 1 JE
Suppliers of hundred charts and number lines as well as many other useful books and resources.

HAMILTON EDUCATION   Tel: 01865 396613   Fax: 01865 399614
Temple Court
107 Oxford Road
Oxford   OX4 2GR
Suppliers of various digit cards, place value cards and leaflets for parents.

BEAM MATHEMATICS   Tel: 0171 457 5535   Fax: 0171 457 5906
Barnsbury Complex   email: beam@rmplc.co.uk
Offord Road
London N1 1QH
Suppliers of number lines and a wide range of books with ideas for teaching all areas of the mathematics curriculum.

NATIONAL NUMERACY PROJECT   Tel: 0118 952 7500   Fax: 0118 952 7507
National Centre for Literacy and Numeracy
London House
59-65 London Street
Reading RG1 4EW
Copies of the Framework for Numeracy are available from this address
'Mathematical Vocabulary' and 'Numeracy Lessons' produced by National Numeracy Project are available from BEAM.

'RAISING ATTAINMENT IN PRIMARY NUMERACY'

Mike Askew, Tamara Bibby and Margaret Brown available from:

Kings College London
School of Education
Cornwall House
1 Waterloo Road
London SE1 8WA

Tel: 0171 872 3088   Fax: 0171 872 3182

'DEVON RAISING ATTAINMENT IN NUMERACY PROJECT'

Ruth Trundley available from:

Devon Curriculum Services
Great Moor House
Bittern Road
Sowton
Exeter EX2 7NL

Tel: 01392 384858   Fax: 01392 384880

'WRITING FRAMES: PHOTOCOPIABLE SHEETS TO HELP SCAFFOLD CHILDREN'S NON-FICTION WRITING IN A RANGE OF GENRES'

Maureen Lewis and David Wray (The Exeter Extending Literacy Project) available from:

The EXCEL Office
Exeter University School of Education
Heavitree Road
Exeter EX1 2LU

'LONG, LONG, LONG, SHORT, SMALL, BIG POEMS'

by Newport Primary School and St Margaret's Primary School available from:
Ruth Trundley

DEVON CURRICULUM SERVICES
Great Moor House
Bittern Road
Sowton
Exeter EX2 7NL

Tel: 01392 384858   Fax: 01392 384880

SLIMWAM II DISK

A suite of programs including 'Counter' and 'Monty' available from:

THE ASSOCIATION OF TEACHERS OF MATHEMATICS
7 Shaftesbury Street
Derby DE 23 8YB

TEL: 01332 346599   FAX: 01332 204357
email: atm-maths@compuserve.com

GLOSSARY OF MATHEMATICAL TERMS

ALGORITHM	A written method or procedure for calculating
ASSOCIATIVE	An operation is associative if it doesn't matter where brackets are put when 3 elements are combined eg $(5 + 3) + 2 = 5 + (3 + 2)$
APPROXIMATION	An inexact but nearly accurate result eg $3.57 + 4.69$ is approximately 8.
AVERAGE	a number that represents or typifies a collection of numbers
BILLION	In Britain this used to be a million million or 10^{12}, but in the USA it is a thousand million or 10^9. It is now becoming this in the UK.
CARDINAL	The aspect of the number that expresses how many. For example, what is often referred to as the 'threeness of 3' is it's cardinality.
CIRCUMFERENCE	The boundary of a circle and the distance around it.
COMMUTATIVE	An operation is commutative if the order in which the operation is performed doesn't matter eg addition and multiplication are commutative because $5 + 3 = 3 + 5$, $5 \times 3 = 3 \times 5$; subtraction and division aren't.
CONSECUTIVE	Numbers are consecutive if they are next to each other in the sequence of counting numbers eg 2, 3, 4 or 99, 100, 101, 102
CUBED	A number cubed means a number multiplied by itself twice eg $5 \times 5 \times 5$ 5 cubed is written 5^3
DECIMAL	A term used to describe our number system of whole numbers and fractions in the base of 10
DECIMAL PLACE	This identifies the various positions after the decimal point in which digits in a decimal number occur, e.g. in the number 3.142 the digit 4 is in the 2nd decimal place and the number 1.20934 has 5 decimal places.
DECIMAL FRACTION	A fraction with a denominator of 10, 100, 1000, ...
DENOMINATOR	This is the bottom part of a fraction and represents the number of parts a whole is divided into
DIVISOR	This is the number that you divide by in a division eg. in the division $523 \div 8$, 8 is the divisor
DODECAHEDRON	A 3 dimensional shape with twelve flat faces
EQUALITY	A statement showing one quantity or expression is equal to another e.g. $5 + 7 = 6 + 6$, $2 + 3 = 5$, $10 = 8 + 2$, $2 \times 5 = 3^2 + 1$.
EQUIVALENT	Fractions are equivalent if they can be cancelled to the same fraction e.g. $\frac{16}{32} = \frac{8}{16} = \frac{4}{8} = \frac{2}{4} = \frac{1}{2}$
FACTOR	A number is a factor if it divides equally into another number eg 2, 3, 4, 6, 12 are all factors of 12
FACTORIAL	Factorial is a way of operating on one number and is calculated by taking the product of all the whole numbers from the a given number down to one. e.g. 5 factorial (written 5!) is found by working out $5 \times 4 \times 3 \times 2 \times 1 = 120$
FRACTIONS	Proper fractions - these are fractions less than 1 e.g. $\frac{3}{8}$ Improper or vulgar fractions - these are fractions greater than 1 e.g. $\frac{9}{5}$
ICOSAHEDRON	A 3 dimensional shape with twenty faces

INEQUALITY	A statement showing one quantity or expression is not equal to another e.g. 5 is less than 10, (written as 5 < 10)
INFINITY	Literally, boundless, vastness, immensity. The counting numbers (1, 2, 3, 4, 5, ...) go onto infinity but so too do the even numbers, the power of 2 and all whole numbers ending in 3. There are a finite number of whole numbers between 1 and 10 but an infinite number of decimals and fractions.
INTEGER	This is the set of positive and negative whole numbers.
INVERSE	Addition is the inverse of subtraction, multiplication is the inverse of division, Knowing the opposite or inverse operation is useful when checking calculations.
ISOSCELES	An isosceles triangle is one in which 2 sides (and two angles) are equal.
KITE	A quadrilateral with 2 pairs of equal sides which are adjacent to each other.
MEAN	This is often called the average and is the sum of a set of numbers divided by the number in the set.
MEDIAN	This is another measure of an average and is the middle number of a set of numbers once they have been placed in order e.g. 1 3 ⑦ 12 15
MULTIPLE	A multiple of a number 'n' is the product of that number and any positive integer eg 3 has the multiples 3, 6, 9, 12, 15, ...etc., 70 is a multiple of 7.
NUMERATOR	This is the top part of a fraction and represents the number of fractional parts.
OCTAHEDRON	A 3 dimensional shape with eight flat faces.
ORDINAL	The aspect of a number which relates to where it is in relation to other numbers e.g. 3 lies between 2 and 4 - this quality of 3 describes it's ordinality.
PARALLELOGRAM	A 4 sided 2 dimensional shape formed by 2 pairs of parallel lines
PARTITION	to split apart or separate a number into its component parts in various ways, eg 256 = 200 + 50 + 6, 52 = 40 + 12
PERCENTAGES	These are fractions where the denominator is 100. 25% is another way of writing $\frac{25}{100}$
PERIMETER	This is the length of the boundary or the distance around the outside of a 2 dimensional, closed shape
PERPENDICULAR	Lines are perpendicular to each other if they cross at right angles
PLATONIC	A platonic solid is one of the following five regular 3 dimensional shapes, cube, tetrahedron, octahedron, dodecahedron, icosahedron.
PLENARY	The closing part of a lesson when pupils feedback on their work and the aims are evaluated
POLYHEDRON	Any solid shape with plane (i.e.flat) faces eg cuboid,tetrahedron, octahedron, etc.
POLYGON	A polygon is any two dimensional shape bounded by only straight sides
POWER	The power of a number is the result of a multiplication using just that number eg 2 x 2 x 2 = 2^3 ('2 cubed'), 5 x 5 x 5 x 5 = 5^4 ('5 to the power of 4')

PRIME	A number is said to be prime if it only has 2 factors, 1 and the number itself. e.g. 11 is prime as 11 and 1 are it's only factors. 1 is not a prime number because it only has 1 factor.
PRISM	A prism is a 3 dimensional shape whose 'end' faces are the same shape and size. e.g. A 'Toblerone' packet is a prism, a brand new unsharpened pencil is a hexagonal prism and a circular prism is usually called a cylinder.
PRODUCT	The result of multiplying two or more numbers together e.g. 6 is the product of 2 and 3.
PYRAMID	A polyhedron with triangular faces meeting at the same vertex, but with any polygon for its base eg square based pyramid.
QUADRILATERAL	Any four sided plane shape (rectangle, square, etc are special cases) where the sides are straight.
RANGE	This is the difference between the smallest and the largest number in a set.
RATIO	The relation between one number and another in terms of division. eg. the two numbers 3 and 12 are in the ratio 1 to 4 (often written 1 : 4). For 2 numbers like 4 and 10 where one number does not divide exactly into the other, the ratio is written as 2 : 5 (i.e. each number has been divided by 2 in order to try to 'capture' the simplest way of expressing the ratio between the 2 numbers).
RECTANGULAR NUMBERS	These are numbers which, when represented by dots or counters, can be Arranged as rectangles, e.g. $\vdots \ \vdots \ \vdots$ 6 is a rectangular number because it is 2 x 3 but 7 is not because the only way you can arrange the dots is in a long line i.e. • • • • • • • (this, is another way of defining prime numbers).
RECURRING	A recurring decimal is one which contains an infinitely repeating set of decimal digits, e.g. 0.333333 .... (written as 0.$\dot{3}$) is a recurring decimal and is equal to $\frac{1}{3}$
RHOMBUS	A parallelogram with all its sides equal e.g.
SCALENE	A triangle where all the edges are of unequal length e.g.
SEQUENCE	Numbers that are in sequence are connected by a rule and follow a pattern eg 4, 6, 8, 10, ...
SQUARE NUMBERS	Square numbers are those formed as a result of numbers being multiplied by themselves eg 5 x 5 = 25. The first 10 square numbers are 1, 4, 9, 16, 25, 36, 49, 64, 81, 100.
SQUARE ROOT	The square root of a number can be thought of as the length of a side of asquare whose area is that number. It is the number which when squared is equal to the original number e.g. the square root of 36 (often written √ 36) is 6.

SYMMETRY

There are 2 kinds of symmetry that solid and plane shapes can have: line symmetry and rotational symmetry. Line symmetry (or reflective symmetry) is the property that a shape has if one side of a shape is the mirror image of the other. The line where the mirror would need to go is called the line of symmetry e.g. A square has 4 lines of symmetry.

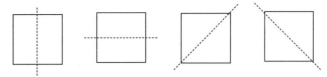

Rotational symmetry is the property that a shape has if when rotated about a certain point for a fraction of a whole turn looks the same.

e.g. An equilateral triangle has rotational symmetry 'of order 3' because after each $\frac{1}{3}$ of a turn it looks the same

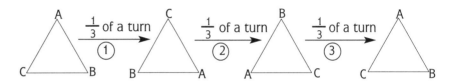

TALLY

A data handling term for the way to record the frequency of an event or items in blocks of 5 e.g. 卌 卌. Also means to add up.

TETRAHEDRON

A polyhedron with four faces where each face is an equilateral triangle

TRAPEZIUM

A four sided shape where one pair of sides is parallel e.g.

VERTEX, VERTICES

A vertex is the point where one or more edges or sides meet.
Vertices is the plural e.g. A square has 4 vertices, a cube has 8.

INDEX OF ACTIVITIES

This is presented in 4 sections to help you find the activity that suits your needs and the age of your children quickly and easily.

INDEX 1   Activities listed alphabetically
                  pages 277 - 278

INDEX 2   Activities listed according to the appropriate year group
                  pages 279 - 284

INDEX 3   Activities listed according to the main area of mathematics covered
                  page 285

INDEX 4   Activities listed according to a particular resource which is used
                  page 286

INDEX 1

About Half	63	Dotty Doubles	102
Add and Adjust	106	Dotty Rectangles	152
Add and Subtract	138	Doubling Patterns	130
Addition Chains	135	Drawing Shapes	166
Aim for the Target	108	Early Blank Lines	65
'Air' Numbers	42	Elastic Shapes	169
Are they the same?	190	Exploring Numbers	144
Around the class	117	Find the Function	124
Around the Hundred Square	133	First in Line	36
Beat the Calculator	129	First to One Hundred	184
Below Zero	44	Fours Fours	198
Blanks	57	Four in a Row	200
Blank Lines	71	Fraction Cards	150
Blank Lines 2	73	Fractions of Shapes	165
Body Maths	15	Grains of Rice	203
Body Multiples	109	Grid Totals	98
Bridging through Ten	107	Grid Totals 2	114
Bridging through Ten 2	136	Grid Totals 3	125
Build a Shape	163	Guess my Shape	160
Calculation Approximation	77	Guess the Number in my Pocket	55
Card Count	18	Halving and Doubling Sticks	92
Caterpillars	188	Hanging out the 'Washing'	33
Clapping Numbers	115	Hidden Numbers	89
Consecutive Numbers	134	Hidden Treasure	164
Consecutive Numbers Extended	195	Higher/Lower	34
Corner Numbers	116	How Close Can You Get?	185
Corner Numbers Investigated	181	How Many?	75
Countdown	96	How Many Boxes?	131
Counting Cards	20	How Many Days in School?	19
Counting Fives	23	How Many Dots?	66
Counting in Tens	21	How Many Dots Now?	69
Counting Races	25	How Many Minutes Have You Lived?	202
Counting Steps for Y3/Y4	22	How Much?	95
Counting Steps for Y5/Y6	26	If I Known This I Also Know	123
Dart Attack	126	Imagine a Line	24
Dartboards	192	Imagine a Number	17
Dartboards 2	186	Imagine a Shape	159
Decimals and Fractions	59	In Between	53
Different Ways	189	It Went Like This	113

Jar of Mung Beans	76	Pile of Cubes	62
Jellyfish Hunt	170	Quick Factors	60
Ladybird Spots	176	Rectangular Numbers	50
Line Jumps	90	Related Numbers	141
Long Division	155	Round the Line	67
Make a Two Digit Number	37	Round the Line Again	72
Match Me	38	Rounding Bingo	68
Memory Game	12	Rounding Bingo 2	74
Matching Number names to Numerals	39	Same Question, Different Solution	137
Mental Jumping	110	Sharing People	104
More Doubles	179	Show Me	13
More Functions	154	Silent Counting	13
More or Less Inequalities	47	So that Means	100
More or Less Moves	93	Spending Money	97
More or Less Towers	32	Split Numbers	143
More than the 3 Billy Goats Gruff	31	Spot the Mistake	14
Multiplication Monsters	127	Spotting Halves and Doubles	142
Multiplying & Dividing by 10 and 100	56	Starting Big	91
Name the Shape	167	Target	149
Negatives	151	Think of a Number	153
Negative Numbers	41	This Container Holds	70
Number Card Pairs	139	That Looks Like	168
Number Detectives	132	Three in a Line	58
Number Pyramids	140	Totalling Up	105
Number Pyramids 2	148	Trigits	54
Number Pyramids Investigated	196	True or False?	111
Number Sequences	49	Two Digit Multiplication	147
Number Stories	11	Two, Twenty, ...	45
Number Talk	99	Unfold a shape	158
Number Tiles 1	16	What Do I Do?	81
Number Tiles 2	16	What Else Do You Know?	146
1, 10, 100 more or less	51	What Number Am I Holding?	112
Odd/even	40	What is it's Value?	52
On the Mat	64	What's the Biggest Number?	35
Ordering Numbers to 100	43	What's that Number?	88
Pairs of Hands	94	What's that Number 2?	101
Partner Counting	20	When the Doorbell Rang	80
Pass the Basket	11	Which is Biggest?	46
Pieces of Number Line 1	25	Which Pair?	145
Pieces of Number Line 2	27		

THINK MATHS!

INDEX 2 (By Year Group)

Nursery and Reception:

Pass the Basket	11
Number Stories	11
Memory Game	12
Silent Counting	13
ShowMe	13
Spot the Mistake	14
Body Maths	15
More than the 3 Billy Goats Gruff	31
More or Less Towers	32
Hanging out the "Washing"	33
Higher/Lower	34
What's the Biggest Number?	35
Pile of Cubes	62
About Half	63
On the Mat	64
When the Doorbell Rang	80
What Do I Do?	81
Unfold a Shape	158
Imagine a Shape	159

Year 1:

Memory Game	12
Silent Counting	13
Show Me	13
Spot the Mistake	14
Body Maths	15
Number Tiles 1	16
Number Tiles 2	16
Imagine a Number	17
Card Count	18
Partner Counting	20
Counting Cards	20
More or Less Towers	32
Hanging out the 'Washing'	33
Higher/Lower	34
What's the Biggest Number?	35
First in Line	36
Make a Two Digit Number	37
Match Me	38
Matching Number Names to Numerals	39
Odd/Even	40
Negative Numbers	41
Pile of Cubes	62
About Half	63
On the Mat	64
Early Blank Lines	65
How Many Dots?	66
When the Doorbell Rang	80
What Do I Do?	81
What's that Number?	88
Hidden Numbers	89
Line Jumps	90
Starting Big	91
Halving and Doubling Sticks	92
More or Less Moves	93
Pairs of Hands	94
How Much?	95
Countdown	96
Spending Money	97
Grid Totals	98
Number Talk	99
Unfold a Shape	158
Imagine a Shape	159
Guess My Shape	160
Build A Shape	163
Ladybird Spots	176
More Doubles	179

Year 2:

Silent Counting   13
Show Me   13
Spot the Mistake   14
Body Maths   15
Number Tiles 1   16
Number Tiles 2   16
Imagine a Number   17
Card Count   18
How Many Days in School?   19
Partner Counting   20
Counting Cards   20
Counting in Tens   21
Higher/Lower   34
What's the Biggest Number?   35
First in Line   36
Make a Two Digit Number   37
Match Me   38
Matching Number Names to Numerals   39
Odd/Even   40
Negative Numbers   41
'Air' Numbers   42
Ordering Numbers to 100   43
Pile of Cubes   62
About Half   63
On the Mat   64
Early Blank Lines   65
How Many Dots?   66
What Do I Do?   81
What's that Number?   88
Hidden Numbers   89
Line Jumps   90
Starting Big   91
Halving and Doubling Sticks   92
More or Less Moves   93
Pairs of Hands   94
How Much?   95
Countdown   96
Spending Money   97

Grid Totals   98
Number Talk   99
So That Means   100
What's that Number 2?   101
Dotty Doubles   102
Sharing People   104
Totalling Up   105
Add and Adjust   106
Bridging Through Ten   107
Aim for the Target   108
Body Multiples   109
Mental Jumping   110
True or False?   111
What Number Am I Holding?   112
It Went Like This   113
Grid Totals 2   114
Clapping Numbers   115
Corner Numbers   116
Around the Class   117
Unfold a Shape   158
Imagine a Shape   159
Guess My Shape   160
Build A Shape   163
Ladybird Spots   176
More Doubles   179
Corner Numbers Investigated   181

Year 3:

Imagine a Number	17
Card Count	18
How Many Days in School?	19
Partner Counting	20
Counting Cards	20
Counting in Tens	21
Counting Steps for Y3/Y4	22
Counting Fives	23
Imagine a Line	24
Pieces of Number Line 1	25
Counting Races	25
'Air' Numbers	42
Ordering Numbers to 100	43
Below Zero	44
Two, Twenty, ...	45
Which is Biggest?	46
More or Less Inequalities	47
Number Sequences	49
Rectangular Numbers	50
1, 10, 100 More or Less	51
What is it's Value?	52
In Between	53
Trigits	54
Guess the Number in my Pocket	55
Round the Line	67
Rounding Bingo	68
How Many Dots Now?	69
This Container Holds ...	70
Blank Lines	71
What Do I Do?	81
How Much?	95
Countdown	96
Spending Money	97
Grid Totals	98
Number Talk	99
So that Means	100
What's that Number 2?	101
Dotty Doubles	102
Sharing People	104
Totalling Up	105
Add and Adjust	106
Bridging Through Ten	107
Aim for the Target	108
Body Multiples	109
Mental Jumping	110
True or False?	111
What Number Am I Holding?	112
It Went Like This	113
Grid Totals 2	114
Clapping Numbers	115
Corner Numbers	116
Around the Class	117
If I Know This I Also Know ...	123
Find the Function	124
Grid Totals 3	125
Dart Attack	126
Multiplication Monsters	127
Beat the Calculator	129
Doubling Patterns	130
How Many Boxes?	131
Number Detectives	132
Around the Hundred Square	133
Consecutive Numbers	134
Addition Chains	135
Bridging Through Ten 2	136
Same Question, Different Solution	137
Add and Subtract	138
Number Card Pairs	139
Number Pyramids	140
Related Numbers	141
Exploring Numbers	144
Imagine a Shape	159
Build a Shape	163
Hidden Treasure	164
Fractions of Shapes	165
Drawing Shapes	166
Name the Shape	167
That Looks Like	168
Corner Numbers Investigated	181
First to One Hundred	184
How Close Can You Get?	185
Dartboards 2	186
Caterpillars	188
Different Ways	189
Are they the same?	190
Dartboards	192

Year 4:

How Many Days in School?	19
Counting Steps for Y3/Y4	22
Counting Fives	23
Imagine a Line	24
Pieces of Number Line 1	25
Counting Races	25
'Air' Numbers	42
Ordering Numbers to 100	43
Below Zero	44
Two, Twenty,...	45
Which is Biggest?	46
More or Less Inequalities	47
Number Sequences	49
Rectangular Numbers	50
1, 10, 100 More or Less	51
What is it's Value?	52
In Between	53
Trigits	54
Guess the Number in my Pocket	55
Multiplying & Dividing by 10 and 100	56
Blanks	57
Round the Line	67
Rounding Bingo	68
How Many Dots Now?	69
This Container Holds	70
Blank Lines	71
What Do I Do?	81
Spending Money	97
Grid Totals	98
Number Talk	99
Add and Adjust	106
Bridging Through Ten	107
Aim for the Target	108
Body Multiples	109
Mental Jumping	110
True or False?	111
What Number Am I Holding?	112
It Went Like This	113
Grid Totals2	114
Clapping Numbers	115
Corner Numbers	116
Around the Class	117
If I Know This I Also Know . .	123
Find the Function	124
Grid Totals 3	125
Dart Attack	126
Multiplication Monsters	127
Beat the Calculator	129
Doubling Patterns	130
How Many Boxes?	131
Number Detectives	132
Around the Hundred Square	133
Consecutive Numbers	134
Addition Chains	135
Bridging Through Ten 2	136
Same Question, Different Solution	137
Add and Subtract	138
Number Card Pairs	139
Number Pyramids	140
Related Numbers	141
Spotting Halves and Doubles	142
Split Numbers	143
Exploring Numbers	144
Which Pair?	145
What Else Do You Know?	146
Two Digit Multiplication	147
Imagine a Shape	159
Hidden Treasure	164
Fractions of Shapes	165
Drawing Shapes	166
Name the Shape	167
That Looks Like	168
Elastic Shapes	169
Corner Numbers Investigated	181
First to One Hundred	184
How Close Can You Get?	185
Dartboards 2	186
Caterpillars	188
Different Ways	189
Are they the same?	190
Dartboards	192
Consecutive Numbers Extended	195
Number Pyramids Investigated	196

THINK MATHS!

Year 5:

Counting Steps for Y5/Y6	26
Pieces of Number Line 2	27
What is it's Value?	52
In Between	53
Trigits	54
Guess the Number in my Pocket	55
Multiplying & Dividing by 10 and 100	56
Blanks	57
Three in a Line	58
Decimals and Fractions	59
Quick Factors	60
Round the Line Again	72
Blank Lines 2	73
Rounding Bingo 2	74
How Many?	75
Jar of Mung Beans	76
Calculation Approximation	77
What Do I Do?	81
Grid Totals	98
Number Talk	99
True or False?	111
What Number Am I Holding?	112
It Went Like This	113
Grid Totals 2	114
Clapping Numbers	115
Corner Numbers	116
Around the Class	117
Number Detectives	132
Around the Hundred Square	133
Consecutive Numbers	134
Addition Chains	135
Bridging Through Ten 2	136
Same Question, Different Solution	137
Add and Subtract	138
Number Card Pairs	139
Number Pyramids	140
Related Numbers	141
Spotting Halves and Doubles	142
Split Numbers	143
Exploring Numbers	144
What Else Do You Know?	146
Two Digit Multiplication	147
Number Pyramids 2	148
Target	149
Fraction Cards	150
Negatives	151
Dotty Rectangles	152
Think of a Number	153
More Functions	154
Long Division	155
Imagine a Shape	159
Drawing Shapes	166
Name the Shape	167
That Looks Like	168
Elastic Shapes	169
Jellyfish Hunt	170
Corner Numbers Investigated	181
Caterpillars	188
Different Ways	189
Are they the same?	190
Dartboards	192
Consecutive Numbers Extended	195
Number Pyramids Investigated	196
Four Fours	198
Four in a Row	200
How Many Minutes Have You Lived?	202
Grains of Rice	203

Year 6:

Counting Steps for Y5/Y6	26	Target	149
Pieces of Number Line 2	27	Fraction Cards	150
In Between	53	Negatives	151
Trigits	54	Dotty Rectangles	152
Guess the Number in my Pocket	55	Think of a Number	153
Multiplying & Dividing by 10 and 100	56	More Functions	154
Blanks	57	Long Division	155
Three in a Line	58	Imagine a Shape	159
Decimals and Fractions	59	Drawing Shapes	166
Quick Factors	60	Name the Shape	167
Round the Line Again	72	That Looks Like	168
Blank Lines 2	73	Elastic Shapes	169
Rounding Bingo 2	74	Jellyfish Hunt	170
How Many?	75	Corner Numbers Investigated	181
Jar of Mung Beans	76	Caterpillars	188
Calculation Approximation	77	Different Ways	189
What Do I Do?	81	Are they the same?	190
Grid Totals	98	Dartboards	192
Number Talk	99	Consecutive Numbers Extended	195
True or False?	111	Number Pyramids Investigated	196
What Number Am I Holding?	112	Four Fours	198
It Went Like This	113	Four in a Row	200
Grid Totals 2	114	How Many Minutes Have You Lived?	202
Clapping Numbers	115	Grains of Rice	203
Corner Numbers	116		
Around the class	117		
Number Detectives	132		
Around the Hundred Square	133		
Consecutive Numbers	134		
Addition Chains	135		
Bridging Through Ten 2	136		
Same Question, Different Solution	137		
Add and Subtract	138		
Number Card Pairs	139		
Number Pyramids	140		
Related Numbers	141		
Split Numbers	143		
Exploring Numbers	144		
What Else Do You Know?	146		
Two Digit Multiplication	147		
Number Pyramids 2	148		

INDEX 3 (by Area of Mathematics)

ADDITION/SUBTRACTION: pages   45, 46, 51, 81, 88, 89, 90, 91, 93, 95, 96, 97, 98, 100, 105, 106, 107, 108, 111, 112, 113, 114, 115, 116, 117, 123, 124, 125, 132, 133, 134, 135, 136, 137, 138, 139, 140, 141, 144, 145, 148, 149, 176, 209

COUNTING FORWARDS AND BACKWARDS: pages   9, 10, 13, 14, 16, 18, 20, 21, 22, 23, 24, 25, 26, 27, 45, 49, 88, 132

COUNTING OBJECTS: pages   11, 12, 13, 17

DOUBLING AND HALVING: pages   92, 102, 117, 142, 179, 186, 188, 192

ESTIMATION OF MEASUREMENT/ROUNDING NUMBERS: pages   65, 67, 68, 71, 72, 73, 74, 77

ESTIMATION OF QUANTITY: pages   62, 63, 64, 66, 69, 70, 75, 76

FACTORS/MULTIPLES/PRIMES: pages   50, 60, 99

FRACTIONS/DECIMALS/PERCENTAGES: pages   22, 24, 26, 27, 53, 58, 59, 63, 72, 73, 74, 141, 150, 165, 190, 202

FUNCTION/FORMULAE: pages   124, 153, 154

INEQUALITIES: page   47

KNOWING NUMBER NAMES AND ORDERING: pages   9, 10, 14, 15, 18, 20, 31, 32, 33, 34, 35, 36, 39

MULTIPLICATION/DIVISION: pages   56, 80, 81, 94, 104, 109, 110, 111, 112, 113, 116, 117, 125, 126, 127, 129, 130, 131, 141, 143, 144, 146, 147, 148, 149, 152, 154, 155, 181, 192, 200, 203, 212, 219

NEGATIVE NUMBERS: pages   21, 22, 24, 26, 41, 44, 151

NUMBER PUZZLES/INVESTIGATIONS: pages   116, 181, 188, 195, 196, 198, 203

ODD AND EVEN NUMBERS: pages   20, 40, 55

PLACE VALUE: pages   19, 37, 38, 42, 43, 46, 52, 54, 57, 185

PROBLEM SOLVING/REAL LIFE CONTEXTS: pages   11, 19, 63, 80, 81, 105, 109, 113, 126, 131, 186, 192, 198, 202, 203

2 AND 3 D SHAPES: pages   158, 159, 160, 163, 165, 166, 167, 168, 169

INDEX 4 (by use of particular resources for number work))

ARROW CARDS: page   38

BASE 10 BLOCKS (EG DIENES):   pages   19, 37, 38

CALCULATOR: pages   21, 41, 56, 129, 190, 202, 209

DICE: pages   36, 125, 129, 179, 184, 185, 192, 209

DIGIT CARDS: pages   13, 14, 32, 38, 47, 54, 58, 99, 150, 185, 209, 217

HTU BASE BOARDS: pages   54, 185, 217

MONEY: pages   37, 95, 97, 105, 209

NUMBER LINES: pages   21, 25, 27, 58, 59, 67, 72, 90, 91, 97, 104, 107, 110, 131, 136, 151, 184, 209, 214, 217

NUMBER SQUARE: pages   20, 21, 23, 27, 88, 93, 101, 106, 109, 132, 133, 134, 184, 198, 219

PLACE VALUE CHART: pages   52, 57